THE LOST BEATLES INTERVIEWS

The Lost Beatles Interviews

Geoffrey and Brenda Giuliano

First published in Great Britain in 1995 by
Virgin Books
an imprint of Virgin Publishing Ltd
332 Ladbroke Grove
London W10 5AH

A catalogue record for this book is available from the British Library.

ISBN 0 86369 886 7

Typeset by Phoenix Photosetting, Chatham, Kent
Printed and bound in Great Britain by
Mackays of Chatham PLC, Chatham, Kent

Contents

Contents

Contents

Contents

Illustrations

Acknowledgements

Senior Editors: Matthew Carnicelli and Mal Peachey
Associate Researcher: Sesa Nichole Giuliano
Intern: Devin Giuliano

The authors would like to thank the following people for their kindness and selfless hard work in helping realise this book: Jagannatha Dasa Adikari; Christine Adair; Dr Mirza Beg; Deborah Lynn Black; Stefano Castino; Vrinda Rani Devi Dasi; Enzo of Valentino; Paul Forty; Robin Scot Giuliano; Sesa, Devin, Avalon and India Giuliano; His Divine Grace B. H. Mangalniloy Maharaja Goswami; ISKCON; Carla Johnson; Sean Kittrick; Dr Michael Klapper; Allan Lang; Leaf Leavesley; Donald Lehr; Andrew Lownie; Mark Studios, Clarence, New York; David Lloyd McIntyre; Michelle Ogden; His Divine Grace A. C. Bhaktivedanta Swami Prabhupada; Steven Rosen; Self Realization Institute of America (SRI); Paul Slovak; Wendell and Joan Smith; Dave Thompson; Edward Veltman; Robert Wallace; Gill Woolcott; Ronald Zucker.

Introduction

THE LURE OF BEATLESPEAK

Re-inventing their persona with the release of almost every new album, the Beatles constantly challenged themselves and thus their listeners to perpetually re-evaluate not only their music but their complete personalities as well. Positioned dead centre as the group's searching spiritual heart, George Harrison became the compassionate conscience of a generation, pushing the perimeters of our own life experience to include the concepts of innate spirituality, the ultimate meaninglessness of worldly acclaim and, perhaps more importantly, the possibility of unquestioning, uncompromising, unalloyed love as a much-needed balm for an isolated, topsy turvy, unenlightened world.

'The more aware I've become the more I realise that all we are doing is acting out an incarnation,' Harrison intoned to *Look* magazine way back in 1968. 'It's just a little bit of time which is both relevant and very irrelevant too. Every moment is surcharged with the possibility of either forgetfulness or surrender to the Divine. All life is worship of God in a way and all we're doing is trying to pass it on to more people. My idea of God is that you're not doing it for yourself particularly but for everyone else. For whoever wants it.' To assimilate such ideas as an impressionable pre-teen back then was for me the foggy outline of everything I myself hoped for and the obtuse beginning of my own internal search. I suspect it was the same for many of you as well.

John Lennon, however, was a different proposition altogether. Pre-Yoko he was still the archetypal working-class, intellectual, upscale acid head, his own inner radar ever on the lookout for deeper yet more meaningful levels of experience to help shape his already generously overloaded sensory framework.

Once Yoko settled in for the duration, however, things quickly changed and Lennon became forever tangled in her wacky, often self-indulgent, artsy, head space.

What isn't generally known is that towards the end John had pretty much rejected Yoko's influence over his work in favour of the straight ahead pop/rock idiom that reached out and grabbed him as a kid back in Liverpool.

Paul McCartney's story meanwhile, is considerably less complex. He caught the showbiz bug early on from his charismatic, piano-playing dad and the old Hollywood movies that sparked into the cluttered front parlour of the McCartneys' humble two-up, two-down. Aside from a brief psychedelic/avant-garde detour in the middle sixties, the wide-eyed entertainer has pretty much stuck to that credo, pro-liferating a long string of pretty, toe-tapping, largely inconsequential ditties tailor-made for the undemanding international top ten. Staunchly denying the deep river that runs through him, McCartney could have been a hell of a musician but settled on triple platinum rock stardom instead. Pity.

All of which brings us to Ringo. Intrinsically much more than the lucky drummer who won the pools when he first sat down to keep time for the savage young Beatles, he remains one of the most well loved bit players in the checkered history of popular music. The consistent twaddle that he is in any way stupid or inept is just that. An engaging little man with a penchant for transforming the mundane into the magical, Starr may turn out to be the most subtly brilliant of the lot. A sparkly bearded buddha playing out his incarnation with humour and compassion.

This book of collected interviews with The Fabs and friends is the end result of over 25 years of peeking in on The Beatles' turbulent lives through any window I could find. A strange way to spend the better part of one's youth, I know, but what's done is done. I just hope it helps the people that sincerely love them to gain a little insight into what it all really means.

As for me, I've travelled down that road about as far as I can. Anyone who wants to carry on will just have to make it on their own. Anyway, let me know how you get on and do enjoy the book. Beatles forever!

All you need is love. Give peace a chance. Power to the people. The farther one travels – the less one knows.

Giuliano
'Skyfield'
Western New York
July 1995

Act One

Where Giants Walk: The Gospel According to John, Paul, George and Ringo

The Mersey Sound

The Mersey Sound is the voice of 80,000 crumbling houses and 30,000 people on the dole.

Daily Worker, 1963

Los Angeles Airport

City of Los Angeles
Department of Airports
#1 World Way
Los Angeles
California 90009
17 August 1964

Mr Brian Epstein
Manager, The Beatles
5/6 Argyll
London W1
England

Delivered to Mr Derek Taylor
Assistant Manager of the Beatles

Dear Mr Epstein:

Due to the dangerous conditions which have been created at airports where the Beatles have landed, the Department of Airports has held conferences with the several agencies responsible for the safety of persons, property and aircraft. Included in these meetings have been representatives of the Los Angeles Police and Fire Departments, the Federal Aviation Agency, the sponsors of the Beatles' Los Angeles appearance, and Airport Security and Operations' personnel.

We therefore advise you, as manager of the Beatles, and as a person vitally concerned with their physical welfare, as well as the safety of the Beatles' youthful fans, of the following conditions and recommendations:

(1) The Los Angeles Police Department cannot guarantee the safety of the Beatles should thousands of youngsters be urged by Beatle publicists to greet them at the airport. Only those officers who can be spared from essential duties throughout this vast city may be made available.

(2) The airport cannot permit a public airport reception here. Children have been crushed and injured at other airports when over-excited at the sight of the Beatles.

Therefore, should you elect to arrive at Los Angeles International Airport, the aircraft, be it a chartered or scheduled airline, will be directed to a restricted area to which there is no public access.

(3) We recommend that you use a charter aircraft to its best advantage for the safety of all concerned. In this area as well as in most other

4

cities, there are numerous airports in which you can land with your destination unannounced.

It is entirely within your jurisdiction to keep both the time and place of arrival unannounced in order to avoid the dangerous congregation of many thousands of children.

You might also want to consider the possibility that unsafe ground conditions brought on by uncontrolled and emotional crowds can force closure of the airport and the diversion of your aircraft.

We sincerely hope you will follow our recommendation. If you do have any questions please contact this office. It is a simple procedure to arrive without fanfare. I'm quite certain fellow airport operators join with us in urging such a policy on your part.

Very truly yours,

Francis T. Fox
General Manager

Paris, 1963

Announcer: This afternoon in our Paris studios we're visiting with four young men and if I mention their first names, Paul, George, Ringo and John, I doubt you'd know about whom we're speaking. But if I said we're here this afternoon with the Beatles? And if we were in England I think we'd get a great big rousing hurrah, wouldn't we, boys?

Paul: I don't know.

Question: Now Paul, tell us, how did the Beatles get going? How did you start?

Paul: It's a funny story really. It was back in the old days. We were all at school together, we grew up at school as teenage buddies. It developed from there.

Question: Did you sing together around school?

Paul: Yeah. George and I were at school together, John was next door and Ringo was at Butlins. We just started playing guitars and things. It went on from there, as far as I'm concerned.

Question: You say those were the olden days. Within the past year you have mushroomed tremendously in popularity. What levered this great rage for the Beatles?

Paul: Well, it's funny really. I think it was the Palladium show, the television show in England. Then following hot in the footsteps we had the Royal Variety Command Performance for the Queen Mother and it all went from there, really. The national newspapers got hold of it and they got hold of Ringo, you know. A lot of columnists got onto the idea and started calling it Beatlemania.

Question: George, what is the status of rock'n'roll in England today? Is that what you call your music?

George: No, not really. We don't like to call it anything. The critics and the people who write about it have to call it something. They didn't want to say it was rock'n'roll because rock was supposed to have gone out about five years ago. They decided it wasn't really rhythm and blues so they called it the Liverpool Sound which is stupid really. As far as we were concerned it's the same as the rock from five years ago.

Question: Can you describe the Liverpool Sound?

George: Oh, it's more like the old rock, but everything's just a bit louder. More bass and bass drum and everybody sort of sings loud and shouts, that's it.

Question: Is the Liverpool Sound, then, the sound in the UK today?

George: Yeah, everybody's making records in that style.

Question: Well, let's ask Ringo here. You're the drummer, we caught your act at the Olympia the other evening. How long have you been beating those skins?

Ringo: About five years now. I've been with the boys about eighteen months and with other groups before that.

Question: Since you boys have gained your current popularity have there been many other organisations trying to imitate you or perhaps take the thunder away from you? Let's ask John Lemon this.

John: Well, I suppose a couple of people have jumped on the bandwagon, but it really doesn't matter because it promotes the whole idea of us if we're away. There's a few little Beatles still going to remind people of us.

Question: Paul, let's go back to you for a moment. When anyone sees your picture, the first thing that strikes them, naturally, is your hairdo. Some people have written that you have a 'sheepdog' cut or, perhaps, an early Caesar. What do you call it?

Paul: To us, it just sort of seems a natural thing. We came out of the swimming baths one day and, you know how it is, your hair sort of flops about afterwards. It stayed that way, you see. Then the papers got hold of it and they called it the Beatles style. I suppose we go along with them now.

Question: Do you go to the barber at all?

Paul: Now and then. Do and don't.

Question: Just to keep it trimmed?

Paul: Yeah, but sometimes we do it ourselves. The thing is, it's really only our eyebrows that are growing upwards.

Question: We've been told that in England today, there's this Beatlemania going on. What would you say Beatlemania is? All the girls scream whenever they see you and perhaps faint waiting in line. Let's be immodest a moment: what's the big attraction?

John: I think it's like a dressing gown. George's dressing gown is definitely a big attraction.

Paul: I don't think any of us really know what it is. We've been asked this question an awful lot of times, but we've never been able to come up with an answer. I think it's a collection of so many different things like: happening to be there at the right time, a little bit of originality in the songs, a different sound. Maybe the gimmick of the haircut as well, the look, getting into the national press at the right time.

John: All these things and more, fab listeners.

Question: I understand you boys write your own material.

Paul: John and I write them. This is Paul speaking.

Question: Do you get together regularly or does an idea pop in your mind and you say, Let's sit down and do it?

Paul: If an idea does pop in your mind then you do sit down and say Let's do it, yeah. If there are no ideas and say we've been told we've got a recording date in about two days' time then you've got to sit down and sort of slug it out. You normally get just a little idea which doesn't seem bad and you go on and it builds up from there. It varies every time.

Question: Paul, we've seen you here at the Olympia; can you compare the French audiences with what you're familiar with back in England?

Paul: There's a lot of difference because in England, you see, the audiences are seventy-five per cent female, here it's seventy-five per cent male. That's the main difference, really. You're still appreciated, but you don't get the full noise and the atmosphere of a place.

John: No screams.

Question: Why is it seventy-five per cent boys?

George: I think they don't let the girls out at night in France.

John: I think it's your dressing gown.

George: Somebody said that they still have chaperones, a lot of them, you see. Whereas in England, they're out. It's the same in Germany, all the boys like rock. It's usually the same on the Continent, I don't really know why.

Question: Paul, we see 'I Want to Hold Your Hand' is number one on the Hit Parade. How did you come to write that?

Paul: Let's see, we were told we had to get down to it. So we found this house when we were walking along one day. We knew we had to really get this song going so we got down in the basement of this disused house and there was an old piano. It wasn't really disused, it was rooms to let. We found this old piano and started banging away.

John: And there was a little old organ.

Paul: Yeah, there was a little old organ too. So we were having this informal jam and we started banging away. Suddenly, a little bit came to us, the catch line. So we started working on it from there. We got our pens and paper out and just wrote down the lyrics. Eventually we had some sort of a song so we played it for our recording manager and he seemed to like it. We recorded it the next day.

Question: Do all of your songs have a basic theme or message?

Paul: No, they don't, but there's one thing that nearly always seems to run through songs. People point it out to us. It's that I, You, Me, always seem to be in the title. 'I Want to Hold Your Hand', 'She Loves You', 'Love me Do' and things like this. I think the reason for that is that we try and write songs which are a bit more personal than others, you see. I, Me and You in the titles make the songs more personal, but that's the only basic message that runs through our songs.

Question: And you coined this 'Yeah, yeah, yeah'. Isn't that sweeping England right now?

John: Well, yeah. That was sort of the main catch phrase from 'She Loves You'. We'd written the song and then suddenly we needed more so we added yeah, yeah, yeah. It caught on, so now they use it if they're trying to be 'with it' or 'hip'.

Question: Paul, what do you think of your trip to the States? I understand in about a week you're going to be on the *Ed Sullivan Show*.

Paul: Yeah, that's right. We're going to do the show in New York and we're taping one for later release. Then we go down to Miami – I can't wait – and we do another Sullivan Show there. Before that, we do Carnegie Hall, don't we?

Question: How were you selected for Ed Sullivan? Was he in England and caught your act or something?

George: We were arriving from Stockholm into London airport and at the same time the Prime Minister and the Queen Mother were also flying out, but the airport was overrun with teenagers, thousands of them waiting for us to get back. And Ed Sullivan was supposed to have arrived at that time and wondered what was going on. Also our manager went over to the States with another singer called Billy J. Kramer and he did a couple of TV shows over there. While he was there our manager got the bookings with Ed Sullivan, but he'd also heard of us from this London airport thing.

Question: Is there a movie in the future?

Paul: Yeah. We've been asked by United Artists to do a feature.

Question: Will it be dramatic or just wrapped around your singing?

Paul: We don't know yet what it's going to be like. I don't think we'll do an awful lot of acting. I think it will be written around the sort of people we are. There'll be four characters in it, very like us.

Question: Do you plan to compose two or three songs specifically for the film?

George: Actually, we have to compose six songs specifically for the film.

Paul: We've got to get down to that too. That's a job.

Question: Then you boys haven't really had much of a chance to see Paris, have you?

George: Not really, no.

Question: How about the French girls compared to the British girls?

Ringo: We haven't seen any yet.

John: Well, I'm married. I didn't notice them.

Question: We'll go back to Paul then. You're single.

Paul: Yeah. I think the French girls are fabulous.

George: We have seen more French boys than French girls, so I mean, we can't really tell.

Question: Perhaps when you get to the *Ed Sullivan Show* there'll be more girls for you.

Paul: I hope so, yeah.

Question: Any of you been to America before?

George: Yeah, me. I went in September, just for a holiday. For three weeks.

Question: Well, I see our time is up, boys. Thank you, Beatles, for being our guests this afternoon.

Paris, 14 January 1964

Question: How important is it to succeed here?
Paul: It is important to succeed everywhere.
Question: The French have not made up their minds about the Beatles. What do you think of them?
John: Oh, we like the Beatles. They're gear.
Question: Do you like topless bathing suits?
Ringo: We've been wearing them for years.
Question: Girls rushed toward my car because it had press identification and they thought I met you. How do you explain this phenomenon?
John: You're lovely to look at.
Question: What about your future?
Ringo: None of us has quite grasped what it is all about yet. It's washing over our heads like a huge tidal wave. But we're young. Youth is on our side. And it's youth that matters right now. I don't care about politics, just people.
George: I wouldn't do all this if I didn't like it. I wouldn't do anything I didn't want to, would I?
Question: Is it true you're only in this for the money?
Paul: Security is the only thing I want. Money to do nothing with, money to have in case you wanted to do something.
John: People say we're loaded with money but by comparison with those who are supposed to talk the Queen's English that's ridiculous. We're only earning. They've got real capital behind them and they're earning on top of that. The more people you meet, the more you realise it's all a class thing.

The Lost Beatles Interviews

British Group Invades US, 1964

'A plague has swept the land, but we have been left whole' was the way one writer reviewed the first invasion of the Beatles, England's mop-haired rock'n'roll sensation. Like most, the writer felt the idols were a fad among teenagers which would pass as quickly as it arrived. How wrong he was!

The Beatles returned in August, stronger than ever. Motel owners found their doors denuded of knobs because adolescent girls believed 'the Beatles had touched them'. An attendant found himself driving an ambulance through seething streets and hidden in the back were the Beatles. 'If those kids had caught them, they'd really have needed an ambulance,' he said. Some fans did require medical aid: one burst blood vessels in the neck, she screamed so hard; another fell and was used as a vantage point by spike-heeled fellow fans.

Some people profited, such as the entrepreneur who bought sheets from the Beatles' hotel beds, and sold them at $1 per square inch!

How did the Beatles take to America? 'Can't say,' Ringo admitted. 'Didn't see much. Luv-ed the money, though.' He was referring to the $2,112,000 the Beatles took home with them.

Washington DC, 11 February 1964

Question: Do any of you have any formal musical training?
John: You're joking.
Question: What do you think of President Johnson?
Paul: Does he buy our records?
Question: What do you think of American girls and American audiences?
John: Marvellous.
Question: Here I am, surrounded by the Beatles and I don't feel a thing. Fellas, how does it feel to be in the United States?
John: It's great.
Question: What do you like best about our country?
John: You!
Question: I'll take that under advisement. Do you have any plans to meet the Johnson girls?
John: No. We heard they didn't like our concerts.
Question: Are they coming to your performance tonight?
Paul: If they do, we'd really like to meet them.
Question: You and the snow came to Washington today. Which do you think will have the greater impact?
John: The snow will probably last longer.
Question: One final question. Have you ever heard of Walter Cronkite?
Paul: Nope.
John: NBC News, is he? Yeah, we know him.
Question: Thanks, fellas. By the way, it's CBS News.
John: I know, but I didn't want to say it as we're now on ABC.
Question: This is NBC, believe it or not.
John: And you're Walter?
Question: No, I'm Ed.
John: What's going on around here?
Question: What do you think of your reception in America so far?
John: It's been great.
Question: What struck you the most?
John: You!
Ringo: We already did that joke when we first came in.
George: Well, we're doing it again, squire!
Question: Why do you think you're so popular?
John: It must be the weather.
Question; Do you think it's your singing?

Paul: I doubt it. We don't know which it could be.

Question: Where'd you get the idea for the haircuts?

John: Where'd you get the idea for yours?

Paul: We enjoyed wearing our hair like this so it's developed this way.

Question: Well, you save on haircutting at least.

Paul: Roar . . .

John: I think it costs more to keep it short than long, don't you?

Paul: Yeah, we're saving our money.

Question: Are you still number one in Europe?

George: We're number one in America.

Question: Where else are you number one then?

John: Hong Kong and Sweden . . .

Paul: Australia, Denmark and Finland.

Question: And you haven't any idea why?

Ringo: We just lay down and do it.

John: In Hong Kong and these other places, suddenly you're number one years after putting out your records. Even here, we've got records we've probably forgotten.

Question: You call your records 'funny records'?

John: 'Funny', yeah, the ones we've forgotten.

George: It's unusual because they've been out in England for over a year. Like 'Please Please Me' is a big hit over here now but it's over a year old.

Question: Do you think they're musical?

John: Obviously they're musical because it's music, isn't it! We make music. Instruments play music. It's a record.

Question: What do you call it, rock and roll?

Paul: We try not to define our music because we get so many wrong classifications off it. We call it music even if you don't.

Question: With a question mark?

George: Pardon?

John: We leave that to the critics.

Question: Okay, that's it. Have a good time in America.

John: Thank you. Keep buying them records and look after yourself.

New York, 12 February 1964

Question: John, is the reaction to the group the same here as in England?

John: I find it's very similar, only over here they go wilder quicker, you know.

Question: Will you sing a song for us?

John: No. Sorry, we need money first.

Question: How much money do you expect to make here?

John: About half a crown. Depends on the tax. How much have you got?

Question: Some of your detractors allege that you are bald and those haircuts are wigs. Is that true?

John: Oh, we're all bald. Yeah. And deaf and dumb too.

Question: What is the Beatle sound?

John: Well, as far as we are concerned, there's no such thing as a Liverpool or even a Beatles sound. It's just a name that people tag on.

Question: One of your hits is 'Roll Over, Beethoven'. What do you think of Beethoven as a composer?

Ringo: He's great. Especially his poems.

Question: Are these your real names?

Paul: Yeah, except Ringo. His name's Richard Starkey. He's called Ringo because of his rings, you know. And Starr, he didn't like Starkey.

Question: Do all the Beatles write songs?

John: Paul and I do most of the writing. George has written a few. Ringo hasn't, because it's hard to write something on the drums, isn't it?

Ringo: Yes.

Question: How do you account for your fantastic success?

Paul: Wish we knew.

John: Good press agent.

Question: Why do millions of Beatles fans buy millions of Beatles records?

John: If we knew, we'd form another group and become their managers.

Question: What do you think of American girls compared to British girls?

Paul: The accents are different, of course. In films American women always seem to be bossing the men, being superior in big business and things. But from what I've seen, they're not. They're very similar to British women, just ordinary people, very nice.

The Lost Beatles Interviews

Question: Where did the name 'Beatle' come from?

George: We were just racking our brains and John came up with the name Beatle. It was good because it was the insect and it was also a pun, you know, 'beat', on the beat. We liked the name and we kept it.

Question: Have you been influenced by any one American artist?

George: In the early days, it was Elvis Presley, Carl Perkins, Chuck Berry, Little Richard and Buddy Holly. But there's no one we tried to copy.

Question: Why do you wear your hair in such an unusual style?

George: Well, I went to the swimming baths and when I came out my hair dried and it was just all forward like a mop. I left it like that. When Ringo joined the group we got him to get his hair like this because by then people were calling it the Beatle cut.

Question: Do you contemplate becoming permanent residents of the US?

George: I love the States, but if we came to live over here everybody would go mad. It's like Elvis, if he went to, say, Australia and then suddenly decided to live there. What would all the American people think?

Question: Paul, what are your ambitions?

Paul: We used to have lots of ambitions. Like number one records; *Sunday Night at the Palladium*; *The Ed Sullivan Show*; to go to America. A thousand ambitions like that. I can't really think of any more. We've lived an awful lot of them.

Question: Paul, what is your aim in life?

Paul: To have a laugh, you know, to be happy.

Question: John, is it a fad?

John: Obviously. Anything in this business is a fad. We don't think we're going to last forever. We're just going to have a good time while it lasts.

Adelaide, 12 June 1964

Question: Did you enjoy your visit to the Rhine?
John: Only standing there in our new coats.
George: Seeing as they got soaked, we didn't mind, did we?
Question: We've got to pay you a tribute coming by open car, because the kids have been waiting all night and they appreciated it.
John: Well, they deserved it, waiting all night.
Question: But you need some dry clothes.
John: We thought it was going to be sunny out.
Question: Who came up with the name The Beatles and how did you derive this particular name with the 'a'?
George: John thought up the name Beatles ages ago and when we needed a name and everyone was thinking of one he just thought of The Beatles.
Question: Why the 'b-e-a' instead of the 'b-e-e'?
John: Forget 'b-e-e'. It was hard enough getting people to understand why it was 'b-e-a', never mind.
Question: What do you expect to find here in Australia?
John: Australians, I should think.
Question: Do you have an acknowledged leader of the group?
John: No, not really.
Question: We heard that you stood on your head on the balcony outside, is that right?
Paul: I don't know where you hear these rumours.
Question: John, has the Mersey Beat changed much since you've been playing it?
John: There's no such thing as Mersey Beat. The press made that up. It's all rock'n'roll.
Question: Do you play the same way now as you did?
John: It's only rock'n'roll. It just so happens that we write most of it.
Question: Did Buddy Holly influence your music?
John: He did in the early days, obviously he was one of the greats.
Paul: So did James Thurber though, didn't he?
John: Yeah, but he doesn't sing as well, does he?
Question: Have you been practising up your Australian accents?
George: No, guvnor, not at all.
Question: Do you think you will be writing any songs with Australian themes?
John: No, we never write anything with themes. We just write the same rubbish all the time.

Question: Do you play the kind of music you want to play or the music you think people want to hear?

John: Well, we've been playing this kind of music for five or six years, something like that. It's all just rock'n'roll. It just happens that we write it.

Question: What do you think made the difference that put you up above other groups?

George: We had a record contract.

Question: What record do you all agree is generally your best recording? Not the best seller, but rather the best musically.

John: We always like the one we just made, don't we? So 'Long Tall Sally'.

George: I like 'You Can't Do That', personally.

Question: What about you, Jimmy? How do you feel being in with the Beatles? A newcomer standing in for Ringo?

Jimmy Nichols: It's a good experience, man.

Question: How is Ringo?

Jimmy: He's much better. He joins us on Sunday.

Question: What do you do then?

Jimmy: I go back to London where they're fixing up a band for me, I'll do some television . . .

John: And he's away.

Question: You're progressing pretty well with your Beatle haircut.

Jimmy: I've been growing it for about three months now.

Question: How long does it take to get a magnificent mane like this?

John: I can't remember being without it.

Question: Do you ever go to the barber's, John?

John: No. I haven't had my hair cut since the film. The woman on the film cut it. I don't trust anybody else.

Question: This is the film, *Beatlemania*, is it?

John: No, it's not called that. That's another one. *Hard Day's Night* it's called.

Question: Are you satisfied with the finished product?

John: Well, it's as good as it can be with anybody that can't act.

Melbourne, 15 June 1964

Question: How do you feel about your responsibilities? I mean teen-agers dwell on your every comment and action. Do you feel very responsible towards this?

Paul: We never used to believe it. We used to open a magazine and it would say So-and-So doesn't drink, doesn't smoke. We just act normally and hope other people don't think we act funny.

Question: I know you say you act normally, but how can you when you're getting so much money? When everywhere you go people go so crazy you can't see anything?

John: Normal in the environment that surrounds us.

Question: John, you started in something called a skiffle group. Now, does this automatically grow into what now is the Beatles or did this come about over a period of years?

John: Over a period of time. See, I met Paul first and he sort of joined us. Then George. It was just us three.

Question: What did you think of the Adelaide reception?

Paul: It was good.

Question: Was it like anything you've ever had before?

Beatles: No.

Question: Do you think it was well conducted?

John: Yes, everyone was well behaved.

Question: Do you ever get this feeling that someone's going to knock you off or something?

Paul: Nah.

Question: How long do you rehearse a new number when you make up a new song?

Paul: Normally with new numbers we don't rehearse them until we record them.

Question: John, I remember the launching of the careers of Frank Sinatra and Johnny Ray, Elvis Presley, but this to my mind is unprecedented by the fantastic build-up and publicity and all the press agents. I'm not detracting in any way from the talent that you obviously have. How much do you attribute to Brian Epstein and his public relations men? And how many are there, to your knowledge?

John: We've never had more than one PR guy and Brian's only got one to each client he's got. So they have their own and they don't work together. We've only ever had one. We didn't even have that one until about six months ago.

Question: Do you think Brian Epstein is going to wave his magic wand sometime and include you as a fifth Beatle or a stand-in drummer for Ringo permanently?

Jimmy: That I don't know.

Question: Jimmy, you've played with many groups indeed. Would you like to tell me quickly, it must be at least a dozen?

Jimmy: Yes, I've played with Soul Stapleton, Oscar Raven, Lee Furry, Lou Brown.

Question: Have any of you ever been involved in any zany publicity stunts?

John: No. We've never had to, actually.

Paul: When we first started up we didn't have a manager or anything so we sat around trying to think of them.

Question: What would be your most exciting moments in show business?

George: I can't remember, there's so many ever since last September. Everything's been exciting. I think when we had got to America and found that they'd gone potty on us. And when we'd got back to Britain last October – we'd been touring Sweden – and when this Beatlemania thing started. We hadn't heard about it because we were away. We just landed in London and everyone was there smashing the place up.

Question: In your wildest dreams did you ever think you'd reach the state you have reached now?

John: No. Nobody imagined anything like this.

Question: What about your act tonight, at the Centennial Hall? How long will it last, your particular segment?

Paul: Thirty minutes, each house.

Question: Are you constantly changing your act?

John: Well, depending on what city or state and which song is more popular. Sometimes we change the order.

Question: What about when you played the Royal Variety Performance for Her Majesty? Same act as always?

Paul: Yeah.

Question: Do you get nervous before any shows?

John: All of them.

Question: Any trouble with the hordes of screaming fans outside of the hotel? Do you sleep through all that sort of thing?

John: They never stay out all night screaming.

San Francisco, 19 August 1964

Question: How was your trip?
John: Like any plane trip, boring.
Ringo: We've been going seventeen hours now.
Question: Did you see more of this town than you did last time?
Ringo: I only saw the airport.
Question: Who is your tailor?
Paul: A fellow called Dougie Millings of London.
Question: Do you know his address?
Paul: Great Portland Street in London.
John: He keeps moving with all the profit he makes.
Question: How frightened were you when you looked at the cage you were to be photographed in upon your arrival?
John: It wasn't bad because somebody had been up there and tested it out.
Ringo: In fact, all the press went up and tested it.
Question: Why did you leave so soon?
Ringo: It got cold.
John: Some people said, 'Climb up on the thing and wave', and then they said, 'Get off'. So we came down.
Paul: We're very obedient.
Question: Why did you start the tour in San Francisco?
Ringo: You'll have to ask someone else. We're never told.
John: We don't plan the tours, they're planned for us, you see. We just say we don't want to go to say, Bobboobooland. We leave the rest of the world open and it's all planned for us.
Question: How do you like not having any privacy?
Paul: We do have some.
John: We just had some yesterday, didn't we, Paul? Tell them.
Paul: Yes, yes.
Question: Ringo, you didn't look too happy when you got off the aeroplane. Was there any reason?
Ringo: If you'd been on it fifteen hours, how would you look?
John: How would he look, Ringo?
Ringo: I don't know. Look at him now.
George: A bit of a fried face, if you ask me.
Question: Where are your cameras? Do you still take pictures?
Ringo: Well, John hasn't sold his. I just forgot mine. They got me up too early.
Question: Which one is married?

Ringo: John is married. We'll all get married in the end.
Paul: We will, in the end?
John: You mean, you're not funny like the rumour says!
Ringo: Two or three years, plenty of time.
Paul: Lots of rumours in America.
Question: Have you been writing now?
John: Yes. I wrote all the way over on the plane.
Question: Now that you've made a movie, do you dig the acting bit?
John: We don't profess to be actors.
Paul: It's American, that 'dig'.
John: Dig?
Paul: Dig your baby, daddy!
John: Oh, I get it.
Paul: 'With it.'
Question: In America, the current slang is: tough, boss and dig.
Paul: They change all the time.
Question: What are some of your hip words in England?
John: They're ever changing, you know, madam. Alec Douglas, that's a big one. 'Wilson', everybody does it.
Paul: Harold Wilson.
George: Always.
Paul: Barry Goldwater.
John: That's a new one over there. It means 'drag'.
Question: What does it mean over there?
John: It means happy days are here again.
Question: Ringo, how do you feel about the 'Ringo for President' campaign?
Ringo: It's marvellous.
Question: If you were President, what political promises would you make?
Ringo: I don't know. I'm sort of politically weird.
John: Are you?
Ringo: No, John, believe me.
Paul: I think you should be President, Ringo.
Question: How about you other guys, how do you feel about Ringo being nominated for President?
John: We think he should win. Definitely in favour.
George: Yes.
Question: Would you make them part of your cabinet?
Ringo: I'd have to, wouldn't I?
George: I could be the door.

Ringo: I'd have George as treasurer.
John: I could be the cupboard.
Ringo: George looks after the money.
Question: Are you going to Miami this year?
George: No. We're going to Florida to do a show in Jacksonville at the Gatorbowl.
Question: What sports do you like?
John: We don't like any sports except swimming. We all swim.
Question: When are you going to work on your next book?
John: All the time.
Question: Do you keep little notes?
John: Yes, here and there.
Question: Ringo, can you show us your rings?
Paul: Go go.
John: Show him.
Ringo: Anybody want to see these? And don't keep saying I change them.
Question: What do you boys plan to do in San Francisco other than sleep?
Ringo: Just play the Cow Palace, that's about it.
Question: You're not going to see the town?
Ringo: No, we're not going to see your beautiful city that we've heard so much about.
Question: Why not?
George: It would take too much organisation, wouldn't it?
Ringo: You won't see anything just speeding along in a car.
Question: I started this whole campaign of you running for President . . .
Ringo: It's very nice, but I don't think I'll win.
Question: We think it would be a relief to have you over here.
Ringo: Okay, you get me in and I'll come over here and we'll sort it all out.

The Lost Beatles Interviews

Seattle, 21 August 1964

Question: Are you people disappointed with the reception you got in Seattle compared to the other cities in the United States?
Paul: No, very nice.
Question: How do you enjoy being mobbed?
John: It's okay if you got the police.
Paul: We've never actually been mobbed. In New Zealand though, they got us.
Question: Your film [*A Hard Day's Night*] received very good reviews right across the country. Are you very pleased?
Paul: Yes, of course. What could we say to that, 'No'?
Question: Somebody said that you're like the Marx Brothers. Can you follow that in the film?
Paul: I'd say Ringo is like Groucho.
Question: Do you wish you'd made your success more on how you sound?
John: We did originally. I mean, when you make a record it first gets heard on the radio before they see you.
Question: Do you wish they'd be quiet and let you sing sometimes?
John: Why? They've got the records.
Paul: They paid to come in and if they want to scream, well they paid.
George: And it's part of the atmosphere now.
Question: It was said in Las Vegas and in Frisco that your performance couldn't be heard because of the noise. Do you consider it might hurt your future concerts?
John: It's been going on for years.
Question: How many more years do you think it will go on?
Paul: Don't know.
John: We're not there yet.
Question: Have you any idea? Three, four? What do you think?
George: Till death do us part!
Question: Do you ever get tired of all this and just want to go some place and relax?
Paul: When you see us we're on tour, but we're not always on tour.
Question: Ringo, how are you feeling?
Ringo: Fine, thank you.
Paul: Originally, dangerously ill.
Question: Haven't had any more throat trouble?
Ringo: No, not yet.
Question: There was a report, Ringo, that you were married. Are you?
Ringo: No.

Question: Any plans?

Ringo: Nope.

Question: John, how does your wife like all these girls making all this fuss over you?

John: She doesn't see them.

Question: Ringo, why do you get the most fan mail?

Ringo: Do I?

Question: You do in Seattle.

Ringo: That's really nice. I don't know, perhaps it's because more people write to me.

Question: John, somebody said you borrowed your bathtub scene, in the film, from *Cleopatra*. Is that true?

John: I haven't seen *Cleopatra*.

Ringo: She used milk though, didn't she?

Question: Paul, what are your plans once your notoriety as a Beatle diminishes?

Paul: We never made any plans as a group. None of us has ever bothered planning. We'll just wait and see what happens.

Question: What would you like to do after you're through singing?

Paul: I don't know. Probably John and I will carry on songwriting.

John: I'm not doing it with you.

Paul: Aren't you? Are the Beatles breaking up? I don't know.

Question: Ringo, what do you plan to do?

Ringo: I haven't thought of it yet.

Question: How far booked ahead are you, gentlemen?

George: A few months, I think.

Question: Another American swing in mind?

John: We've got nothing to do with it. We just say, 'Where are we?'

Question: Is there one particular artist or type of music that you fellas follow more closely?

John: Just rock'n'roll, really.

Question: Who are the previous groups that you most like?

Paul: Buddy Holly had a good group.

Question: Did you ever meet him?

John: No.

Question: I understand you took a junket on the way up. Did you take a look at Boulder Dam?

Paul: So that's what it was.

George: I heard about that in school.

Question: Of all your imitators, which one do you have the most respect for, or give the biggest chance of making it?

John: None of the imitators have really done anything at all.

Paul: There's two groups, but they're not imitating really. They're just people who've got longer hair in England now. They're not imitating us, they had long hair before us. Especially in prehistoric days.

Question: Who would be the biggest American stars in Great Britain now?

John: Elvis.

Question: John, have you written a poem after you got back to the United States?

John: No, I never write anything like that.

Paul: Don't you?

John: Oh, no. I never do, you know.

Paul: I wish you would.

Question: Ringo, is there a story behind all the rings on your fingers?

Ringo: That's from me mother, that's from me grandfather. It's a wedding ring, but I'm not married. And these are from two different girls. I've had these on for three years now.

Question: You don't change rings?

Ringo: No. I've got a few more, but I never wear them.

Question: Could you tell us how much you make . . .

John: A lot.

Question: Do you like Donald Duck?

Ringo: No.

Question: Why?

Ringo: I can't understand him.

Paul: I can't either.

Question: George, what do you think England has over America and America over England?

George: It depends on the individual. I might like things about England that you may detest so I think the qualities depend on each individual. Thank you.

New York, 28 August 1964

Question: How do you like this welcome?
Ringo: So this is America. They all seem out of their minds.
Question: Why are your speaking voices different from your singing voices?
George: We don't have a musical background.
Question: Do you like fish and chips?
Ringo: Yes, but I like steak and chips better.
Question: How tall are you?
Ringo: Two feet, nine inches.
Question: Paul, what do you think of columnist Walter Winchell?
Paul: He said I'm married and I'm not.
George: Maybe he wants to marry you!
Question: How did you find America?
Ringo: We went to Greenland and made a left turn.
Question: Is it true you can't sing?
John: (*points to George*) Not me. Him.
Question: Why don't you smile, George?
George: I'll hurt my lips.
Question: What's your reaction to a Seattle psychiatrist's opinion that you are a menace.
George: Psychiatrists are a menace.
Question: What's this about an annual illness, George?
George: I get cancer every year.
Question: Where would you like to go if all the security wasn't necessary?
John: Harlem.
Question: How do you feel about other Beatle-type groups?
John: The Rolling Stones are personal friends of ours. They are most creative and beginning to write good songs.
Question: Do you plan to record any anti-war songs?
John: All our songs are anti-war.
Question: When you do a new song, how do you decide who sings the lead?
John: We just get together and whoever knows most of the words sings lead.
Question: How does it feel, putting on the whole world?
Ringo: We enjoy it.
Paul: We aren't really putting you on.
George: Just a bit of it.

John: How does it feel to be put on?

Question: What's your reaction to composer Aaron Copland who found the Beatles' music interesting and Richard Rodgers who found it boring?

Paul: I like anyone who says he likes our music. I don't mind Richard Rodgers saying he finds it boring, but I must add that I find Richard Rodgers' music boring. And I'm not being nasty, Richard.

Question: George, how do you feel about a nightclub, Arthur, named after your hairstyle?

George: I was proud, until I saw the nightclub.

Question: What do you consider the most important thing in life?

George: Love.

Paul: I once knew a fellow on the Dingle who had two dads. He used to call them number one dad and number two dad. Now apparently number one dad wasn't nice. He used to throw the boy on the fire, which can develop a lot of complexes in a young lad.

Ringo: I remember my uncle putting a red-hot poker on me, and that's no lie. He was trying to frighten me.

Paul: Tell me, Ringo, do all your relatives go round applying red-hot pokers to you?

John: It's the only way they can identify them.

Paul: You see, Ringo comes from a depressed area.

John: Some people call it the slums.

Ringo: No, the slums are farther.

Question: How important is politics to the Beatles?

John: I get spasms of being intellectual. I read a bit about politics but I don't think I'd vote for anyone. No message from any of those phoney politicians is coming through to me.

Question: Is it fun being a Beatle?

George: We've always had laughs. Sometimes we find ourselves hysterical, especially when we're tired. We laugh at soft remarks the majority of people don't get.

Question: What frightens you most?

John: The thing I'm afraid of is growing old. I hate that. You get old and you've missed it somehow. The old always resent the young and vice versa.

Ringo: I'd like to end up, sort of, unforgettable.

Question: Ringo, why are you always so quiet?

Ringo: I don't like talking. It's how I'm built. Some people gab all day and some people play it smogo. I don't mind talking or smiling. I just don't do it very much. I haven't got a smiling face or a talking mouth.

Question: What will you do when the Beatles disband?
John: We're not going to fizzle out in half a day. But afterwards I'm not going to change into a tap-dancing musical. I'll just develop what I'm doing at the moment, although whatever I say now I'll change my mind next week. I mean, we all know that bit about, 'It won't be the same when you're twenty-five.' I couldn't care less. This isn't show business. It's something else. This is different from anything that anybody imagines. You don't go on from this. You do this and then you finish.

Sullivan Riding a Fad

The end of television's 'Beatle' infestation is not in sight. Ed Sullivan, whose CBS variety hour seems to be a wholesale importer of Liverpool singing groups, has signed Gerry and the Pacemakers for a second appearance Sunday and taped a third turn.

Still another group, Billy J. Kramer and the Dakotas will appear on the show next month.

Elderly (i.e.: over 21 years of age) television viewers may be comforted by a statement of Robert Precht, Sullivan's son-in-law, who is the show's producer.

'In our minds, this British thing is something of a phenomenon which has been occurring in the past three or four months,' he said. 'They are extraordinarily attractive with the younger viewers and we felt we should go along with it.'

Precht said that it has always been the policy of the show to present singers whose record sales were near the top of popularity lists – which is where 'the Beatles' and their British brethren are perched.

'We certainly don't want viewers to get the impression that the show is simply a vehicle for rock'n'roll,' Precht said. 'It is one of those fads, and will pass.'

Milwaukee, 4 September 1964

Question: How are you feeling tonight, fellas?

Derek Taylor: We're all ill, the lot of us.

Question: Do you think the pandemonium you cause is ridiculous?

Paul: Nothing's ridiculous when people enjoy themselves. We're not idols, you know. That's what the press makes us out to be, but it's all rubbish. We're just chaps.

Question: Was there any need, from a safety point, to have avoided the fans at the airport?

Paul: We don't think so, no. The police told us we couldn't go past them. It's mean not to let them have a wave. It's a lousy deal . . . a dirty trick.

Question: But the police say it was your manager's decision to duck out.

Paul: It's a lie. Our manager wasn't even on the plane.

George: It was a dirty lying policeman who said that.

Catholic priest: What deficiency in American youth are you supplying?

Paul: There's nothing like that. They just like our records.

Priest: What is your appeal?

Ringo: Our appeal is that we're normal lads.

Priest: What are you rebelling against?

Paul: We're not rebelling against anything.

Priest: Don't you hate your parents?

Paul: No.

Priest: Well, don't you think all teenagers rebel against their parents?

Paul: Well, it's the thing to do at a certain age. Didn't you when you were young?

Priest: Do you hate the press?

Paul: Not at all. They're chaps. They've got a job to do.

Priest: Do you enjoy putting the press on?

Ringo: We're not putting on the press. We're just being ourselves.

Priest: How do the Beatles keep their psychic balance?

George: There's four of us so if one goes a little potty, it's all right.

Priest: Do you prefer to see girls in dresses?

Paul: Yes. Especially if they don't have the figure to take slacks, you know.

Bellaire Store Announces:
NEWEST THING, BEATLE WALLPAPER

President Lincoln's famous quotation, paraphrased roughly that 'for a person who likes that sort of thing, that is the sort of thing they would like', applies aptly to a wallpaper display at the Sherwin-Williams Co. store at 3394 Belmont St in Bellaire.

George Rykoskey, store manager, has learned that there are people, mostly young and mostly female, who 'like that sort of thing', and there are people, mostly old and mostly male, who 'don't like that sort of thing'. There seems to be no middle ground.

The wallpaper is a new item manufactured in England and containing, of all things, pictures of the 'Beatles' in 'living color' and their autographs.

The most pithy comment on the display was by a man who said that its only redeeming feature is that at least the wallpaper doesn't sing.

Kansas City, 17 September 1964

Question: Paul, have the receptions in the United States been what you hoped?

Paul: They've been better, actually. Somebody told us they'd be good, but these have been marvellous, fantastic.

Question: What has pleased you most about the receptions?

Paul: The bigness of them.

Question: Was there any place in America you wanted to see, but didn't get to?

John: New Orleans.

Question: Did you ever date a fan?

John: Yes, I have done, honestly. What more can I say?

Question: Do you fellas hear what you're playing when the screams get going, and how do you keep together?

George: We've heard it all before.

John: It sounds louder to people who haven't been to the shows. We're immune.

Question: Do you do much rehearsing on your tours?

Paul: No, only new numbers.

George: And when we change the act.

Question: You have inspired Beatles hairdos. Do you appreciate seeing these styles on other people?

Ringo: It's quite good. We always change them when we see someone else with them.

Question: Do you plan to change your hairstyle any time soon?

Ringo: Not our hair, just our clothes.

Question: Are you concerned about a poll in Britain which indicates that a group called the Rolling Stones . . .

Ringo: There's many polls. They just won one of them . . .

George: They won that one last year as well.

John: That's their poll. It doesn't make any difference.

Ringo: We don't read the papers.

Question: With the recent anti-smoking campaign, are you trying to give up smoking?

John: No, I never even thought of it. When you got to go, you got to go.

Question: Have you written any new songs lately?

Paul: John and I have written two since we've been here.

Question: On the plane?

Paul: In Atlantic City, actually.

Question: What's the most annoying thing about this whole thing?

Ringo: Not being able to see the fans at the airport.
Paul: Too much security.
Ringo: The plane goes to the far end of the field and we just get put in a car. Away we go, without seeing anybody.
John: Away we go.
Ringo: They blame us. You see, it's not us, it's them.
Question: George, what caused you to throw a Scotch and Coke at a reporter in Los Angeles?
George: He was a very nasty young man.
John: Old man.
George: He'd been told to leave anyway, you see. He insisted on jumping around trying to take pictures and we couldn't see with somebody flashing us in front. So I thought I'd baptise him.
Question: What do you plan to do after the break-up of the Beatles?
Paul: No one's made any plans, but John and I will probably carry on songwriting and George will go into basketball.
George: Or roller skating. I haven't really decided yet.
Question: Ringo, would you show us your grey hair?
Ringo: No. I don't want to be messing it all up as we're on television.
Question: What do you do about the barber?
John: We never go to one.
George: We don't do anything about them when we're not on tour.
Question: Is this the highest guarantee you've had in the United States?
John: I think so, yes.
Derek Taylor: The highest ever in the world, we're told. It may not be so, but we're told.
Question: What care does your hair get?
Paul: Just a bit of combing and washing.
Ringo: Nothing special.
George: We never put any hair oil on it because it makes it go funny, you see.
Question: It was rumoured a couple of days ago you tried to get reservations at a hotel in Springfield and were turned down repeatedly.
John: We don't make them anyway and the ones that have turned us down, well, that's their privilege.
Question: What is the one question you would like to be asked at a press conference?
Paul: I think everything's been asked.
Question: George, whatever became of your car wreck in London? What kind of accident was it?
George: I only just tapped into some fella and knocked the headlamp

in. But the further away you are the worse the damage appears. Over here, I mean, the car was a write-off, but actually it wasn't.

Question: Did you have to pay for anything?

George: No. The other fella's insurance paid because it was his fault. I'm a good driver.

Question: Are you considering making America your home?

Paul: We like the place, but not to live here.

Question: Is there any other particular city you enjoyed visiting?

John: New York.

Paul: New York.

George: Hollywood.

Ringo: Hollywood.

Question: Do you have any favourite entertainers?

John: American soul.

Paul: And Sophie Tucker.

Question: We heard you play cards between performances. What kind do you like?

Ringo: Poker and Crazy Eights.

Question: I'd like to ask Paul how his feud with Walter Winchell is doing.

Paul: It's not a feud, he's just soft. I give up talking to him.

Question: How much hysteria do you feel is real and how much is pretended by the little girls that adore you?

John: Doesn't matter.

Paul: There's a lot of it in the papers that's not real. There's also a lot, I think, that is.

Question: What's the origin of the name Beatles? Why did you choose that?

John: I thought of it. There's no reason, same as you pick a name for anything, really.

Question: John, how does your wife feel about girls screaming and running after you?

John: She knows they never catch me.

Question: Ringo, I heard you were having trouble with your throat. Is it all right now?

Ringo: Yes. It's fine. I haven't had any trouble for the last two months.

Question: Have you ever measured your hair to see who's got the longest?

Beatles in unison: No.

George: I think mine is, anyway, because it grows faster than the others.

John: I'm usually a close second.

Question: Ringo, are you going to have your tonsils taken out, and have you had that offer yet from a girl to send her the tonsils?

Ringo: We got the telegram, but I don't think I'm going to give them to her.

John: We're going to auction them off.

Paul: That's disgusting.

Question: We'd like to know if there's any truth to the rumour, John, that you might leave the group?

John: No. I don't know where it started, it just appeared somewhere.

Ringo: We can hardly get rid of him anyway.

Question: Did you make any new records while you were in Hollywood?

Paul: We did do an album for a souvenir, but it's not for general release. It was so terrible, that's why.

Question: Paul, how do you feel about reports that say you are conceited?

Paul: They're true.

Question: Is there anything you wanted to do in Kansas that you didn't get a chance to, anyone in particular you wanted to see? Mrs Truman?

John: Not particularly, no.

Question: Have you bought any new clothes in the United States?

John: A guy on the radio yesterday described this as a typical Liverpool outfit. I got it in Key West.

Question: Do you ever wear a tie?

John: Me? Yeah, when I find it.

George: I've got one of his suits.

John: I can never find my stuff.

Question: Which do you like more, the fans or the money?

John: We'll still have the money and we'll miss the fans, they'll be the ones who'll have gone. The money will still be there thankfully.

Question: I can't find out who the opening acts are with you.

Paul: The Exciters, Clarence Frogman Henry, the Bill Black Combo and Jackie De Shannon.

Question: Another English group is going to play Kansas City, the Dave Clark Five. Are you going to play with them?

Ringo: We know them.

Question: How did they come out in the poll?

Ringo: The *Melody Maker*, you're talking about?

Paul: They didn't win.

John: It varies. Each little paper has its own readership so the votes go one way or another every year.

Question: Did you talk with Charlie Finley when he was in Frisco?
George: I met him this morning. Brian Epstein was the only one who saw him in San Francisco.
Question: He said he was very fond of you men. What's your reaction?
Ringo: Oh, we're fond of him now.
George: We like his baseball.
Question: Ringo, what do you do when you're confined to your hotel room?
Ringo: We just sit around, watch telly, radio . . .
John: Watch the radio!
Ringo: . . . or play cards. Anything at all. We even talk to each other.
Question: How much are the American tax authorities earning off you?
Beatles in unison: Nothing!
Question: How about the British government?
John: They're getting a lot.
Ringo: We'll end up with about ten dollars when they get through.
Question: Is it true you all are writing books and, if so, what's the subject matter?
Paul: No, John's the only one who writes.
Ringo: We haven't learned how yet.
Question: Since your return to America this time have you been asked to appear on Ed Sullivan's programme?
Derek: Yes, they were, but it hasn't been fitted in yet.
Question: You were saying earlier that the two of you might continue on and the rest of you break up the act. Is there a date you are going to break up?
Paul: If it's got to happen, John and I would probably carry on song-writing, we didn't mean singing.
Question: How long do you think it will be before it does happen?
John: Just another role to me.
Paul: No idea really. It could happen tomorrow after the Kansas show.
Question: When you were in Florida did you talk with Cassius Clay?
John: We only met him once with the kind of publicity stunt that he's best at.
Paul: It was organised by the newspapers down there. They asked us. He's a good fella, isn't he? Big!
Question: Do you like baseball?
John: Not particularly, no.
George: Very good game, Mr Finley. Very nice, Mr Finley.
John: Only on TV.

George: Great game.

Ringo: Nice holiday, throw the ball, have a cigarette and throw a ball, ten minutes later throw another ball.

Question: Did Charlie Finley ask you to wear Kelly green and gold baseball outfits?

George: No. We wouldn't wear them anyway. Not even for three hundred thousand.

Question: Are you going to do another picture?

George: Next February, but nothing else has been decided.

Question: No date, no title?

George: No date, no title, no script, no other people to act in it.

John: No nothing, just us.

Question: Would any of you care to give us your views, I don't mean to be smart by this, on religion or politics?

John: We're not interested in either.

Question: Is it being planned to do a movie of your whole life, school, the Cavern Club . . .

John: No. They couldn't put that kind of thing on the screen. Not yet, anyway.

Question: One of you said you didn't like politics, it was like beer, you didn't like the taste. And in Chicago you made the comment that if you were for anyone in the election you'd be for LBJ.

John: We said Eisenhower, actually.

Question: What about in your own country? You're going back to a general election campaign.

Ringo: We're not going to vote over there.

Paul: None of us do.

John: If we can find out which one takes the least tax I'll vote for them.

Question: In New Orleans you met Fats Domino. Could you tell us how that came about?

John: Frogman Henry said he'd try and arrange for us to meet him, we've always liked him. He brought him round with a friend, stayed about an hour and had some shots taken for his kids.

John: He's marvellous, we sang a song with him.

Question: Paul, you lost your driver's licence, how did you do it?

Paul: I lost it a year ago. I just got it back, actually. For speeding three times. If they catch you three times you lose it. Got caught!

Ringo: He wasn't fast enough!

Question: Why did you want to go to New Orleans?

John: Well, it's the clubs and that, the sounds, man.

Question: Ringo, what do you think of Jayne Mansfield?

Ringo: She's a drag.

Paul: Ringo!

George: I second him.

Derek: It's the word D - R - A - G and it means simply, bore.

John: It's American.

Question: What about Mamie Van Doren?

George: We never met her. Her publicist wasn't as good as Jayne Mansfield's.

Question: What is your reaction to girls who come up to your hotel and tear up the sheets and anything you've discarded, like cigarette butts?

John: If they do it after we leave, it's all right.

Ringo: Not if they're ripping them while we're still asleep.

Question: With all these girls chasing you all over the world, who's the most exciting woman you've ever met?

John: Ringo's mother was pretty hot. I'm only joking.

Question: Do you smoke American cigarettes and, if so, what kind?

George: Yeah, we like American ciggies and we smoke filters, but we're not advertising anybody's cigarettes unless they give us a few million free.

Question: Do you do anything for free?

John: Yeah, charity shows.

Question: George, I heard that in the Lafayette Hotel a girl climbed eight storeys up the side of the building and jumped in the window, grabbed you in your nightclothes and was then arrested.

George: No. It's untrue. I heard a noise in the next room and it was the policemen chasing her around. She jumped on Ringo, actually.

Ringo: That bird was running round the room and I was chasing her!

Question: How many of your records have been sold?

John: We were told eighty-three . . .

Ringo: Eighty-five.

John: Eighty-five, sorry.

Question: Million?

John: Yes.

The Lost Beatles Interviews

Dallas, 18 September 1964

Question: Although you haven't seen much of Dallas, how do you like it?

Paul: Well, it's mighty fine, partner. Mighty fine.

Question: Ringo, do you have any political affiliations?

Ringo: No, I don't even smoke.

Question: What kind of girls do you prefer?

Ringo: My wife.

Question: What kind of girl is she?

Ringo: A nice girl.

Question: What kind of girl do you like, Paul?

Paul: John's wife.

John: Nobody likes a smart aleck.

Question: Do you have any books coming out?

Ringo: John's the one with the books.

John: I've got one coming out next year, but I haven't written it yet.

Question: What's the name of it?

John: I don't know. I haven't written it.

Question: What kind of books do you like to do?

John: Ah . . . rubbish.

Ringo: I'm writing a detective novel.

John: Yeah, he's writing a detective book.

Question: Last night, you had a lot of trouble getting into the Cabana. Did any of you get hurt at all?

George: I got punched in me face a few times. But, I mean, that's part of life, isn't it?

Question: One of the reviews of your book [*In His Own Write*] says that you're being an anarchist. Would you say you are one?

John: I don't even know what it means.

Question: Comparing the receptions you've received all over the United States and taking into consideration the time of night, how was the reception here in Dallas?

Paul: It was hectic, but nice.

Question: Do you like your cowboy hats?

John: Hey, sure do!

Question: Ringo, in California the girls ate some grass you walked on. How do you feel about that?

Ringo: I just hope they don't get indigestion.

Question: What is your opinion of Mods and Rockers?

John: They should be locked up.

Question: How does it feel to make over a thousand dollars a minute?
George: It's one of the very best feelings in life.
Question: What do you think of American girls?
Ringo: Well, there's sure lots of them.
Question: Ringo, are you going to give the young lady your tonsils when you have them out?
Ringo: They're no good to me any more.
Question: Which one of you is most anxious to get home?
John: Probably me, I'm married.
Question: Is there ever any jealousy between you, during the act happening on stage?
Ringo: No, not yet.
Question: How do you like Texas?
John: Swell.
Question: Have you ridden a horse yet?
Paul: No, but we plan to. Don't worry.
Question: George, are you trying to make your black curl a youth symbol like Ringo's rings or Paul's eyes?
George: Yeah, that's why I'm wearing one now.
Question: When do you have time to write your songs?
John: We write them in hotel rooms after the show sometimes.
Paul: Any time we've got to spare, really.
Question: Have you had any fish'n'chips since you've been in the States?
Paul: No, not even a cup of tea.
Question: How long y'all gonna sing for us tonight?
John: We do about thirty minutes, cousin.
Question: Are you disappointed in your American tour because you've been forced to spend so much time in seclusion because of your fans?
George: We expect any tour we do to be secluded and not having much of a chance to see the cities and things. . . .
John: Because we're here to work.

Beatles Select Gifts in Private

LONDON – Harrods, the London store where Queen Elizabeth II goes shopping, allowed the Beatles to do their Christmas shopping after hours behind locked doors Thursday night.

That privilege has never before been granted, not even to the Queen, Jacqueline Kennedy or visiting royalty and nobility. They all had to jostle with Harrods' regular customers.

Queen Elizabeth Friday spent two hours picking out presents, but other shoppers were there at the time.

The management feared that mob scenes might erupt if they allowed the Beatles to shop during normal opening hours.

John Passes L-Test

Beatle John Lennon passed his driving test first time at Weybridge, Surrey, today. He drove his white Austin Mini. 'I left the Rolls at home,' he said.

John had only seven hours' tuition before taking his test, taken by Weybridge's senior examiner, Mr Scrine.

His instructor, Mr Paul Wilson, said: 'He was one of the most apt pupils I have had to teach in my 30 years' experience of driving instruction. He has done very well in such a short time. He has been very quick.'

Afterwards, John said: 'I'm very pleased I passed.'

John's wife, Cynthia, passed her test at the second attempt last October.

The Lennons live at St George's Hill, Weybridge.

15 February 1965

Beatles in Birthday Honours List

Queen Elizabeth has included the Beatles in her birthday honours list, naming them members of the Most Excellent Order of the British Empire. They are the first group of pop singers to make the honours list. Henceforth, they may use the initials MBE after their name.

Daily Mail, 11 June 1965

Beatle Critic Dumps 12 Medals

LONDON – A colonel set a record for anti-Beatleism today by sending 12 medals back to Queen Elizabeth II.

Col Frederick Wagg, 74, veteran of two world wars, joined the protest movement against the award of the MBE – Member of the Order of the British Empire – to the long-haired pop quartet.

He also resigned from Prime Minister Harold Wilson's Labour Party and cancelled a $33,600 bequest to it.

'Decorating the Beatles,' said the colonel, 'has made a mockery of everything this country stands for.

'I've heard them sing and play and I think they're terrible.'

MBE holders have mailed their heavy silver crosses back to Buckingham Palace.

Wagg's jesture dwarfed them all. Along with protests to the Queen, the Queen Mother and Prime Minister Wilson he sent:

The Mons Star, the General Service Medal and the Victory Medal from World War I; the North West Frontier Medal from Indian Army service between the wars; the 1939–40 Star, Battle of the Atlantic Star, North Africa Star, Defence Medal and Victory Medal from World War II; and the Belgian Order of Leopold and the French Croix de Guerre and Croix de Résistance.

He said he sent back the foreign decorations because they were granted with royal approval. Britons may not accept foreign medals without royal permission.

The only medal he is keeping, he said, is the Croix de Lorraine which Gen. Charles de Gaulle handed to him personally after World War II.

Hundreds of letters about the Beatles award cascaded into the Prime Minister's office at No. 10 Downing Street, and Buckingham Palace, officials said, but some of the opposition came from supporters of rival pop groups.

London, 1965

Question: Well, gentlemen, first of all, many congratulations on receiving your MBE. The whole country seems very delighted indeed. How do you feel about it, Paul?

Paul: Delighted, indeed. I'm delighted everyone's delighted. I love it.

Question: Is it fun for you?

Paul: Yeah. Of course. It would be for you too, wouldn't it? My uncle woke up one morning and said, 'MmmBbbEee'. You know, it's great.

Question: Ringo, how did you first hear about it?

Ringo: Um, well, we heard about it six weeks ago. We got the forms to fill in and then we knew we were going to get it two days ago.

Question: How did these forms come? Straight through the post, or what?

Ringo: Just in brown envelopes delivered by hand, I think, to one of Brian's secretaries.

George: I'll tell him. They were sent from the Prime Minister at 10 Downing Street to our manager's office; and they were delivered from there to Twickenham where we were filming.

John: *Help!*

George: A day later, when we found them we thought we were being called up for the army and then we opened them and found out we weren't.

Question: Why is the MBE awarded?

Paul: I don't know. In fact I know nothing about it, just that we've got it and it's very nice to have. I don't think about it. Maybe people may think of it. But it doesn't make me any more respectable. I'm still a scruff.

Question: Well, I was wondering about that, Ringo. How do you feel about going to the Palace in your morning suit and all that?

Ringo: I don't mind. It'll be all right, when I buy one.

Question: You haven't got one then?

Ringo: No, not yet. I've got an evening suit. If that will do.

Question: Oh, I don't think it will.

Ringo: Well then, I'll just go in me pyjamas.

Canadian MP Returns MBE

Hector Dupuis, a member of the Canadian House of Commons representing a Montreal district, has announced he is returning his MBE
medal because the Queen has awarded one to the Beatles. He claimed
English royalty has placed him on the 'same level as vulgar nin-
compoops'. Mr Dupuis received his medal for his work as director of
the selective service in Quebec.

Montreal Gazette, 14 June 1965

London, 1965

Question: What was your reaction when you heard the news about your MBEs?

Ringo: There's a proper medal as well as the letters, isn't there? I will keep it to wear when I'm old. It's the sort of thing you want to keep.

John: I thought you had to drive tanks and win wars to get the MBE.

George: I didn't think you got this sort of thing for playing rock'n'roll.

Paul: I think it's marvellous. What does this make me, dad?

Question: What do you say about Hector Dupuis turning in his medal?

George: If Dupuis doesn't want the medal, he had better give it to us. Then we can give it to our manager, Brian Epstein. MBE really stands for 'Mr Brian Epstein'.

Question: Why do you think you got the medal?

John: I reckon we got it for exports, and the citation should have said so. Look, if someone had got an award for exporting millions of dollars' worth of fertiliser or machine tools, everyone would have applauded. So why should they knock us?

The Royal Investiture, 26 October 1965

The Queen: (*to Paul*) How long have you been together now?
Paul: Oh, for many years.
Ringo: Forty years.
The Queen: (*to Ringo*) Are you the one who started it?
Ringo: No, I was the last to join. I'm the little fellow.
The Queen: (*to John*) Have you been working hard lately?
John: No, we've been on a holiday.

[*Outside Buckingham Palace*]

Paul: We've played many palaces including Frisco's Cow Palace. But never this one before. It's a keen pad and I liked the stuff. Thought they'd be dukes and things but they were just fellas.
Question: What about the Queen?
Paul: She's lovely, great. She was very friendly. She was just like a mum to us.
Question: Were you nervous?
John: Not as much as some of the other people.
Question: How did the other medal recipients act towards your award?
John: One formally-dressed, middle-aged winner walked up to us after the ceremony and said, 'I want your autographs for my daughter but I don't know what she sees in you.' So we gave him our autographs.
Question: How did you know what to do during the ceremony?
John: This big fellow drilled us. Every time he got to Ringo he kept cracking up.
Question: What will you do with your medals?
Paul: What you normally do with medals. Put them in a box.

Toronto, 17 August 1965

Question: What do you think about your fans reading *Playboy*?
Ringo: Our young fans aren't supposed to read *Playboy*.
John: It's you, their fathers, who should hide it from them.
Ringo: If their fathers read it, send us the back issues.
Question: Everybody has a theory on why you affect crowds the way you do. Do you have one?
Paul: No, not at all.
Question: Does marriage agree with you?
Ringo: Yes it does.
John: Yes.
Question: How did you propose to your wife?
Ringo: Same as anybody else. Are you married? If you're not you'll find out.
Question: I want to get married and I want to do it right.
Ringo: You want to do it right?
Question: How do I do it?
John: Use both hands.
Question: Ringo, would you still like to be a disc jockey?
Ringo: Oh yeah, yeah.
Question: I'd like to ask Mr Lennon why he took up writing and who's your biggest influence in that field?
John: I don't know why I took it up and I haven't got a hero. Well, I suppose maybe Lewis Carroll.
Question: Which film did you enjoy doing more, *Help*! or *A Hard Day's Night*?
George: We enjoyed both of them actually. I think the new one we liked a bit more because we knew more about the film business, you see.
Question: Do you prefer the shorter tour this year as opposed to last? Does it give you more time to rest?
Ringo: Yes.
Question: What kind of shampoo do you use?
Ringo: Anything we can borrow.
Question: I'd like to know what happened to the colour of John Lennon's hair.
John: It's covered in sweat, you see, so it looks darker than it is.
Question: Recently, on the *Musical Express* winners' concert and at Shea Stadium, you wore military-type uniforms. Did you design them yourselves?

Paul: No, we were in the Bahamas and I had nothing to wear so I borrowed a soldier's outfit off the film and somebody said, 'Wow, that's okay'. So I said, 'Right'.

John: That's how it happened.

George: Then we had them made.

Question: Would you boys ever like to do a tour with completely English acts over here?

Ringo: We usually do in Britain. There's quite a lot of them over there.

Question: Do you think that travelling with women companions hurts your image?

Paul: We're not travelling with women companions and anyway, we haven't got an image.

Question: Of all the countries you've travelled, which audience has been the most responsive?

John: Gravelbede!

Question: Where?

Paul: America, actually, because there's more people. It's the biggest place.

Question: Paul, are you planning to marry Jane Asher?

Paul: I haven't got any plans. That's all there is, but everyone keeps saying I have. So maybe they know more than me.

Question: Would you like to visit Niagara Falls?

George: We've seen the photographs.

Question: What was your reaction to your greeting in Rome?

John: We had a good greeting, contrary to rumours over here. There was nobody at the airport because we arrived at five in the morning, but the show was a sell-out. So sit down!

Question: Did you boys have any difficult moments during the filming of *Help!*?

George: Only trying to get up to the studio on time.

Question: Have you had a chance to enjoy your success?

Ringo: Yeah, all the time. (*Laughs.*)

Question: Are you bored with this life, or do you still find it exciting?

John: We still like it or we wouldn't be touring.

Question: Are you going to have any more Beatles' Christmas Shows?

John: Ask Mr Christmas Epstein.

George: Mr Epstein, may I have a Mr Epstein Christmas Show?

John: I'll give him something to work on.

Question: Do you plan to continue writing, and if so, do you have a medium in mind?

John: Yeah, because I think we're under contract now, but I've got nothing in mind. It will be the same stuff, only backwards.

Ringo: Nothing in his mind, you get that?

Question: Individually, how do you like being the Beatles?

Ringo: Simply wonderful to be here.

John: We like it or we'd be the Rolling Stones.

Question: How long do you plan to continue doing concert tours?

Paul: It's up to Brian and the people who buy the tickets.

John: Until people stop coming to see us.

Question: Will Paul tell us a little bit about his marriage plans?

Paul: You've just asked me. The thing is, you see, everyone keeps saying I'm married or I'm divorced or I've got fifty children, but I haven't . . .

Ringo: You've only got forty.

Paul: I haven't said anything, people keep making it up, so if you'd like to make it up, I'll sue you.

Question: Have any of you boys had a mental block on stage?

John: It happens, yes.

Paul: What?

John: I didn't know what key I was in last night.

Question: Ringo, Gerry Shotberg, the photographer, questioned whether or not you were still taking pictures. You said, 'No, because I'm bored and all I can take pictures of is hotel rooms.' Do you feel you boys have to stay in too much?

Ringo: The question is, why have I really stopped taking photographs!

Question: Well, I realise it just gets boring staying in the hotel room.

Ringo: It's not boring staying in the hotel room, it's boring taking photos in a hotel room.

Question: We realise that John and Paul are both prolific songwriters and we get the impression that their songs are written very quickly. How far in advance do you compose them?

Paul: It depends. If we feel like writing a lot then we'll get ahead of what we've got to do, but mainly we just write to order if we're doing a new film or LP. [Brian] makes us work.

Question: Do you mind that you can't hear yourself think when you're singing?

John: How do you know we can't hear ourselves think? You weren't in our minds, were you? We can hear ourselves think or we would forget what we were doing.

Paul: The thing about singing, it doesn't matter because people pay to come in and know what they want. They don't pay to come in and do what other people want them to do. They're having a good time, so leave them alone. Up with the workers!

Question: Do you call what they do having a good time?

Paul: Why not? It's only you who don't!

John: They must be or they wouldn't be coming again and again. If they were having a bad time like you they wouldn't come.

Question: Do you realise a lot of English groups are stealing your limelight?

John: Yeah, it's terrible.

Question: Ringo, are you Jewish?

Ringo: Stand up that man or woman.

John: He's having his Bar Mitzvah tomorrow.

Ringo: No, I'm not Jewish.

Question: If there had been National Service in England would the Beatles have existed?

Ringo: No, because we would have all been in the army.

Paul: Unless we all got in the same hut.

Question: Would Ringo consider changing his hairstyle?

Ringo: For what? I'm quite happy.

Question: What do you think of the news media keeping you in front of the public?

John: They're doing very well and without them people wouldn't know what we're doing, so that's it.

Question: I was talking to Bill Haley at the start of this show and he was mentioning getting a gig together via Telstar with all the English and American groups. Who do you think would win in such a challenge?

John: By the fans at the moment, the English would win. But if we judged it, the Americans would probably win.

New York, 1965

Question: Were you worried about the oversized roughnecks who tried to infiltrate the airport crowd on your arrival?

Ringo: That was us!

Question: How do you add up success?

Beatles, in unison: Money.

Question: What will you do when Beatlemania subsides?

John: Count the money. I don't suppose I think much about the future. I don't really give a damn. Though now we've made it, it would be a pity to get bombed. It's selfish, but I don't care too much about humanity; I'm an escapist. Everybody's always drumming on about the future, but I'm not letting it interfere with my laughs, if you see what I mean.

Question: What is your opinion on the atom bomb?

Paul: It's disturbing that people should go around blowing up, but if an atom bomb should explode I'd say, 'Oh well'. No point in saying anything else, is there? People are so crackers. I know the bomb is ethically wrong, but I won't go around crying. I suppose I could do something like wearing those 'ban the bomb' things, but it's something, like religion, that I don't think about. It doesn't fit in with my life.

Question: Are you ever in any danger during your concerts?

Paul: I was got once by a cigarette lighter. Clouted me right in the eye and closed my eye for the stay. In Chicago a purple and yellow stuffed animal, a red rubber ball and a skipping rope were plopped up on stage. I had to kick a carton of Winston's out of the way when I played. And I saw a cigarette lighter go flying past me in Detroit's Olympia Stadium.

Question: Don't you worry about all that?

Paul: It's okay, as long as they throw the light stuff, like paper.

Question: Would you ever accept a girl in your group if she could sing, play an instrument and wear the Beatle haircut?

Ringo: How tall is she?

Question: Beatle-licensed products have grossed millions and millions of dollars in America alone; Beatle wigs, Beatle hats, Beatle T-shirts, Beatle egg-cups, Beatlenut ice-cream . . .

Ringo: Any time you spell beetle with an 'a' in it, we get some money.

Question: What are your favourite programmes on American television?

Paul: '*News en español*' from Miami. '*Popeye*', '*Bullwinkle*'. All the cultural stuff.

John: I like American TV because you can get eighteen stations, but you can't get a good picture on any one of them.

Question: George, is the place you were brought up a bit like Greenwich Village?

George: No. More like the Bowery.

Question: Do any of you have ulcers?

George: None that we've noticed.

Question: How come you were turned back by Immigration?

John: We had to be deloused.

Question: Who in the world would the Beatles like to meet more than anyone else?

Ringo: Santa Claus.

Question: Paul, you look like my son.

Paul: You don't look a bit like my mother.

Question: Why aren't you wearing a hat?

George: Why aren't you wearing a tie?

Question: Is it true that on one flight the stewardess broke up a pillow fight among you guys and got clobbered on the head?

George: I'm not really sure where she got hit. She did make us break it up, though. Remember that house we stayed in at Harlech?

Paul: No. Which one?

George: Yes you do! There was a woman who had a dog with no legs. She used to take it out in the morning for a slide.

Question: Do teenagers scream at you because they are, in effect, revolting against their parents?

Paul: They've been revolting for years.

John: I've never noticed them revolting.

Question: Do you have any special messages for the Prime Minister and your parents?

John: Hello, Alec.

George: Hello, Mudda.

Ringo: Hello, fellas.

Question: Did you really use four-letter words on the tourists in the Bahamas?

John: What we actually said was, 'Gosh'.

Paul: We may have also said, 'Heavens!'

John: Couldn't have said that, Paul. More than four letters.

Question: Why don't all four of the Beatles ever sing together?

George: Well, we try to start out together, anyway.

Question: What does each Beatle consider his most valued possession?

John: Our lives.

55

Question: What do you do with your money?

Ringo: We bury it.

George: We hide it.

Paul: We don't see it. It goes to our office.

John: We pay a lot of taxes.

Question: Do you wear wigs?

John: If we do they must be the only ones with real dandruff.

Question: How do you feel about teenagers imitating you with Beatle wigs?

John: They're not imitating us because we don't wear Beatle wigs.

Question: Where did you get your hairstyle?

Paul: From Napoleon. And Julius Caesar too. We cut it any time we feel like it.

Ringo: We may even do it now.

Question: Are you wearing wigs or real hair?

Ringo: Hey, where's the police?

Paul: Take her out!

George: Our hair's real. What about yours, lady?

Question: What would happen if you all switched to crewcuts?

John: It would probably be the end of the act.

Yank Who Makes Beatle Films Funny is Sold on the Boys as Individuals

NEW YORK — The Beatles are being exploited by Walter Shenson, but they don't mind a bit.

Mr Shenson, an American ex-film publicist, produced the Liverpudlians' first and very successful movie, *A Hard Day's Night*, and their second, *Help!*, which deserves equal success. His exploitation of the Beatles consists in making their films as funny as possible.

'In Hollywood,' Mr Shenson said, 'there is a tendency to say goodbye to actors when filming is done. I exploit the Beatles to the fullest, and they are willing because we all care.'

'After a picture is finished, we find places where we can add 20 per cent or more humour to it. So we dub dialogue to fit.

'With both pictures, we have brought the boys to the studio and shown them a rough assemblage of the film.

'Then we'll find a spot where something is needed and say: "How about something funny?" They go up to an open mike and start building something right there. They are very quick, sharp boys.'

Mr Shenson, whose first production after he quit being a publicist was *The Mouse That Roared* with Peter Sellers, is a big Beatle fan.

He enjoys talking about the boys, as follows:

'They are so bright and perceptive. After their first picture was so well received, they came to my office with their manager Brian Epstein. I asked them if there was anything they wanted for the second picture.

'They said, "Well, we know what we don't want." They decided *A Hard Day's Night* was in black and white, their next should be colour.

'The last picture had a lot of screaming fans, so they didn't want any in this. The last picture showed them singing before audiences, and this time they didn't want that.

'The Beatles are not a four-headed monster, they are individuals who dig each other. These boys really love each other.

'There is absolutely no competition among them, no desire to top each other. If one boy makes a joke, the others fall down laughing.

'But despite their difference in personality, there are a lot of adjectives that describe them all. They are witty, outrageous, bright, terribly talented, rude. They are scary because they have all this and are still in their early twenties.

'Yet when you are a generation older, as I am, and you are with them, you become their age, they are so compelling.

'They are so close they have developed a shorthand language so that they can be talking about you in your presence and you won't know it.

'Unlike you and me, they can't go out shopping or to a movie. They love movies, so I would give them private screenings of all the latest. Now each one has his own projector and I lend them prints.

'They can't really go out without being recognised. Paul says he can occasionally, if he sticks his hair under a cap and dresses casually.

'We had one scene for *Help!* in which the boys run into a store. We decided to film it on location, using a good Bond Street store. We picked a Sunday and the boys did their scene.

'While the crew was changing camera locations to shoot the scene again, the boys stayed in the store. John took one look around – he is furnishing a new house – and said, "I'll take that and that and that".

'In the seven minutes it took for the new set-up, John bought a desk, a grandmother clock (he was very proud that it was a grandmother and not grandfather clock) and leather-bound sets of George Bernard Shaw and A.A. Milne.

'The deal the Beatles and I have with United Artists calls for three pictures. It's always a challenge to find something new to do for these boys.

'I don't want to sound pompous, but I feel a great obligation not to louse them up. We'll have a meeting as soon as they get back from their American tour, to discuss their next film.

'They have bought a book by Dick Condon called *A Talent for Loving*. It's a Western satire, and that may be their next picture. They have already asked me if I can find someone to teach them the "fast draw".

'This is part of kids loving Westerns, and they are kids. Ringo has also announced to me that he wants to wear all black.

'The Beatles come to my house. I have two little boys and they die because they can't call their friends and tell them who is visiting. Ringo even taught my older boy, who is 12, how to play the drums.

'My older boy is a classical music bug, but he has pictures of the Beatles all over his walls. However, in one corner, as his rebellion, he has a picture of Beethoven.

'You know what I like about the Beatles? After they finished both pictures, each one came up to me, after seeing the finished product, and said, "Don't worry. No matter what the critics or public say about the picture, we love it."

'Maybe security comes with success, but most successful performers don't say things like that to the producer. That incident sums up the warmth and niceness of these boys.'

Rolling Stones Succeed
BEATLES TOP POPS NO MORE

LONDON – The Beatles, winners of the 1964 *Top of the Pops* championship, dropped to third place in the 1965 competition. The championship table is computed by the *New Musical Express* which awards 30 points for a top spot in the weekly charts, down to one point for an entry at number 30.

Although the Beatles occupied the top spot in the charts for 15 of the 52 weeks of 1965, the Rolling Stones lingered longer at lower positions to clinch the 1965 honours.

The Rolling Stones collected 836 points, followed by the Seekers with 813 and the Beatles coming in third with 760.

Sandie Shaw in fifth place was the only girl in the top ten. Most popular Americans were Bob Dylan and Gene Pitney at 11 and 12. Elvis Presley crept in at 18.

The record of the year was 'Tears', a 1920s' ballad, by comedian Ken Dodd, which sold more than a million copies in Britain and has been in the parade for 18 weeks.

The Lost Beatles Interviews

John *vs.* Jesus *vs.* the World, 1966

'In the only popularity poll in Jesus' time, he came out second to Barabbas . . .'

The Rt Rev. Kenneth Maguire,
Angelica Bishop of Montreal

'Christianity will go. It will vanish and shrink. I needn't argue about that; I'm right and will be proved right. We're more popular than Jesus now; I don't know which will go first, rock'n'roll or Christianity. Jesus was all right, but his disciples were thick and ordinary. It's them twisting it that ruins it for me.' (John)

'John Lennon's remarks were taken out of context and did not accurately reflect the article or the subject as it was discussed. What actually occurred was a lengthy conversation between me and John in which the subject of Christianity was discussed. He observed that the power of Christianity was on the decline in the modern world and that things had reached such a ridiculous state that human beings – such as the Beatles – could be worshipped more religiously by people than their own religion. He did not mean to boast about the Beatles' fame.' (Maureen Cleave, journalist)

'Beatle-burning teenagers, joined by a surprising number of adults, turned a huge pile of Beatle lore, records and pictures into a pile of ashes near Radio Station KLUE Friday night. Tony Bridge, station owner, joined the campaign along with staff members. Lowell Wolfe, station manager, aided Donna Woods, of Longview, at the bonfire, spreading kerosene on the pile.' (*Longview Texas Morning Journal*)

'I've nothing really against the ideas of Christianity and their ways. I suppose I wouldn't make that Jesus remark today. I think about things differently. I think Buddhism is simple and more logical than Christianity, but I've nothing against Jesus.' (John)

'I will revoke the membership of any member of my church who agrees with John Lennon's remarks about Jesus.' (Reverend Thurman Babbs, Cleveland, Ohio)

'Deport the Beatles. They are unworthy of a decent American reception. They should be fumigated. They are undesirables and enemy agents to the Christian cause. They have been a corrupting influence. Parents in our country have no time for their lousy, low and lewd forms of so-called entertainment. Let them go back to Britain!' (Carl L. Estes, newspaper publisher)

'I'll let Julian learn all about Jesus when he goes to school, but I'll also tell him there have been lots of other Jesuses. I'll tell him about the Buddhist ones; they're good men as well.' (John)

'When I heard in *Datebook* that John Lennon was playing the role of Christ in *The Jesus Saga*, I nearly died. I have always admired the Beatles, but this has shaken my loyalty to the core. It was shocking enough to hear John announce that heaven-shaking boast that the Beatles were bigger than Jesus, but now to hear that that hypocrite is actually playing the role of the greatest man on earth, well, it's enough to make the angels wipe their glasses and clean out their ears! For John's sake I do hope John has repented that statement a million times.' (Jennifer, Waco, Texas)

The 'Say Sorry' Press Conference

John: Look, I wasn't saying the Beatles are better than God or Jesus. I said 'Beatles' because it's easy for me to talk about Beatles. I could have said 'TV' or 'the cinema', 'motorcars' or anything popular and I would have got away with it. My views on Christianity are directly influenced by *The Passover Plot* by Hugh J. Schofield. The premise is that Jesus' message had been garbled by his disciples and twisted for a variety of self-serving reasons by those who followed, to the point where it has lost validity for many in the modern age. The passage which caused all the trouble was part of a long profile Maureen Cleave was doing for the *London Evening Standard*. Then, the mere fact that it was in *Datebook* [magazine] changed its meaning that much more.

Question: What was your own formal religious background?

John: Normal Church of England, Sunday School and church. But there was actually nothing going on in the church I went to. Nothing really touched us.

Question: How about when you got older?

John: By the time I was nineteen, I was cynical about religion and never even considered the goings-on in Christianity. It's only in the last two years that I, all the Beatles, have started looking for something else. We live in a moving hothouse. We've been mushroom-grown, forced to grow up a bit quick, like having thirty- to forty-year-old heads in twenty-year-old bodies. We had to develop more sides, more attitudes. If you're a busman, you usually have a busman's attitude. But we had to be more than four mopheads up there on stage. We had to grow up or we'd have been swamped.

Question: Just what were you trying to get across with your comments then, sir?

John: I'm not anti-God, anti-Christ or anti-religion. I was not saying we are greater or better.

Question: Mr Lennon, do you believe in God?

John: I believe in God, but not as one thing, not as an old man in the sky. I believe that what people call God is something in all of us. I believe that what Jesus, Mohammed, Buddha and all the rest said was right. It's just that the translations have gone wrong.

Question: Are you sorry about your statement concerning Christ?

John: I wasn't saying whatever they're saying I was saying. I'm sorry I said it, really. I never meant it to be a lousy anti-religious thing. From what I've read, or observed, Christianity just seems to me to be shrinking, to be losing contact.

Question: Why did you subject yourself to a public apology in front of television cameras?

John: If I were at the stage I was five years ago, I would have shouted we'd never tour again, packed myself off and that would be the end of it. Lord knows, I don't need the money. But the record burning, that was a real shock, the physical burning. I couldn't go away knowing that I'd created another little pocket of hate in the world. Especially with something as uncomplicated as people listening to records, dancing and enjoying what the Beatles are. Not when I could do something about it. If I said tomorrow I'm not going to play again, I still couldn't live with somebody hating me for something so irrational.

Question: Why don't you tell your fans all this?

John: But that's the trouble with being truthful. You try to apply truth talk, although you have to be false sometimes because this whole thing is false in a way, like a game. But you hope sometimes that if you're truthful with somebody they'll stop all the plastic reaction and be truthful back and it'll be worth it. But everybody is playing the game and sometimes I'm left naked and truthful with everybody biting me. It's disappointing.

Question: We've been hearing a great deal regarding your comments on God versus Jesus. Would you tell us what you really meant by that statement?

John: I'll try and tell you. I was just talking to a reporter, who also happens to be a friend of mine and all of us at home. It was a sort of in-depth series she was doing and so I wasn't really thinking in terms of PR or translating what I was saying. It was going on for a couple of hours and I said it just to cover the subject. I didn't mean it the way they said it. It's just so complicated, it's gone way out of hand, you know. I wasn't saying that the Beatles were any better than Jesus, God or Christianity. I never thought of any repercussions. I knew she was interviewing me but I wasn't thinking that it meant anything.

Question: What's your reaction to the repercussions?

John: Well, when I first heard it I thought, It can't be true. It's just one of those things like bad eggs in Adelaide. But when I realised it was serious I was worried stiff because I knew how it would go on. All the nasty things that would get said about it and all those miserable-looking pictures of me looking like a cynic. And they'd go on and on and on until it would get out of hand and I couldn't control it. I really can't answer for it when it gets this big, it's nothing to do with me now.

Question: A disc jockey in Birmingham, Alabama, who actually started most of the repercussions, has demanded an apology from you.

John: He can have it, I apologise to him. If he's upset and he really means it, you know, then I'm sorry. I'm sorry I said it for the mess it's made, but I never meant it as an anti-religion thing, or anything. You know, I can't say any more than that. There's nothing else to say really, no more words. I apologise to him.

Question: Do you really think Christianity is shrinking?

John: It just seems to me to be shrinking. I'm not knocking it or saying it's bad. I'm just saying it seems to be shrinking and losing contact.

Paul: And we deplore the fact that it is, you know, that's the point about it all.

John: Nothing better seems to be replacing it so we're not saying anything about that.

Paul: If it is on the decline in any way and you say it is then it must be helpful.

John: It's silly going on saying, 'Yes, it's all fine and we're all Christians. Yeah, yeah. We're all Christians and we're all doing this,' and we're not.

Paul: We're going to get blamed for the rise and fall of Christianity now.

Question: Mr Lennon, are you a Christian?

John: Well, we were all brought up to be. I don't profess to be a practising Christian. And Christ was what he was and anything anybody says great about him I believe. I'm not a practising Christian, but I don't have *unChristian* thoughts.

Question: Was there as much reaction to your statements throughout Europe and other countries around the world as there was here in America?

John: I don't think Europe heard about it, but they will now! It was just England and I sort of got away with it there. Inasmuch as nobody took offence and saw through me. Over here it's just as I said, it went this way.

Question: Some of the wires this morning said that Pan American Airlines had provided each of you with free Bibles.

John: We never saw that.

Question: If Jesus were alive today in a physical form, not a metaphysical one, he would find 'Eleanor Rigby' a very religious song, a song of concern with human experience and need. I'm curious about our expression of that.

John: Well, I don't like supposing that if Jesus were alive now knowing what he'd like to say or do. But if he was the real Jesus, the Jesus as he was before, well 'Eleanor Rigby' wouldn't mean much to him, but if it did come across his mind he'd think that, probably.

Question: There have been Beatle boycotts nationwide, record burnings, even threats against your life. Does this bother you?
Paul: Well, it's bound to bother us, isn't it?
Question: Mr Lennon, do you feel you are being crucified?
John: No, I wouldn't say that at all.

John: I can't express myself very well, that's my whole trouble. I was just commenting, in my illiterate way of speaking. It was about how Christ's message had been garbled by disciples and twisted for various selfish reasons by those who followed, to the point where it lost validity for many today. Actually, if I am going to blame anyone, it's myself for not thinking what people a million miles away were going to say about it. I've just had a reshuffling of all the things pushed into my head. I'm more of a Christian than I ever was. I don't go along with organised religion and the way it has come about.

Jesus says one thing and then all the clubs formed, telling their versions, and the whole thing gets twisted. It's like a game of having six people in a line and I whisper something to the guy next to me, maybe 'Love thy neighbour' or 'Everything ought to be equal.' By the time it gets to the end of the line it's altogether something else.

The Lost Beatles Interviews

New York, 23 August 1966

Question: How do you manage to have such a weird effect on teenagers?
George: Enthusiasm, I guess.
Question: Do you worry about smoking in public? Do you think it might set a bad example for your younger fans?
George: We don't set examples. We smoke because we've always smoked. Kids don't smoke because we do. They smoke because they want to. If we changed, we'd be putting on an act.
Ringo: (*loud whisper*) We even drink.
Question: What careers would you individually have chosen had you not become entertainers?
Ringo: A hairdresser.
George: I had a short go at being an electrician's apprentice, but I kept blowing things up so I got dumped.
Paul: I don't know . . . maybe something with art in it.
John: No comment.
Question: Which of you is really bald?
George: We're all bald. And I'm deaf and dumb.
Question: What are your feelings on the 'hints of queerness' American males found in the Beatles during the early days of your climb to popularity?
Paul: There's more terror of that hint of queerness – of homosexuality – here than in England where long hair is more accepted. Our whole promotion made us look silly. But we've had a chance to talk to people since then and they can see we're not thick little kids.
Question: What's it like being Beatles?
George: We've got to know each other quite well. We can stand each other better now than when we first met.
Question: Has success spoiled the Beatles?
John: Well, you don't see us running out and buying bowler hats, do you? I think we've pretty well succeeded in remaining ourselves.
Paul: The great thing about it is that you don't have big worries any more when you've got where we have, only little ones, like whether the plane is going to crash.
Question: Can we look forward to any more Beatle movies?
John: Well, there'll be many more. But I don't know whether you can look forward to them or not.
Question: Is your popularity beginning to taper off?
Paul: I agree that our popularity has hit a peak. But I also agreed with a man who said the same thing last year. And we were both wrong.

Question: How do you feel about bandleader Ray Block's statement that the Beatles won't last a year?

John: We'll probably last longer than Ray Block.

Question: Sorry to interrupt you while you are eating, but what do you think you will be doing in five years' time when all this is over?

John: Still eating.

Question: What will you do when the bubble bursts?

George: Take up ice hockey.

Paul: Play basketball.

Question: Aren't you tired of all the hocus-pocus? Wouldn't you rather sit on your fat wallets?

Paul: When we get tired, we take fat vacations on our fat wallets.

Question: Do you get much fan mail?

Ringo: We get two thousand letters a day.

John: We're going to answer every one of them.

Question: What is the biggest threat to your careers, the atom bomb or dandruff?

Ringo: The atom bomb. We've already got dandruff.

Question: How long will your popularity last?

John: When you're going to go, you're going to go.

Question: What do you think you've contributed to the musical field?

Ringo: Records.

George: A laugh and a smile.

Question: Do you care what the public thinks about your private lives?

Ringo: There's a woman in the United States who predicted the plane we were travelling on would crash. Now a lot of people would like to think we were scared into saying a prayer. What we did actually – we drank.

Question: What do you think of space shots?

John: You see one, you've seen them all.

Question: What about the recent criticism of your lyrics?

Paul: If you start reading things into them, you might just as well start singing hymns.

Question: Do you plan to record any anti-war songs?

John: All our songs are anti-war.

Question: What do you think of the Vietnam war?

John: We think of it every day. We don't like it. We don't agree with it. We think it is wrong. But there is not much we can do about it. All we can do is say we don't like it.

Question: What is your opinion of Americans who go to Canada to avoid the draft?

John: We're not allowed opinions.
Paul: Anybody who feels that fighting is wrong has the right not to go in the army.
John: We all just don't agree with war. There's no need for anyone to kill for any reason.
George: 'Thou shalt not kill' means that — not 'Amend Section A.' There's no reason whatsoever. No one can force you to kill anyone if you don't want to.
Question: Why are you disinterested in politics?
John: We're not. We just think politicians are disinteresting.
Question: You've admitted to being agnostics. Are you also irreverent?
Paul: We are agnostics, so there is no point in being irreverent.
Question: How do you stand in the draft?
John: About 5 feet, 11 inches.
Question: Are you afraid military service might break up your careers?
John: No. There's no draft in England now. We're going to let you do our fighting for us.
Question: What do you think about the pamphlet calling you four Communists?
Paul: Us, Communists? Why, we can't be Communists. We're the world's number one Capitalists. Imagine us Communists!
Question: What do you consider the most important thing in life?
George: Love.
Question: What is your personal goal?
George: To do as well as I can at whatever I attempt. And someday to die with a peaceful mind.
Question: But you really don't expect that to happen for a long time yet, do you?
George: When your number's up, it's up.
Question: What about your future?
John: It looks nice.
Question: Are you scared when crowds scream at you?
John: More so in Dallas than in other places, perhaps.
Question: Would you like to walk down the street without being recognised?
John: We used to do this with no money in our pockets. There's no point in it.
Question: What would you do if the fans got past the police lines?
George: We'd die laughing.
Question: If you could have any wish you wanted at this moment, what would it be?

John: No more unscheduled public appearances. We've had enough. We're going to stay in our hotel except for concerts.
Question: Won't this make you feel like caged animals?
John: No. We feed ourselves.

Seattle, 25 August 1966

Question: John, could you please tell me something about your new movie [*How I Won the War*]?

John: I don't really know anything except that I'm in it and it's about the last World War.

Question: Mr McCartney, would you please confirm or deny reports of your marriage to Jane Asher in Seattle this evening.

Paul: It's tonight, yeah.

Question: What time and where?

Paul: I can't tell you that, can I?

Question: You are confirming the report, then?

Paul: No, I'm not really. It was a joke. Who started this, anyone know? I just got in and found out I was getting married this evening. No, she is not coming in tonight as far I know. And if she is, we are going out anyway. So we'd miss her.

Question: Do you believe you represent a different type of morality, than, say, a group like the Rolling Stones or the other protest groups?

Paul: No, we don't represent anything like that.

John: Are the Stones a protest group? I thought it was the Circle.

Question: I'd like to know if your motivation in this is money. I'd like to think you're having as much fun as you seem when you're doing it.

John: Well, when I look as though I'm having fun, I am. When I'm not, I'm not usually.

Question: I have a prediction that in twenty-five years, you're going to be a great writer.

John: I don't know where I'll be in twenty-five years.

Question: What about the Beatles' next movie? There's been a lot of stories but nothing's confirmed.

John: Somebody gave us a good idea, so we told him to go and to turn it into a script. But we won't be able to tell whether or not we're going to make the film until we've read it.

Question: The audience your music attracts has changed from, say, thirteen-year-old girls to more the college age. Do you like it better that way?

George: I think it's probably got a bit older but I don't know how old.

Question: Paul, since you've denied the marriage rumours, what are you doing after the show?

Paul: Marrying you, probably.

Question: How is the attendance on this tour compared to past American tours?

Paul: There's apparently been more people at the shows than in the past.

Question: John and Paul, I'd like to know if all the songs written by Lennon/McCartney are composed by the two of you or do you ever write one by yourselves?

John: We do them separately and together.

Question: Your music used to be composed mostly of guitar backgrounds, but recently you've come around to using strings, harpsichords and a lot of weird things like that. Is there any particular purpose in this evolution?

John: No, just to use something besides guitar. It's not necessarily that we are coming around to them. It's finding them again.

Question: George, where can people generally get a sitar?

George: In India.

Question: I hear you're the world's greatest sitar player. Paul, you've said that sometimes you 'have' to write. Could you explain what you mean by that?

Paul: I just meant that when there's an LP due we write songs. We do it like that more than write all the time. We write more to order. You know, if we've got fourteen tracks to fill, then we've got fourteen songs to write. That's what I meant.

Hollywood, 28 August 1966

Question: How do you compare movie work to concert tours or recording sessions?
John: We don't.
Question: Would you rather play the Hollywood Bowl again instead of Dodger Stadium?
George: We don't really mind.
Question: Maybe we can start another controversy here. One of your countrymen said on his arrival in England that he thought American women were out of style for not wearing mini-skirts and as they didn't wear them their legs were ugly. I'd like to ask you what you think of American women's legs.
Ringo: Well, if they don't wear mini-skirts how does he know their legs are ugly?
Question: Regarding your album jacket which was banned here [the butcher cover of *Yesterday And Today*], whose idea was it and what was it supposed to mean?
John: Ask the photographer who took it [Robert Whitaker].
Question: John, how did you decide to make *How I Won the War*?
John: Because he [Richard Lester] asked me and I just said yes.
Question: Do you consider that now, since you've been in the United States for almost a week, that this religious issue is answered once and for all?
John: I hope so.
Question: Would you clarify and repeat the answer you gave in Chicago?
John: I can't repeat it because I don't know what I said.
Question: Well, would you clarify the remarks that were attributed to you?
John: You tell me what you think I meant and I'll tell you if I agree.
Question: Some of the remarks attributed to you compared the relative popularity of the Beatles with Jesus Christ and intimated that the Beatles were more popular. This created quite a furore in this country, as you are aware.
Paul: Did you know that, John? You created a furore!
Question: Now, would you clarify the remark?
John: I've clarified it about eight hundred times. I could have said 'TV' or something. And that's just as clear as it can be. I used Beatles because I know about them a bit more than TV. I could have said any number of things, but it wouldn't have got as much publicity.

Question: Do you think the controversy has hurt your careers, or helped?

George: It hasn't helped or hindered, I don't think. I think most sensible people took it for what it was. It was only the bigots that thought it was on their side. They thought, 'Ha ha, here's something to get them for.' But when they read it they saw there was nothing wrong with it really. They thought by John saying we were more popular than Jesus that he must be arrogant.

Question: John, what stimulates you in your work?

John: Just anything, you know.

Question: What's your favourite group in the US?

John: I've got a few. The Byrds, the Lovin' Spoonful, Mamas and Papas, I suppose.

Paul: Beach Boys.

John: The Miracles are the other side of it.

Question: I was wondering if you still have an arrangement with the US Internal Revenue Department to pay your taxes to England? How much money have you grossed on your current US tour?

George: Money's got nothing to do with us.

Paul: Brian does that.

George: And we don't particularly care about it.

John: They just tell us what we get in the end, you know.

George: We pay tax, but we don't know how much we've made, because if we worried about that we'd be nervous wrecks by now.

Question: I'd like to direct this question to Messrs Lennon and McCartney; a recent article in *Time* magazine put down pop music and referred to 'Day Tripper' as being about a prostitute and 'Norwegian Wood' as about a lesbian. I want to know what your intent was when you wrote them and what your feeling is about *Time*'s criticism of the music that is being written today?

George: We were just trying to write songs about prostitutes and lesbians. That's all.

Question: Do you have any plans to work separately in the future?

George: All together, probably.

Question: Mr Lennon, aren't you doing a picture alone?

John: Yeah, but that's only in the holiday bit, in between Beatles.

Question: I'd like to ask a question you've never been asked before.

John: Go ahead, Fred.

Question: What are you going to do when the bubble bursts?

John: That's a personal 'in' joke. He used to ask it at every press conference just to keep the party going.

Question: Do you think we'll have another tour again next year?

George: Could be, Fred, Brian does that.

Question: In Hollywood tonight, you had to arrive in an armoured truck which was swarmed by adoring fans. Do you ever have an opportunity to walk out on the streets without being recognised? Can you walk into a theatre to see a movie by yourself?

John: If you go in when the lights are down.

Paul: We can do that in England. It's easier than it is here because we know England.

Ringo: Also it would be easier to do it if we weren't on tour. Because when we're on tour people know where we are and that's why we have a crowd.

Question: Paul, many of the top artists in the pop field have said the Beatles have been a major influence on their music. Are there any artists who have had an important influence on you?

Paul: Oh yes, nearly everyone. We pinch as much from other people as they pinch from us.

Question: Ringo, do you carry wallet pictures of your baby with you?

Ringo: I don't carry photos of anything.

Question: May I ask about the song 'Eleanor Rigby'? What was the inspiration for that?

John: Two queers.

Question: John, did you ever meet Cass of the Mamas and the Papas?

John: Yes and she's great. I'm seeing her tonight.

Question: Have you ever used Beatle doubles as decoys?

Paul: No, we tried to get Brian Epstein to do it, but he wouldn't.

Question: Ringo, how much did you contribute to 'What Goes On'? And are you contributing to any other Lennon/McCartney compositions?

Ringo: About five words to 'What Goes On'. I haven't done a thing since.

Question: I'd like to address this to John and Paul. You write a lot of stuff that other people steal from you and also purchase from you, as with Ella Fitzgerald and the Boston Pops. How do you feel about your pieces being changed around?

John: It depends how they do it.

Paul: Once we've done a song and it's published, anyone can do it. So whether we like it or not depends on if they've done it to our taste.

Question: Then let's ask it this way: who do you think does it the best?

Ringo: Us!

Question: For those of us who have followed your career from the early days of Liverpool and Hamburg and the pride in you being awarded the MBE and the dismay over the unwarranted adverse publicity of late, the question is: individually, what have been your most memorable occasions and what have been the most disappointing?

George: I think Manila was the most disappointing.

John: And the most exciting is yet to come.

Ringo: Maybe the most disappointing.

Question: Gentlemen, there was quite a ruckus when you went on the stock market with your stock. How is your stock doing?

John: Fine, thank you.

Ringo: It went down, but it's coming up again.

George: It's gone down.

Ringo: It's the same as any other stock.

John: It goes down every time the LPs drop out. They all think they're buying bits of records.

Question: Leonard Bernstein likes your music; how do you like Leonard Bernstein's?

Paul: Very good. He's great.

John: One of the greatest.

Question: George, before you left England you made a statement that you were going to America to be beaten up by Americans. Do you mean to say that you feel the American fan is more hostile than in Britain?

George: No, not at all. Actually, I said that when we were just back from Manila. They said, 'What are you going to do next?' And I said, 'We're going to rest up before we go get beaten up over there.' Really, we just got shoved around. Jostled around in cars . . .

Ringo: It was a joke.

Question: Do you think that's more an enthusiastic fan than a hostile fan? Would you say?

Paul: If anyone beats us up they're not really fans, are they?

George: I think they proved it themselves that there are a lot of fans who are great. And all the ones we've lost we don't really mind anyway, because if they can't make up their minds, who needs them!

Question: How has your image changed since 1963?

George: An image is how *you* see us so you can only answer that.

John: You're the only one that knows.

Question: Oh, I want to get your opinion. Is it a little tarnished now or more realistic? I know I have my opinion.

John: Everybody attacks our opinion.

Paul: We can't tell you our image. Our image is what we read in the newspapers and that's the same as you read. We know our real image which is nothing like our image. What I meant to say was . . .

Ringo: Take two bricks.

Question: Who is the young man with the lengthy haircut to your right?

John: That's good old Dave, isn't it? That's Dave [Crosby] from the Byrds. A mate of ours. Ahoy, mateys.

Paul: He's shy.

Question: Do you ever plan to record in the United States, and why haven't you yet?

Paul: We tried actually, but it's a financial matter. We had a bit of trouble over that one. We tried, but it didn't come out.

Ringo: It's all a bit of politics and dice.

John: No comment.

Question: Mr Lennon, is it true you're planning to give up music for a career in the field of comparative religion?

John: No. Is that another joke going around?

Question: I'm sure you've heard about the many Beatle burnings and Beatle bonfires. Do you think American girls are fickle?

Ringo: All girls are fickle.

John: The photos that we saw of them were of middle-aged DJs and twelve-year-olds burning a pile of LP covers.

Question: This question is directed to Paul and John. You have written quite a few numbers for Peter and Gordon and I understand they don't like it because they think it's your writing the songs that makes them popular. Do you plan to write any more songs for them?

Paul: They don't mind it. They like it, but people come up and say, 'Ah, we see, you're just getting in on the Lennon/McCartney bandwagon.' That's why they did that one with our names not on it, 'Woman'. Because everyone thinks that's the reason they get hits. It's not true, really.

Question: Gentlemen, what do you think would happen to you if you were to do an appearance without the armoured truck and the police?

Ringo: We'd get in a lot easier.

John: We wouldn't make it.

Paul: It depends. Sometimes we could have made it much better without the armoured truck. But today we probably wouldn't have.

Question: Do you think you'd be physically harmed?

Paul: Oh, yeah, probably.

John: What do you think?

Question: The *New York Times Magazine* of Sunday July 3rd carried an article by Maureen Cleave in which she quotes one of the Beatles, not by name, as saying, 'Showbusiness is an extension of the Jewish religion.' Would you mind amplifying that?

Paul: Did she say that?

John: I said that to her. No comment.

George: Ah, come on, John. Tell me what you meant.

John: You can read into it what you like. It's just a little old statement. It's not very serious.

Question: Paul, are you getting married? And if yes, to whom?

Paul: Yes, but I don't know when. I've got no plans.

Question: John, under what conditions did you write *In His Own Write*? Those sort of wild, kinky words, how did you piece them together?

John: I don't know.

Question: Do you have any more books coming out?

John: Well, ah, yes and I can't answer that. It's just the way it happens.

Paul: Any more books coming?

John: I didn't think: Now how can I do this?

Paul: Just like an author.

Question: I understand there's a suit pending against the Beatles by Peter Best who claims to be a former member of the group. Is that true?

John: I think he's had a few, but we don't bother with those.

Question: Are all of your news conferences like this? I'm talking about all of the reporters or would-be reporters or semi-reporters that show up. Are you besieged by these kind of people throughout your travel here in the United States?

John: You can't always tell the would-bes from the real thing. So we never know.

Question: Is it this way when you travel in Europe?

John: Yes.

Paul: But what's wrong with a crowd?

Question: Nothing, I'm just wondering if you have this many reporters everywhere you go.

Paul: No, not always.

George: Some of them are just onlookers.

Question: 'Tomorrow Never Comes' is the last cut on the second side of your latest LP, right?

George: 'Tomorrow Never Knows'.

Question: Could you give me a vague idea of some of the tape manipulations you used when your voice drops into the track? Is that sung backwards, by any chance, and then recorded forwards?

The Lost Beatles Interviews

Paul: No, it's not sung backwards.
George: It would be hard to do that, wouldn't it?
Paul: It's recorded pretty straight. There's nothing, there's tape loops on it which are a bit different and the words are from *The Tibetan Book of the Dead*. So there.
George: There, nearly.

John Buys a Rolls

Beatle John Lennon took delivery of his rainbow-coloured Rolls yesterday.

His £11,000 car has been painted mainly yellow with bunches of flowers on the door panels, blue, red, green and white have been used in the colour scheme. The car also has the sign of the zodiac on the roof.

The work was done by a firm of coach builders and paint sprayers at Chertsey, Surrey.

Mr John Fallon, aged 50, the firm's managing director, said: 'It took about five weeks to do.'

He refused to reveal the cost.

26 May 1967

On *Sgt Pepper*

Most songs [on *Sgt Pepper's Lonely Hearts Club Band*] we did we had to do as if we were recording live, like mono. We spent hours getting drum, bass and guitar sounds, then balancing them and doing the take. That was in effect a backing track and then we later added overdubs. Nowadays you can overdub individually with each person having his own channel to record on. Then we'd have to think of all the instrumental overdubs, say, a guitar coming in on the second verse and a piano in the middle and then a tambourine. And we'd routine all of that, get the sound and the balance and the mix and do it as one performance. And if one person got it wrong we'd have to back up and do the entire overdub of all the parts again.

We had old microphones and pretty antiquated machines, but we'd find new meanings in old equipment, and I think that it was largely because of the times and the state of mind everyone was in that it was exciting to try and come up with ideas. (George)

We were being influenced by avant-garde composers. For 'A Day in the Life', I suggested we should write all but fifteen bars properly so that the orchestra could read it, but where the fifteen bars began we would give the musicians a simple direction: 'Start on your lowest note and eventually, at the end of the fifteen bars, be at your highest note.' How they got there was up to them, but it all resulted in a crazy crescendo. It was interesting because the trumpet players, always famous for their fondness for lubricating substances, didn't care, so they'd be there at the note ahead of everyone. The strings all watched each other like little sheep: 'Are you going up?' 'Yes.' 'So am I.' And they'd go up. 'A little more?' 'Yes.' And they'd go up a little more, all very delicate and cosy, all going up together. You listen to those trumpets. They're just freaking out. (Paul)

John Lennon brought a television set because he felt that television was very important to him at this stage. I had thought they would bring teddy bears, things like that, but it went into a whole other dimension. There are a number of myths as a result. The flowers, for instance. My concept was that it was a municipal flowerbed, so that you would have the letters spelled out in flowers like the Boy Scouts' [logo] on the clock at Edinburgh.

There was a young boy helping who asked if he could do a guitar in hyacinths and it was such a gentle sort of idea we said, 'Yes, certainly', so the sort of white shape at the front of the cover is actually a guitar and one of the myths that arose is that you could read that as 'PAUL?' When the stories that Paul died arrived, this was taken to be a sign that Paul had indeed died, but it was never intended to be Paul; it was simply a guitar.

Another myth is that the plants around the edge were marijuana plants and for a time I thought someone had played a joke on me and put some in, but they're not marijuana plants at all, just plants from a regular nursery. (George Martin)

Robert Fraser, a friend of the Stones, owned the gallery I was with. A cover for *Sgt Pepper* designed by The Fool already existed and was very psychedelic – swirly orange and green and purple – there were a lot of others like it. Robert thought it would be interesting to have the first cover done by a Fine Artist as opposed to a record-cover designer. A certain amount had already been established: the concept of their being a band within a band, for instance. They'd had their uniforms made already. I think my contribution was to talk a great deal to them about the concept and try to add something visual to it. Paul explained that it was like a band you might see in a park. So the cover shot could be a photograph of them as though they were a town band finishing a concert in a park, playing on a bandstand with a municipal flowerbed next to it. I think my main con- tribution was to decide that if we had the crowd a certain way the people in it could be anybody. I think that was the thing I would claim actually changed the direction of it: making a life-sized collage incorporating real people, waxworks, photographs and artwork . . .

All the figures you see behind the Beatles only filled a space about two feet deep and then there was a line of figures in front of them which were the waxworks. The actual Beatles stood on a platform about four feet deep. So that from front to back the whole thing was only about fifteen feet deep. People were asked to put in favourite objects. In a way this didn't work; maybe I didn't explain it well enough, so Paul, for instance, decided his favourite objects were musical instruments and hired a great number of them and came with a vanload of French horns and trumpets and beautiful things and I think that would have empha- sised it too hard, so we only used one or two.

I couldn't be more thrilled to have worked on it. It was very exciting, of course it was. (Peter Blake, on the *Sgt Pepper* cover)

[The Fool] hadn't somehow checked on the album size and their design was just out of scale. So they said, 'Oh, okay, we'll put a border on it,'

so we now had this design which was too small and a border being
added just to fill up space. I said to the fellows, 'What are we selling
here, a Beatles album or a centrefold with a design by The Fool which
isn't even ready? Hadn't we better get a picture taken of the four of you
and stick that in so we can see who you are?' So they posed for a picture
and that went in the middle. The back took some time and had to be left
till last because we were printing lyrics and they had to be designed and
we had to have a running order and we couldn't have that until everyone decided on it. I remember Paul and I walking along, I think on Kin-
gly Street in the West End, trying to work out some clever word using
the initial letter of each song – the first would have to be S for Sgt Pepper and then we'd try and get a vowel, say – but we couldn't get it right,
so the running order was decided in another way. But it all worked out
and we made it on time. (Neil Aspinall)

One of the few opera triumphs of the recording century. They were
giving an example around the world that guys can be friends. They had
conveyed a realisation that the world and human consciousness had to
change.

After the apocalypse of Hitler and the apocalypse of the Bomb, there
was here an exclamation of joy, the rediscovery of joy and what it is to
be alive . . . They showed an awareness that we make up our own fate,
and they have decided to make a cheerful fate. They have decided to be
generous to Lovely Rita, or to be generous to Sgt Pepper himself, turn
him from an authority figure to a figure of comic humour, a vaudeville
turn.

Remember, this was in the midst of the sixties; it was 1967 when
some of the wilder and crazier radicals were saying 'Kill the pigs'. They
were saying the opposite about old Sgt Pepper. In fact the Beatles themselves were dressing up in uniforms, but associating themselves with
good old-time vaudeville authority rather than sneaky CIA, KGB, MI5
or whatever. It was actually a cheerful look round the world . . . for the
first time, I would say, on a mass scale. (Allen Ginsberg)

It was six in the morning and we went down the King's Road to see
Cass Elliott of the Mamas and Papas. We had the album with us, finished at last. She had a great sound system. Her flat was in a block of
houses, back to back, really close together, and we put the system on a
window ledge and the music blasted throughout the neighbourhood.
'We're Sgt Pepper's Lonely Hearts Club . . .' It sounded great. All the
windows around us opened and people leaned out, wondering. It was

Act One: Where Giants Walk

obvious who it was in a second. Nobody complained. A lovely spring morning. People were smiling and giving us the thumbs up. Then we piled on to a bus and went off. John had a new song in his head. I don't know which one, but he said he had a new sound. Nice. (Neil Aspinall) I knew there was some possible connection with cannabis in the studios — 'smells' were noted — but I never pursued it. I had a pretty close relationship with the Beatles, largely because they were so successful. I knew them better than I did most of the pop artists and the situation developed when they were refused something by EMI's management, which was quite often — some disagreement about a minor thing maybe — Lennon and McCartney would come to me.

Just about the time the record was issued I got an invitation and I went, rather unusually for me, to a dinner party with a very rich group of middle-class older ladies and I never met with such an atmosphere, they were absolutely thrilled with this record. Most of us sat on the floor for hours after dinner, singing extracts from it. This to me was a new experience, the music had spread so widely. (Sir Joseph Lockwood, Chairman of EMI, 1967)

The Happy Dream Ends with a Tragedy

The Beatles, mourning the death of their manager Brian Epstein yesterday, have cut short their weekend of meditation at Bangor and drove back to London early today.

They have been attending a course given by the International Meditation Society at Bangor Normal College.

Paul McCartney, accompanied by his girlfriend Jane Asher, was the first to leave in a chauffeur-driven car.

The other three waited for cars to arrive from London to collect them before they, too, left at 1.50 a.m.

Before getting into the cars, the Beatles and their companions were handed flowers by 'disciples' of the Himalayan mystic Maharishi Mahesh.

A Scotland Yard spokesman said today that there are no suspicious circumstances surrounding the death yesterday of 32-year-old Beatle manager Mr Brian Epstein, at his London home.

Mr Epstein, the man who launched the Beatles on the road to fame, was found dead yesterday afternoon by his housekeeper who became worried when she could get no reply from his locked bedroom.

Since Friday the four Beatles, together with John Lennon's wife Cynthia, Pattie Harrison and her sister Jennie Boyd and Jane Asher, had been meditating at the feet of the Maharishi Yogi.

Just before the news yesterday afternoon of Mr Epstein's death, two of them described how much more relaxed they were as a result of their meditation.

Paul McCartney confirmed that the Beatles were no longer going to take drugs. 'You cannot keep on taking drugs forever,' he said. 'You get to the stage where you are taking fifteen aspirins a day without having a headache.

'We were looking for something more natural. This is it.

'It is not weirdy or anything, it is dead natural. Meditation will be good for everyone, it is something which one does normally anyway.'

And Ringo Starr said: 'I hope the fans will take up meditation instead of drugs.'

Earlier, the four Beatles and their companions had all been initiated into the society. Paul said: 'There is no black magic or anything like that about initiation.

'At the moment I am finding what I am searching for by meditation. I hope I will get more out of meditation, so that I will have no need for drugs.'

It has been a weekend of comings and goings at Bangor with first of all Mick Jagger leaving on Saturday morning, followed on Sunday by Marianne Faithfull.

But the size of the party, staying in students' rooms at the Bangor Normal College, did not go down because during the night Cynthia Lennon arrived by car and Jane Asher later by train.

And so Sunday afternoon there was a social call for Paul McCartney from his father, Mr Jim McCartney, his stepmother and his seven-year-old stepsister, Ruth, who had travelled from Gayton.

London, 1967

Ringo: The four of us have had the most hectic lives. We have got almost anything money can buy. But when you can do that, the things you buy mean nothing after a time. You look for something else, for a new experience. We have found something now which fills the gap. Since meeting His Holiness, Maharishi Mahesh Yogi, I feel great.

Paul: I now realise that taking drugs was like taking an aspirin without having a headache.

John: If we'd met Maharishi before we had taken LSD, we wouldn't have needed to take it.

George: We haven't really started yet. We've only just discovered what we can do as musicians, what thresholds we can cross. The future stretches out beyond our imagination.

John: The main thing is not to think about the future or the past, the main thing is just to get on with now. We want to help people do that with these academies. We'll make a donation and we'll ask for money from anyone we know with money, anyone that's interested, anyone in the so-called Establishment who's worried about kids going wild and drugs and all that . . .

With Brian dying it was sort of a big thing for us. And if we hadn't had this meditation it would have been much harder to assess and carry on and know how we were going.

George: We've all come along the same path. We've been together a long time. We learned right from the beginning that we're going to be together.

John: We'd dropped drugs before this meditation thing. George mentioned he was dropping out of it and I said, 'Well, it's not doing me any harm, I'll carry on.' But I just suddenly thought, I've seen all that scene. There's no point and if it does do anything to your chemistry or brains . . .? Then someone wrote to me and said that whether you like it or not, whether you have no ill-effects, something happens up there. So I decided if I ever did meet someone who could tell me the answer, I'd have nothing left to do it with.

George: There's still the craze. Usually the people who establish something that becomes a craze, well, they're usually very sincere people. It's just when all the publicity comes, then it turns bad.

John: There's a big academy of this meditation scene out in California and if even just two hundred of them try it, just because of what we say, they'll turn the next two hundred on themselves as soon as they've done it, and that might have been worth all the Haight-Ashbury and all the drop-outs. The point about how the English are taking it now seems to me to be better. It's not drop out, it's drop in and change it.

John and Paul, New York, 1968

Question: Why did you leave the Maharishi?
John: We made a mistake.
Question: Do you think other people are making a mistake as well?
John: That's up to them. We're human.
Question: What do you mean, you made a mistake?
John: That's all you know.
Paul: We thought there was more to him than there was, but he's human and for a while we thought he wasn't.
Question: Could you tell us about your newest corporate business venture [Apple]?
John: It's a business concerning records, films and electronics and, as a sideline, manufacturing or whatever. We want to set up a system whereby people who just want to make a film about anything don't have to go on their knees in somebody's office, probably yours.
Paul: We really want to help people, but without doing it like charity or seeming like ordinary patrons of the arts. I mean, we're in the happy position of not really needing any more money, so for the first time the bosses aren't in it for the profit. If you come to see me and say, 'I've had such and such a dream,' I will say, 'Here's so much money. Go away and do it.' We've already bought all our dreams, so now we want to share that possibility with others. There's no desire in any of our heads to take over the world, that was Hitler. There is, however, a desire to get power in order to use it for the good.
John: The aim of this company isn't really a stack of gold teeth in the bank. We've done that bit. It's more of a trick to see if we can actually get artistic freedom within a business structure, to see if we can create nice things and sell them without charging three times our cost.
Question: How will you run your new company?
John: There's people we can get to do that. We don't know anything about business.

Beatles to Record for Their Own Apple Label

Apple Records, a branch of the music division The Beatles Apple Corps Ltd, announces that contracts have been signed between Apple and Capitol Records (for the USA and Canada) for Capitol to manufacture and distribute all record product for North America in New York and Los Angeles.

The deals were concluded this week after prolonged negotiations between the Beatles and their representatives and the heads of Capitol. The Beatles themselves will henceforth be released on their own label, 'Apple'.

Apple press release, London, 1968

Closing Down the Baker Street Shop

Paul McCartney says tonight:
We decided to close down our Baker Street shop yesterday and instead of putting up a sign saying 'Business will be resumed as soon as possible' and then auctioning off the goods, we decided to give them away. The shops were doing fine and making a nice profit on turnover. So far, the biggest loss is in giving the things away but we did that deliberately. We're giving them away – rather than selling them to barrow-boys – because we wanted to give rather than sell.

We came into shops by the tradesman's entrance but we're leaving by the front door. Originally, the shops were intended to be something else, but they just became like all the boutiques in London. They just weren't our thing. The staff will get three weeks' pay but if they wish they'll be absorbed into the rest of Apple. Everyone will be cared for. The King's Road shop, which is known as Apple Tailoring, isn't going to be part of Apple any more but it isn't closing down and we are leaving our investment there because we have a moral and personal obligation to our partner John Crittle who is now in sole control. All that's happened is that we've closed our shop in which we feel we shouldn't, in the first place, have been involved.

Our main business is entertainment, communication. Apple is mainly concerned with fun, not frocks. We want to devote all our energies to records, films and our electronics adventures. We had to re-focus. We had to zoom in on what we really enjoy, and we enjoy being alive, and we enjoy being Beatles.

It's 1968; already, it's 1968. Time is short. I suppose really what we're doing is spring cleaning in mid-summer. The amazing thing is our giving things away. Well, the answer is that it was much funnier to give things away.

Well, it's just that the Beatles are the Beatles are the moptops are the moptops are the Beatles are the moptops . . . are whatever you see them to be, whatever you see us to be. Create and preserve the image of your choice. We are yours with love, John Lennon, Paul McCartney, George Harrison and Ringo Starr.

Apple Boutique press release, London, 1968

Businessman Klein Steps In

The Beatles have asked Mr Allen Klein of New York to look into all their affairs and he has agreed to do so, it was announced from their headquarters at Apple, 3 Savile Row, London W1, today Monday, 3 February 1969.

Miami Audio Expert Finds Three Pauls

At the urging of a Miami disc jockey, Dr Henry M. Truby, director of the university's language and linguistics research laboratory, put the McCartney riddle to a 'sound fingerprint' test.

After 20 hours of running experiments on dozens of Beatles records dating from the early 1960s, the professor said there is 'reasonable doubt' that three voices popularly attributed to McCartney are produced by the same set of vocal chords.

'I hear three different McCartneys,' Truby said.

Speculation that McCartney died in an automobile accident in November 1966 has touched off a worldwide controversy in pop music circles.

The furor prompted Apple Ltd, the Beatles' London office, to report Paul as saying: 'I am alive and well and unconcerned about the rumors of my death. But if I were dead, I would be the last to know.'

But Truby, an audio expert, insists, 'I heard three different McCartneys.'

Truby said experiments on a sound spectograph machine indicated there were six different voices on the records he tested. Three were clearly identified as those of Beatles John Lennon, George Harrison and Ringo Starr. The three others sound 'roughly' like the same person, the professor said, but the spectograph – which makes sound 'fingerprints' – shows a different authorship.

'I cannot conclude that the same voice appears in these early and late passages,' said Truby, who has spent 20 years in scientific audio studies.

Disc jockey David Century of WEDR-FM radio asked Dr Truby Thursday to make the tests.

Truby said his study has some built-in difficulties stemming from the fact that McCartney's solos have musical accompaniment in the background.

'But after spending 20 hours listening to Beatle recordings,' Truby added, 'it seems to me there is reasonable doubt that McCartney is one and the same person. There appear to be three voices attributed to him.'

1969

His Divine Grace A.C. Bhaktivedanta Swami Prabhupada with John, Yoko and George, Ascot, Berkshire, 11 September 1969

Swami Prabhupada (*to Lennon*): You are anxious to bring about peace in the world. I've read some of your statements, and they show me you're anxious to do something. Actually, every saintly person should try and bring peace, but we must know the process. What kind of philosophy are you following? May I ask?

Yoko: We don't follow anything. We are just living.

George: We've done meditation. Or I do my meditation, mantra meditation.

Prabhupada: Hare Krishna is also a mantra.

John: Ours is not a song, though. We heard it from Maharishi. A mantra each.

Prabhupada: His mantras are not public?

John: No, it's a secret.

Yoko: If Hare Krishna is such a strong, powerful mantra, is there any reason to chant anything else?

Prabhupada: There are other mantras, but Hare Krishna is especially recommended for this age.

John: If all mantras are just the name of God, then whether it's a secret mantra or an open mantra, it doesn't really make much difference, does it, which one you sing?

Prabhupada: It does make a difference. For instance, in a drug shop they sell many types of medicines for curing different diseases. But still you have to get a doctor's prescription in order to get a particular type of medicine. Otherwise, the druggist won't supply you. You might go to the drug shop and say, 'I'm diseased. Please give me any medicine you have.' But the druggist will ask you, 'Where is your prescription?' Similarly, in this age, the Hare Krishna mantra is prescribed in the scriptures. And the great teacher Sri Chaitanya Mahaprabhu, whom we consider to be an incarnation of God, also prescribed it. Therefore, our principle is that everyone should follow the prescription of the great authorities.

Yoko: If the mantra itself has such power, does it matter where you receive it?

Prabhupada: Yes, it does matter. For instance, milk is nutritious. That's a fact everyone knows. But if milk is touched by the lips of a serpent, it is no longer nutritious. It becomes poisonous. If you don't receive the mantra through the proper channel, it may not really be spiritual.

John: But what if one of these masters who's not in the line says exactly the same thing as one who is? What if he says his mantra is coming from the Vedas and seems to speak with as much authority as you?

Prabhupada: If the mantra is actually coming through a bona fide disciplic succession, then it will have the potency.

John: But the Hare Krishna mantra is the best one?

Prabhupada: Yes. We say that the Hare Krishna mantra is sufficient for one's perfection, for liberation.

George: Isn't it like flowers? Somebody may prefer roses, and somebody may like carnations better. Isn't it really a matter for the individual devotee to decide? One person may find that Hare Krishna is more beneficial to his spiritual progress, and yet another person may find that some other mantra may be more beneficial for him.

Prabhupada: But still there is a distinction. A fragrant rose is considered better than a flower without any scent. You may be attracted by one flower, and I may be attracted by another, but among the flowers a distinction can be made. There are many flowers that have no fragrance and many that do. Therefore, your attraction for a particular flower is not the solution to the question of which is actually better. In the same way, personal attraction is not the solution to choosing the best spiritual process. You've been speaking of the Maharishi. Hasn't he written some book on Bhagavad-Gita [a sacred Vedic text]?

John: Yes, that's the one we've read.

Prabhupada: So, why is he using Krishna's book to put forward his own philosophy? Bhagavad-Gita is Krishna's book. Why is he taking Krishna's book?

George: Well, he didn't. He just translated it.

Prabhupada: Why? Because Krishna's book is very well respected.

John: I've also read part of another translation by Paramahansa Yogananda.

Prabhupada: Yes, all these men take advantage of Krishna's book to lend an air of authority to their own speculations. Vivekananda has done it, Sri Aurobindo has done it, Dr Radhakrishan has done it, Mahatma Gandhi has done it. Thousands of them have done it. But why do they use Bhagavad-Gita as the vehicle for their own ideas?

George: In the versions I've read, the authors all claim theirs is the best. And sometimes I get something from one which I didn't get from another.

John: I found that the best thing for myself is to take a little bit from here and a little bit from there.

Yoko: I mean, we're not just saying that. We want to ask your advice.

In other words, what is your answer to this question of authority?

Prabhupada: If we don't take the Gita from the authorised disciplic succession, it won't help us. In our introduction to Bhagavad-Gita we have carefully explained that aside from Krishna there is no authority. Krishna is the authority, because Bhagavad-Gita was spoken by Krishna. Can you deny that?

John: What about Yogananda, Maharishi and all these other people who have translated the Gita? How are we to tell that their version isn't also Krishna's word?

Prabhupada: If you seriously want to understand this, you should study the original Sanskrit text.

John: Study Sanskrit. Oh, now you're talking!

George: But Vivekananda said that books, rituals, dogmas and temples are secondary details anyway. He said they're not the most important thing. You don't have to read the book in order to have the perception.

Prabhupada: Then why did Vivekananda write so many books?

John: Who says who's actually in the line of descent? I mean, it's just like royalty, Yogananda also claims to be in a line, he talks about his guru's guru's guru's guru, like that. Maharishi claimed that all his gurus went way back. I mean, how are we to know?

Prabhupada: Whatever Maharishi may be, his knowledge does not extend up to Krishna, not up to His personal feature.

John: That's what he used to say in exactly the same way about everybody else.

Prabhupada: But factually he cannot be an authority, because he does not know anything about Krishna. If a postman comes and does not know anything about the post office, what kind of postman is he?

Yoko: But he does talk about his post office.

Prabhupada: No, you cannot create your own post office. There is only one post office, the government post office. If a postman comes and says, 'I belong to another post office,' then at once you can know he is unauthorised.

John: In the Bible or any other holy book, they talk about one God. So it's just the one Being everywhere, in all the books. So why isn't Hare Krishna or something similar in the Bible?

Devotee: It is in the Bible. In Psalms it says, 'Praise the Lord with every breath. Praise the Lord with drum and flute.'

John: But they haven't got very good tunes. They haven't been passing on any good chants, have they? I mean, would it be effective to chant, 'Lord Jesus, Lord Jesus, Hail Lord Jesus?'

Prabhupada: Lord Jesus says that he is the Son of God. He's not God, but the Son of God. In that sense, there is no difference between Krishna Consciousness and Christianity. There is no quarrel between God and God's Son. Jesus says to love God, and Krishna, the Supreme Personality of Godhead, says, 'Love me.' It's the same thing. All right?

His Divine Grace A. C. Bhaktivedanta Swami Prabhupada, a lifelong proponent of the yoga of devotion (Bhakti) and founder of the Hare Krishna Movement, was sometime spiritual adviser to the Fab Four. He died in India in 1977.

Act Two

Gods of the Apple: Music and Myth

On God and Getting High

God is in everything, God is in the space between us. God is in the table in front of you. (Paul, 1967)

My life belongs to Lord Krishna now. I'm just the servant of the servant of Krishna. I've never been so humble in all my life, and I feel great! (George, 1974)

You're just left with yourself all the time, whatever you do, anyway. You've got to get down to your own God in your own temple. It's all down to you, mate. (John, 1969)

I still practise Transcendental Meditation and I think it's great. Maharishi only ever did good for us, and although I have not been with him physically, I never left him. (George, 1992)

It is one of our perennial problems, whether there is actually a God. From the Hindu point of view each soul is divine. All religions are branches of one big tree. It doesn't matter what you call Him as long as you call. Just as cinematic images appear to be real but are only combinations of light and shade, so is the universal variety a delusion. The planetary spheres, with their countless forms of life, are naught but figures in a cosmic motion picture. One's values are profoundly changed when he is finally convinced that creation is only a vast motion picture; and that not in, but beyond, lies his own ultimate reality. (George, 1973)

I won't go to funerals because I don't believe in them. I believe your soul has gone by the time you get into the limo. She or he's up there or wherever it is. I can't wait to go half the time. (Ringo, 1980)

In one way I feel pessimistic. When you see the rate that the world is being demolished – people polluting the oceans and chopping down all the forests – unless somebody puts the brakes on soon, there isn't going to be anything left. There's just going to be more and more people with less and less resources. In that respect, I feel very sad. But at the same time, I have to be optimistic.

At the bottom line, I think that even if the whole planet blew up, you'd have to think about what happens when you die. In the end, 'Life goes on within you and without you.' I just have a belief that this is only one little bit, the physical world is one little bit of the universe. So in the end it doesn't really matter. (George)

With life and all I've been through, I do have a belief in goodness, a good spirit. I think what people have done with religion is personified good and evil, so good's become God with 'o' out, and evil's become Devil with a 'd' added. That's my theory of religion. (Paul, 1989)

Through Hinduism, I feel a better person. I just get happier and happier. I now feel that I am unlimited, and I am more in control of my own physical body. The thing is, you go to an ordinary church and it's a nice feeling. They tell you all about God, but they don't show you the way. They don't show you how to become Christ-conscious yourself. Hinduism, however, is different. (George, 1972)

Watching the wheels? The whole universe is a wheel, right? They're my own wheels, mainly. But watching myself is like watching everybody else. And I watch myself through my child, too. Then, in a way, nothing is real. As the Hindus or Buddhists say, it's an illusion, meaning all matter is simply floating atoms. The agreed-upon illusion is what we live and the hardest thing is facing yourself. It's easier to shout 'Revolution' or 'Power to the people' than it is to look at yourself and try to find out what's real inside you and what isn't. That's the hardest one.

I used to think the world was doing it to me and that the world owed me something. That either the Conservatives, the Socialists, Fascists, Communists, Christians or the Jews were doing something to me; when you're a teeny-bopper, that's what you think. But I'm forty now and I don't think that any more, because I found out it doesn't fucking work! The thing goes on anyway, and all you're doing is jacking off, screaming about what your mummy, daddy or society did, but one has to go through that. Most arseholes just accept what is and get on with it, right? But for the few of us who did question what was going on . . . I have found out personally – not for the whole world! – that I am responsible for it. I am part of them. There's no separation; we're all one, so in that respect, I look at it all and think, 'Ah, well, I have to deal with me again in that way. What is real? What is the illusion I'm living or not living?' And I have to deal with it every day. The layers of the onion. But that is what it's all about . . . You make your own dream. That's the Beatles' story, isn't it? That's what I'm saying now: Produce your own dream . . . I can't wake you up. I can't cure you. You can cure you.

It's fear of the unknown. The unknown is what it is. And to be frightened of it is what sends everybody scurrying around chasing dreams, illusions, wars, peace, love, hate, all that – it's all illusion. Accept that it's unknown and it's plain sailing. Everything is unknown – then you're ahead of the game. That's what it is. Right? (John, 1980)

Satya Sai Baba is not my guru, we're just good friends. (George)

I really didn't like that. Unfortunately, John was driftin' away from us at that point, so none of us actually knew. He never told us; we heard rumours and we were very sad. But he'd embarked on a new cause, which really involved anything and everything. Because John was that kind of guy – he wanted to live life to the full as he saw it. He would often say things like, 'If you find yourself at the edge of a cliff and you wonder whether you should jump or not – try jumping.' (Paul, 1986, discussing John's heroin use)

I keep [my religious beliefs] to myself unless somebody asks me about it. But I still feel the same as I felt back in the sixties. I lost touch with the Krishnas when Prabhupada died. I used to go and see the old master, A.C. Bhaktivedanta, quite a lot. He was real good. I'm still involved but it's something which is more a thing you do inside yourself. You don't actually do it in the road. It's a way of just trying to get in touch with yourself. I still write songs with [Krishna] in there in little bits and pieces. Lots of songs that are unfinished say various things but maybe I say it in different ways now. There's a song on [Cloud Nine] which is straight out of Yogananda, 'Fish on the Sand' it's called. (George, 1990)

I know the only time we ever took drugs was when we were without hope. And the only way we got out of it was through hope. If we can sustain that, then we won't need drugs, liquor, or anything. (Paul)

[LSD] went on for years. I must have had a thousand trips. I used to just eat it all the time. (John, 1970)

Up until LSD, I never realised that there was anything beyond this normal waking state of consciousness. But all the pressure was such that, as Bob Dylan said, 'There must be some way out of here.' I think for me it was definitely LSD. The first time I took it, it just blew everything away. I had such an incredible feeling of wellbeing, that there was a God and I could see Him in every blade of grass. It was like gaining hundreds of years' experience within twelve hours. It changed me and there was no way back to what I was before. It wasn't all good though, because it left quite a lot of questions as well. (George, 1987)

I'm a tidy man. I keep my socks in the socks drawer and stash in the stash box. Anything else they must have brought. (George, 1969, discussing his arrest for possession of cannabis)

The very first time we took LSD, John and I were together. And that experience and a lot of other things that happened after that, both on LSD and on the meditation trip to Rishikesh, we saw beyond each other's physical bodies, you know. That's there permanently, whether he's in a physical body or not. I mean this is the goal anyway: to realise the spiritual side. If you can't feel the spirit of some friend who's been close, then what chance have you got of feeling the spirit of Christ or Buddha or whoever else you may be interested in? If your memory serves you well, we're going to meet again. I believe that. (George)

I don't recommend it [acid]. It can open a few doors but it's not any answer. You go out and get the answers yourself. (Paul, 1968)

We smoke pot. We like it. We think it's harmless. Just like drainpipe trousers used to be. I had a real suburban upbringing in Liverpool and I can see the other point of view, but it can't change the person I've become.
  My dad didn't like it when I wore narrow trousers. Now his are sixteen inches and mine thirty inches. You can see what I'm getting at.
  And I guess it'll be like that with drugs. I don't go round preaching the gospel, just live my life quietly. (Paul)

John Lennon Fined £150 on Drug Charge

John Winston Lennon, aged 28, of the Beatles, was fined £150 with 20 guineas costs at Marylebone Magistrates Court yesterday when he pleaded guilty to the unauthorised possession of 219 grains of cannabis resin found when detectives, accompanied by dogs, searched his flat at Montagu Square, Marylebone, on 18 October.

Appearing with him on remand was Mrs Yoko Ono Cox, aged 34, artist, of the same address, who denied charges of unauthorised possession of the drug and wilfully obstructing Detective Sergeant Norman Pilcher when he was exercising his powers under the Dangerous Drugs Act.

She was discharged and Mr Lennon was also discharged on a similar charge of obstructing the officer, which he denied. The prosecution offered no evidence on those three counts.

Mr Roger Frisby for the prosecution told Mr John Phipps, the Magistrate, that although the flat appeared to be in the joint occupation of the couple, Mr Lennon had taken full responsibility for the drugs and said Mrs Cox had nothing to do with it.

Mr Frisby said that when the officers got into the flat and told Mr Lennon that they had a search warrant they found a large quantity of drugs properly prescribed by Mr Lennon's doctor. When asked if he had any he should not have, such as cannabis, Mr Lennon shook his head.

Mr Frisby said a cigarette-rolling machine found on top of a bathroom mirror, a tin originally containing film found in a bedroom and a cigarette case all bore traces of cannabis resin. In an envelope in a suitcase was found 27.3 grains of the drug and 19.8 grains were in a binocular case nosed out by a dog, on the mantel in the living room.

29 November 1968

Yoko is Named in Divorce Bid

Beatle John Lennon is being sued for divorce.

His wife, 27-year-old Cynthia Lennon, has filed a petition in which she alleges her husband has committed adultery.

The woman named in the petition is 34-year-old Japanese actress Yoko Ono.

Solicitors acting for both 27-year-old John and Yoko have entered an appearance denying Mrs Lennon's allegations.

John and Cynthia were married in 1962 and have a five-year-old son.

Their home at St George's Hill, Weybridge, Surrey, is up for sale at £40,000.

Yoko is married to American film producer, Anthony Cox.

The hearing of the petition is expected to be before the end of the year. Meanwhile solicitors for John and Cynthia are negotiating financial settlements.

1968

Beatle Paul to Marry

Paul McCartney, aged 26, is to marry Miss Linda Eastman today at Marylebone Registry Office, W1. They first met two years ago when Eastman, a professional photographer, took photographs of the Beatles in America.

Mr McCartney is the only unmarried member of the Beatles group. Miss Eastman, who is 27, is a member of the Eastman Kodak family. She has a daughter, Heather, by her first marriage.

Last night a group of teenage girls waited outside Mr McCartney's home in Cavendish Avenue, NW8. When he arrived in his car three police cars accompanied him. A policeman said they had been asked to clear the pavement but there was no trouble.

12 March 1969

The Lost Beatles Interviews

Pattie Harrison Clapton on the 1969 Drug Bust

It was Paul and Linda McCartney's wedding day and [we were invited to a] party . . . I was at home on my own, getting ready, when there was a knock on the door . . . I thought it must be just a gang of friends coming to our house on the way. I was about to answer the front door when the back door bell rang at the same time and I had a very uncanny feeling that all was not well. I opened the door and there they were: about six policemen, a policewoman and two dogs. A piece of paper was handed to me by Sgt Pilcher, who was gunning for everybody at the time. I knew exactly what it said without really reading it and I answered, 'Look, we don't have any dangerous drugs,' and then I went to answer the back door and they all came flooding in and proceeded to search the house and the greenhouse. I phoned George and said, 'Guess what's happened?' . . .

. . . Finally Sgt Pilcher said, 'Look what our dog Yogi has found,' and he produced this huge block of hash which I'd never seen before. I said to him, 'Where on earth did you find that?' and he said, 'In George's shoe' . . . It was preposterous and I said, 'Well, if you're looking for grass, it's on a table in the sitting room, in a little box.' I also said, 'I don't understand why you're doing this, because obviously it's going to attract a lot of publicity and many Beatles fans might start smoking and I thought the idea was to try and stop people taking drugs.' And he said, 'I want to save you from the evils of heroin!'

. . . Eventually George and Derek turned up and we all went to Esher police station and the police there were very sweet . . . When we got back to the house the vibes there were so bad I said, 'Look, we've got to go to the party, I can't bear it, the idea of the police going through everything.' So we got ready and off we went . . . As we went downstairs George saw Lord Snowdon and said, 'I'm going to talk to him, maybe he can stop this bust,' and I was casually looking around, when suddenly I spotted my younger sister Paula puffing on a joint which she then proceeded to offer Princess Margaret . . . I couldn't believe it, it was the early evening of the same day that we'd just been busted and there was my sister trying to hand Princess Margaret a joint!

Beatle Name Change

Beatle John Winston Lennon today changed his name to John Ono Lennon at a brief ceremony on the roof of the Beatles' Apple Company Headquarters at 3 Savile Row, London W1. The change of name was effected by Señor Bueno de Mesquita, Commissioner for Oaths.

Yoko Ono Lennon

John Ono Lennon

John says: 'Yoko changed hers for me. I've changed mine for her. One for both, both for each other. She has a ring. I have a ring. It gives us nine 'O's between us, which is good luck. Ten would not be good luck. Three names is enough for anyone. Four would be greedy.'

22 April 1969

Canada Puts Wet Blanket on Lennon 'Bed-in'

TORONTO, 26 May – Beatle John Lennon and his wife Yoko arrived here Sunday from the Bahamas, reporting it was too hot there for their 'bed-in for peace'. But immigration officials made it hot for them here, too.

Lennon, Yoko and her five-year-old daughter, Kyoko, were detained for 2½ hours at Toronto International Airport when they arrived on their way to Montreal.

Lennon and Yoko first planned to bed down in the United States, but he says the US government barred him because of the marijuana conviction. US immigration officials say he withdrew his visa application.

Paying $1200 in excess baggage charges, the affluent peace crusader arrived in the Bahamas Saturday with his wife, her daughter and four sound technicians. They planned to settle down in a $180-a-day suite, receiving admirers and photographers in bed from 10 a.m. to 10 p.m. for a week, and broadcasting to the US on the theme: 'If everyone stayed in bed for a week, there'd be no killing.'

After one night, Lennon said it was too hot and the Bahamas were 'farther from the United States than I thought. They'll hear me better from Canada.'

1969

John and Yoko Take a Trimming and Beatlemaniacs Mourn

AALBORG, Denmark, 21 Jan. – Very short, yeah, yeah, yeah. That was the verdict today on Beatle John Lennon's new close-cropped hairstyle.

The once shaggy Beatle and his wife, Yoko, both were shorn of their locks in a North Jutland barn Tuesday.

But mourning Beatlemaniacs need not despair. The hair is being kept in plastic bags – although for what purpose was not known.

Aaga Rosendahl Nielsen, head of the new experimental college Mr Lennon has joined, said Mr Lennon told him he sent for a hairdresser 'because I just felt like shedding all that hair and because a new haircut might enable me to move about anonymously.'

Looking at the crowd of newsmen and photographers, Mr Rosendahl Nielsen added:

'Of course, there is something symbolic in the haircut, but anyone is free to guess what the symbolism may be. Personally I like him better with the new haircut. It makes his personality come out much more strongly.'

Mr Lennon and Yoko came to Aalborg at Christmas to see her daughter, Kyoko, who has been living at the experimental college with her father, American movie producer Anthony Cox.

The last time Mr Lennon had his hair cut short was in 1967, for a role in Richard Lester's anti-war movie, *How I Won the War*.

1970

Solo Projects Indicate Beatle Break-up Coming

LONDON – Beatle Paul McCartney announced yesterday a series of independent projects which close friends say would almost certainly mean the end of the Beatles as a group.

The announcement, issued through McCartney's attorney and brother-in-law John Eastman of New York, said the private ventures will keep McCartney from directly working with the remainder of the Beatles quartet indefinitely.

'It is now highly unlikely they will ever even record together again,' one business source said.

The announcement said the first solo venture for McCartney would be the release this month of an album, *McCartney*. Eastman said McCartney wrote all 14 songs, played all the instruments, sang all the vocals, produced the record and collaborated on the cover design with his wife.

McCartney's plans to branch out on his own came in the wake of reported squabbles among the group and disagreement about their legal and business representation.

1970

Beatles Seen Treading Separate Paths

LONDON – The Beatles will be going more and more their separate ways in the months to come, friends said yesterday.

Projects that will divide the four more deeply than any of their individual undertakings in the past include:

– A long-playing record album designed to establish Beatle drummer Ringo Starr as a singer of popular 'standard' melodies.

– A major campaign by guitarist George Harrison, 'the quiet Beatle', to make his name as a musician in his own right.

– A determination by John Lennon to pursue his international campaign for peace.

Lennon told associates he and his wife Yoko have got the word 'peace' into more front page headlines than any statesman he can name.

All of this does not rule out the probability that records featuring the four will continue to appear for some time to come, friends said.

Another long-playing record album, a movie and a Beatle book will keep them together through next summer, the friends said.

John Lennon has confided to associates he can even imagine the day when he might not want his music on the same record with fellow Beatles Paul McCartney – his co-composer since the Beatles began – and George.

1970

Apple Bottoms Out

Earlier this week the Apple Press Office was closed down and the two remaining employees dismissed. Since the break-up of the Beatles their Apple empire has diminished to little more than a centre for collecting their royalties and dealing with their private affairs.

4 August 1970

Yoko Ono Gives Reason for Beatles Break-up

LONDON – The official biographer of the Beatles said yesterday the major cause of the break-up of that top quartet appeared to be John Lennon's marriage to Japanese artist Yoko Ono.

'If there was one single element in the split, I'd say it was the arrival of Yoko,' said Hunter Davies, author of *The Beatles, An Official Biography*.

While he was writing the book, Davies was the most intimate confidant of the Beatles outside their own music and business organisation.

Writing in the *Sunday Times*, Davies said that after Lennon and Yoko got together, 'the rest of the Beatles didn't matter any more.' Lennon and Yoko were married in Gibraltar in March last year.

Long rumoured differences among the Beatles came out in the open in a statement from Paul McCartney saying he was splitting from the group, and 'time will tell' whether temporarily or permanently.

Davies said that since the Beatles hadn't performed together in person since 1966, McCartney's statement 'was pretty pointless'.

McCartney himself, in an interview with Raymond Palmer in the *News of the World*, said: 'No matter how much we split, we're still very linked. We're the only four people who've seen the whole Beatlemania bit from the inside out, so we're tied forever, whatever happens.'

McCartney did not clarify in detail his reasons for breaking away from the group.

But Davies maintained that under Yoko's influence, Lennon began taking charge at Apple, the Beatles' business headquarters, and this 'was a blow to Paul's pride . . . Paul fell by the wayside and . . . they were no longer bosom buddies . . . George Harrison and Ringo Starr (the other two Beatles) are not exactly dotty over (endeared to) Yoko either.'

With Yoko, Lennon has mounted campaigns for world peace, held zany art exhibitions, made radical movies, formed a wild rock and roll band and issued non-Beatle records. None of these activities included the other Beatles.

So far Lennon, Harrison and Ringo have kept silent about McCartney's breakaway. McCartney himself didn't make his reasons much clearer than his original vague announcement.

Asked by Palmer what sort of things he might try on his own, McCartney replied: 'Anything and everything. There's no point in restricting yourself . . .

'The only danger is that once you get into this kind of machine where you make a lot of money – where you can get a nice house, a car and stuff – the danger is in believing that is what life is all about.

'Now, having a lot of money, I can see it for what it is, just like stones or shells or cows or whatever it is that the Zulus and the Basuto use for trading.

'There's still just as much ambition. But the ambition is just to do whatever comes along now . . .

'There are things like love and peace which matter as well . . .

'After you've gone through the whole bit of performing and showing everyone how famous you are, you realise that you don't need to show anyone any more.'

Despite the break-up, another Beatles record is to be issued next month, and Davies said Apple had another 12 hours of recorded material to be released.

1970

John Blames Paul for the Bust-up

Beatle John Lennon, in a frank interview in the US pop music journal *Rolling Stone*, blames Paul McCartney's attempts to dominate the group for leading to its break-up and claims the other Beatles insulted his Japanese-born wife, Yoko Ono.

Lennon also had some outspoken things to say about the solo albums recently issued by his former colleagues – Ringo: 'Good, but I wouldn't buy any of it.' McCartney: 'Rubbish.' George Harrison: 'Personally, at home, I wouldn't play that kind of music.'

Lennon, who has just issued his own solo album, said: 'I prefer myself, I have to be honest, you know.

'Ringo was all right, so was Maureen [Ringo's wife], but the other two really gave it to us. I'll never forgive them.'

Lennon said all the Beatles got 'fed up of being sidemen for Paul.'

Lennon listed his experiences with drugs and said he stopped LSD because he just could not stand the bad trips.

He said he started taking LSD in 1964 and made about a thousand trips.

Lennon said he started on pills at 17 and was on pills when he made his first film, *A Hard Day's Night*, and had turned to marijuana when he made the second film, *Help!*

Paul McCartney yesterday started High Court proceedings to end the Beatles partnership.

In a writ issued in the Chancery Division yesterday, he claimed a declaration that the partnership 'The Beatles and Co.,' formed in April 1967, 'ought to be accordingly dissolved.'

January 1971

'That was a band I was with . . .'

Don't ever call me 'ex-Beatle McCartney' again. That was a band I was with. Now I'm not with them. (Paul)

Touring's like the army, whatever the army's like. One big sameness which you have to go through. One big mess. I can't remember any tours. We've had enough of performing, forever. I can't imagine any reason which would make us do any sort of tour again. (John)

Yes, I was in the Beatles. Yes, we made some great records together. Yes, I love those boys. But that's the end of the story. (Ringo)

John Lennon's Aunt Mimi
with a favourite cat

(left toright) Paul McCartney,
Pete Best, George Harrison,
John Lennon. The Beatles
enjoy a pint at The Grapes,
Mathew St, Liverpool

Playing for the Ready
Steady Go cameras

Leather and quiffs:
with Stuart Sutcliffe in
Liverpool, early 1960

Jackets and ties:
The Beatles smarten up
with Ringo, circa 1962

The Beatles advertise
Vox amplifiers, 1963

Answering the
press, circa 1964

The rear view of
the haircuts that
scandalised America

The Beatles minus
mop-tops – a photo
joke from 1963

John Lennon crops the
mop for real, circa 1967

Mr Ringo and
Mrs Maureen Starkey,
circa 1965

Mr John and Mrs
Cynthia Lennon arrive
in style, circa 1965

Mr George and
Mrs Patti Harrison
leaving court in
Esher after facing
charges of possessing
marijuana, 1969

Mr John Ono and Mrs
Yoko Ono Lennon
on top of the world,
Ma, in London

Mr Paul and Mrs
Linda McCartney
out on the town, 1975

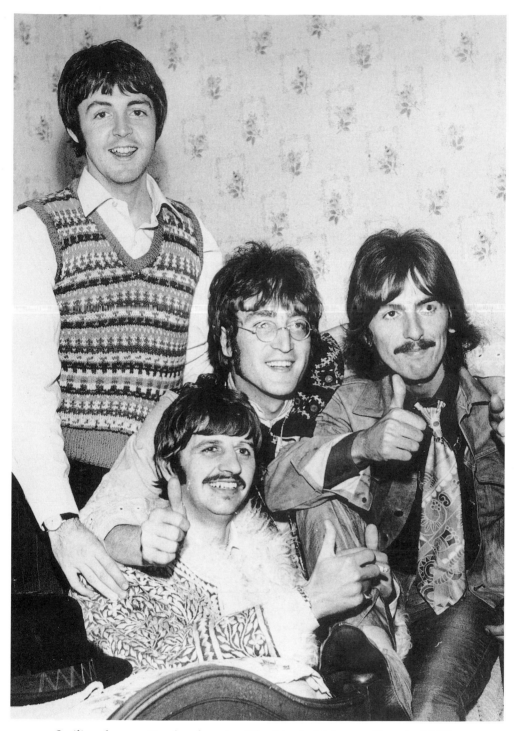

Smiling, happy, Beatles shooting The Magical Mystery Tour in 1967.
They were never to be this happy together again . . .

The end of the Beatles. UPI urgent wire to all newspapers of December 8 1980

8766
U R G E N T

LENNON-SUB

(NEW YORK)-- NEW YORK POLICE SAY FORMER BEATLE JOHN LENNON IS IN

CRITICAL CONDITION AFTER BEING SHOT THREE TIMES AT HIS HOME ON

MANHATTAN'S UPPER WEST SIDE. A POLICE SPOKESMAN SAID "A SUSPECT IS IN

CUSTODY," BUT HE HAD NO OTHER DETAILS. A HOSPITAL WORKER SAID--

QUOTE-- "THERE'S BLOOD ALL OVER THE PLACE. THEY'RE WORKING ON HIM

LIKE CRAZY."

UPI 12-08-80 11:35 PES

The Beatles are Alive and Well

Spring is here and Leeds play Chelsea tomorrow and Ringo and John and George and Paul are alive and well and full of hope.

The world is still spinning and so are we and so are you.

When the spinning stops – that'll be the time to worry, not before.

Until then, the Beatles are alive and well and the beat goes on, the beat goes on.

Final Beatles Press Release, 10 April 1970

John and Yoko, Amsterdam, 1969

Question: Some people are equal, but some are *more* equal than others, as you know.

John: Yes. But they all have equal possibility.

Question: You are to talk without philosophy because I'm not much of a philosopher.

John: Me either.

Question: You see this whole roomful of reporters, photographers and filmers . . .

Yoko: It'll come through.

John: I think there's something beautiful about it because on all the Beatle tours there's always people who had laughs! The field reporters had a good time when they got the right photograph or the right interview. We always had a laugh because some photographer fell over, got the wrong picture or something. It's a happening.

Yoko: And there's plenty people in the world who are sensitive enough. When you report, they will see what we're doing and it's good.

John: But it means this is a mad house. Everything's too serious.

Question: But you're sitting here singing, 'Those were the days, my friend,' and you give some kind of impression that you are very sensible and have a grown-up approach . . .

John: Well, I'm pretty old now and she's pretty old, but we have a sense of humour and that's what this is about, partly.

Yoko: The world needs a sense of humour, I think, more than anything, because the world is getting more and more violent and tense.

Question: This flabbergasts a Dutchman a bit. Is Holland a honeymoon country?

John: It's a beautiful place. Amsterdam's a place where a lot of things are happening with the youth. It's an important place.

Yoko: A romantic place.

John: Everywhere is important, but Amsterdam is one of them. There's a few centres in the world and Amsterdam is one of them for youth.

Yoko: Many vitally alive youth, with high ideas and everything for the world.

John: The Provos with their white bicycles.

Question: Are those ideas that appeal to you, by the way?

John: Yes, the peaceful ideas that the youth have. If we have any influence on youth at all we'd like to influence them in a peaceful way.

Yoko: Communicate with them and each other.

John: Say hello to them. We're here to say hello to people in Amsterdam or Holland.

Question: What do you see in a conformist institution such as marriage?

John: Intellectually, we know marriage is nowhere; that a man should just say, 'Here, you're married,' when we've been living together a year before it. Romantically and emotionally it's something else. When our divorce papers came through, it was a great relief. We didn't realise how much of a relief it was going to be until Peter [Brown] came up and said, 'It's over.' It was only a bit of paper. We'd made the marriage over by living together when we were still married to the other two people. Just the fact that somebody said it was a relief and the fact that we got married was another kind of joy. It was very emotional, the actual marriage ceremony. We both got very emotional about it and we're both quite cynical, hard people, but very soft as well. Everyone's a bit both ways. And it was very romantic.

Question: I should like to have your reactions on this, Mrs Lennon.

Yoko: I got this ring and, of course, to many people in the contemporary world that's old-fashioned. I sort of broke down. I felt so good about it. When I think about it, it's an old ritual, but very functional. It has a lot to do with sex [*slipping the ring on and off her finger*] . . .

John: Stop it, stop it!

Yoko: Ahh . . .

John: I'm joking, I'm joking.

Question: It's kind of loose, though.

John: Pardon? Yes, we're having it fitted here.

Question: You were talking about marriage as an institution; now, the $64,000 question: what about the kiddies?

John: We're thinking it might be nice if we conceive one in Amsterdam. We might call it 'Amsterdam' or 'Peace' or 'Hair' or 'Bed-In' or something. It would be beautiful.

Question: How do you feel about English linen?

Yoko: Yes, it would be nice to conceive a child in this bed, actually, wouldn't it?

John, Bed-in, Montreal, 1969

Question: Do you condemn civil rights demonstrations?

John: I don't condemn them; I'm *with* them. I'm just saying: Isn't it about time they thought of something else? There have been marches for sixty years. It's ineffective. Someone asked us, 'What would you suggest we do?' I said, 'You've got women, use sex.' Every day in the popular papers, they have bikini-clad girls. Use sex for peace!

Question: Do you condemn campus violence and building takeovers?

John: Sit-ins are okay. I don't see why they have to destroy the building to take it over, though. Either sit in and take it over or leave. Take no notice of it. You don't need the building.

Question: The Americans are very interested in what happens in Harvard, Berkeley and City College. Are you condemning them and the methods used?

John: If you're successful, we congratulate you. If not, think of something else. Be like the Indians and retreat. I know they lost and that, but the philosophy was right. Violence begets violence. The successful revolutions were in Russia, France and England. They were successful and the new people took over power and built up all the buildings they brought down, had more babies and became the Establishment. So we see where violence gets us.

Question: Some of the people seem to think you're kind of revolutionary and the Establishment seems to fear they won't let you in and give you visas and everything. You're standing right in the middle now between two factions of two opposing philosophies. Have you found this kind of antagonism amongst your previous friends?

John: It's not antagonism, it's just about Yoko and me. We're in two different bags. She was avant-garde and I was pop. We met, fell in love, but that didn't solve the problems of our personalities and our previous work and all that. We had to destroy each other's games and preconceived concepts and what avant-garde was. We had to find out what we really were. That's all we're doing with these people and that's what they're doing to us. They're saying, 'What do you think you're doing?' That's the only way to communicate. If two lovers deeply in love still have to destroy each other's games to get through to each other then we must do it with the world as well.

John Returns his MBE

John Lennon has returned his MBE award in protest against Britain's involvement in the Nigerian and Vietnamese conflicts. In identical letters addressed to Her Majesty the Queen, the Prime Minister and the Secretary of the Central Chancery, John Lennon writes, 'I am returning this MBE in protest against Britain's involvement in the Nigeria–Biafra thing, against our support of America in Vietnam and against "Cold Turkey" slipping down in the charts.' The letter is signed, 'With love, John Lennon' in his handwriting. Typed underneath is 'John Lennon of Bag.' The letters are written on notepaper headed 'Bag Productions, 3 Savile Row, London W1.' Bag is the company set up by Lennon and his wife Yoko Ono to handle their films, records and other merchandise. John Lennon and the other three Beatles were awarded the MBE in the Queen's Birthday Honours List in the summer of 1965.

Apple press release, 1969

Lennon on Returning his MBE

We had to do a lot of selling-out then. Taking the MBE was a sell-out for me. Before you get an MBE the Palace writes to ask if you're going to accept it, because you're not supposed to reject it publicly and they sound you out first.

I chucked the letter in with all the fan mail, until Brian asked me if I had it. He and a few other people persuaded me that it was in our interest to take it, and it was hypocritical of me to accept it.

But I'm glad, really, I did accept it, because it meant that four years later I could use it to make a gesture.

We did manage to refuse all sorts of things people don't know about.

For instance, we did the Royal Variety Show once, and we were asked discreetly to do it every year after that, but we always said, 'Stuff it.'

So every year there was always a story in the newspapers saying: 'Why No Beatles For The Queen?' which was pretty funny, because they didn't know we'd refused it.

It always embarrassed me. I was a hypocrite to take it, but I was on the make. I've been thinking about giving it back for a long time. I discussed it and thought about it and put it off like you do anything, like getting a haircut, something like that, or getting your teeth fixed. I was always going to do it, whenever I remembered it or somebody put it on a letter. I use to flinch because I'm basically a socialist.

I set the alarm for eight o'clock and then just lay there. I thought, well, if anyone wants me they'll phone. The phone went lots of times, but that's the one I never answer. My own phone didn't go at all. So I just lay there.

The Queen isn't upset over me returning my MBE. She's too intelligent.

John and Yoko, Denmark, 1970

John: All right, you rumourmongers, let's get going.

Question: We've all heard a lot of rumours about you.

John: So have I.

Question: Can we get some truth about your visit here in Denmark?

John: Well, I've just heard a new one in the *Daily Express* that I've bought seventy acres of land here. Every paper seems to think I'm going to buy seventy acres of land. I've been to Greece recently and they thought I was going to buy land there, and Canada, wherever. I've got no other land except some in England and Ireland. We came to see Kyoko. And Tony and Melinda, of course, but Kyoko was the access point and we've had a nice seven days of peace.

Question: What kind of man are you really?

John: I'm a nervous guy, you know.

Question: Do you and Yoko believe in peace in our time?

John: Yeah. The thing is, we have this poster that says WAR IS OVER IF YOU WANT IT. We all sit round pointing fingers at Nixon and the leaders of the countries, saying, 'He gave us peace,' or 'They gave us war.' But it's *our* responsibility what happens around the world, in every other country as well as our own. It's our responsibility for Vietnam and Biafra and the Israeli War and all the other wars we don't quite hear about. It's *all* our responsibility and when we all want peace we'll get it. I support humanity, I don't belong to any left wing, right wing, middle wing, Black Panthers, White Christians, Protestants, Catholics or nothing. People have said we're naive for trying to sell peace like a bar of soap. But I want to ask you, is Mr Ford naive? Or is the soap powder factory naive? They're selling the same old soap that's been around for two thousand years, but suddenly it's *new blue soap*. So we're selling *new blue peace* and we hope some of you buy it. The war is here now and there's two ways of looking at it. Some people say, 'Why did you spend your money on posters or peace campaigns? Why didn't you give it to the Biafran children, or something like that?' And we say, 'We're trying to prevent cancer, not cure it.'

Question: Did you spend all your money?

John: No. The people around us made more money than the Beatles ever did, I'll tell you that. None of the Beatles are millionaires. But there's a lot of millionaires who became millionaires around the Beatles, however. You know the story.

Question: Where are you going from here?

John: I don't know. We play everything by ear. We try not to make plans. I don't really like knowing what I'm going to do for the next eight months, and we'll just stay until it's time to go back and work.

Question: Are you feeling comfortable out here?

John: Oh, it's beautiful. All the snow. We go walking in the garden and all that. It's beautiful, all the colours in the sky and the mist. It's just a fantastic place with good vibes, as they say in this generation. Very good vibes around and just the people we've met. We've met very few, but they're straight. They're not as paranoid as in the big cities or other countries. People are less paranoid in Denmark.

FBI Memo

Airtel to New York
RE: John Winston Lennon
100-469910

In view of subject's intention to engage in disruptive activities surrounding RNC [Republican National Committee], New York Office will be responsible for closely following his activities until time of actual deportation. Afford this matter close supervision and keep Bureau fully advised by most expeditious needs warranted.

NOTE:
John Lennon, former member of Beatles singing group, is allegedly in US to assist in organising disruption of RNC. Due to narcotics conviction in England, he is being deported along with wife Yoko Ono. They appeared at Immigration and Naturalisation Service, New York 3/16/72, for deportation proceedings, but won delay until 4/18/72 because subject fighting narcotics conviction and wife fighting custody child case in US. Strong possibility looms that subject will not be deported any time soon and will probably be in US at least until RNC. Information developed [blank out] that subject continues to plan activities directed toward RNC and will soon initiate series of 'rock concerts' to develop financial support, with first concert to be held Ann Arbor, Michigan, in near future. New York Office covering subject's temporary residence and being instructed to intensify discreet investigation of subject to determine activities vis à vis RNC.

John, New York, 1976

Question: What were you thinking and feeling when you were fifteen?
John: I was thinking if only I could get out of Liverpool I might get a break. I wanted to be a famous artist. Possibly I would have to marry a rich old lady, or man, you know, to look after me while I did my art. But then, rock'n'roll came along, and so I didn't have to marry anybody.
Question: How do you feel now about your music with the Beatles?
John: Beatle records stand up in any period unless the music really changes. We were all used to groups like the Grateful Airplane. We [the Beatles] were always ourselves. You could pick any Beatle record and a few of them are obviously of an era. But most of them still sound pretty current, like 'Hey, Jude', or songs like 'Eleanor Rigby'. It doesn't matter what period or what era, they would go down well.
Question: What were the Beatles really trying to do? And why all the hostility when you broke up?
John: When it gets down to the nitty gritty, it's the song, you know. And, if anything, the Beatles were figureheads. I could speak [about them] more succinctly later on when I thought about it. When we split up, you know. I call it a divorce, right? But when I thought about it, obviously, you know, I could change my mind.
Question: What did the Beatles actually contribute to their generation?
John: I have a picture of it now. There was a ship sailing to the new world. I saw this group on the ship, maybe the Stones were up there too, but I just said, 'Land Ho!' So we were all part of it. We [the Beatles] were in the crow's nest. We contributed whatever we could. I can't designate what we did or didn't do, how each individual was impressed by the Beatles physically or whatever. And we were all on this ship together, our generation. What we did was wake up the avant-garde in music and film. I mean, not just the Beatles, but rock'n'roll itself, you know. And this so-called avant-garde was asleep, and we were going around in circles.
Question: What is your goal these days?
John: I'm now thirty-four. And a lot of things one knew before but you couldn't live them. So now I'm trying to live out all the things I've learned in thirty-four years, to apply every day. All those things from the psychedelic era to Maharishi or Janov, or anybody like that.
Question: Do you like people?
John: I do like people, but I become whoever I'm with and so if I am with a madman, I become mad. If I'm with somebody I love, I become lovely. Right? So really, I'm like a cloud in the wind.

Question: Do you want to clear up the idea that the Beatles were responsible for the drug scene?

John: Hey! Actually that's a dumb question. Who gave the drugs to the Beatles? I didn't invent those things, I just bought them. We never invented the stuff. The big story about the Beatles and LSD started in the British press after they interviewed Paul on TV. They asked him if he felt any responsibility announcing that he had taken LSD. So he said, 'Okay, well, just don't put the film out then.' How dare they say that we propagated it.

Paul, Press Conference for *Give My Regards to Broad Street*, 1984

Question: Did you have a hard time picking the old songs to re-record?
Paul: I pulled out about fifty songs that I fancied singing and I gave a list of those to the director and said, 'Let's just choose.' So some of them got chosen for pure story reasons. Like 'Yesterday' was included on the director's request because he wanted to set up the thing that happens toward the end of the movie where I become a busker. But something like 'For No One', that was just because I love that song and I realised I hadn't sung it since the twenty years ago we're talking about. I never ever did it in public. I did it only once on the record. And I thought, 'Well, it's a pity that songs can just come and go that quickly.' I wanted that one in just for my own pleasure. And then 'Ballroom Dancing', for instance, was put in because it's a very visual number. So it was a mishmash of reasons . . .

Why shouldn't I sing 'em? Just because I once recorded them with the Beatles? They're not sacred, not to me, anyway. I wouldn't say I do a better version of those. Maybe those are the definitive versions, maybe not. You know, I think 'Long and Winding Road' in this is better than the original version. Just that particular song. So that was it really, I fancied singing them and didn't see why not.

John and I once tried to write a play when we were just starting out, even before we wrote any songs. We got two pages and just couldn't go any further, we just dried up. It would have been great, actually, because it was like a precursor to *Jesus Christ Superstar*. It was about this guy called Pilchard who you never actually saw. He was always upstairs in a room, praying. And the whole play was about the family saying, 'Oh God, is he prayin' again?' It was quite a nice idea, but we could never get him out of that room and downstairs.

Question: There are so many books out on the Beatles. Do you have any plans to write an autobiography?
Paul: The only thing that would make me do it is that round about this age, you do start to forget, you know. After twenty years, you don't remember it so well. And that would be the motivating factor, to actually get it down. But I haven't actually thought of doing it, really. But it's beginning to sneak into my mind that maybe I ought to get it down even if it isn't going to be like Mick's. It's more a publicity stunt rather than a book.

Question: In the early press accounts, you were the good guy. But in later biographies, you're cast as the bad guy. Do you feel a need to give your side?

Paul: Well, like anyone, I wouldn't mind being understood rather than misunderstood. It's very tempting when someone like John was slagging me off in the press. There was a period there when he was really going for me. It's very tempting to answer back, but I'm glad I didn't, I just thought, 'the hell with it, he's going over the top like he does.' He was a great fella, but he had that about him. He'd suddenly throw the table over and on to a new thing. And I was the table. But, I mean, a lot of it was talk and I think John loved the group. I think, though, he had to clear the decks for his new life. That was my feeling at the time. And there's nothing really you could say. But I don't think I was the bad guy or the good guy. I think originally what happened is that I'm from a very close, warm family in Liverpool, and I was very lucky to come from that kind of family. John wasn't. John was an only child. His father left home at three. His mother was killed when he was sixteen. My mum died when I was fourteen, so we had that in common. But when it came to meet the press and I saw a guy in the outer office shaking, I'd go in and say, 'Want a cup of tea?' because I just didn't like to be around that tension, that nervousness. So it fell to me to go and chat to the guy and put him at ease. Which then looked like PR. So I became known as the sort of PR man in the group. I probably was. The others would say, 'I'm not bloody doing that interview, you do it.' So I tended to look a bit the good guy in the media's eyes, because that's who I was being nice to. And I suppose the others may have resented that a little. But eventually, I've got this wild, ruthless ambition kind of image. If you do well, you get a bit of that. I don't really think it's that true. I think everyone was just as ruthless and ambitious as I was.

Question: What do you think of the exploitation of Lennon's death?

Paul: I think it's inevitable. You're talking about the West and capitalism. Exploitation's part of the game, really. I prefer to remember him how I knew him. I was in Nashville and saw a John Lennon whisky decanter. AARGH! He didn't even drink it. So, yeah, it's a bit yucky. But you can't do anything about it. This is America, folks.

Question: There have been reports you might bid upwards of $60 million for Northern Songs. How important is it to you to regain control of your old material?

Paul: I'd really like to do it. Just because it seems natural that I should be allowed to own my own songs eventually. And I figure whoever's been publishing them has made a lot of money on me. But if you sign 'em away, you sign 'em away. That's the law of the land. And I signed 'em away, so I can't really blame the fella who bought them. But I'd like to get them back just because they're my babies, John's and my babies.

Like 'Yesterday', I think if you tell the man in the street that Paul doesn't own 'Yesterday', it would surprise him. And the trouble is having to ask permission to sing it in the movie. That gets you. But actually, the publishers were quite fair. I think they only charged me a pound. I think they saw the irony too.

Question: Your current work will always be compared to your past work with the tendency to devalue the current. Is that difficult to live with? Do you ever just want to get rid of the Beatles?

Paul: Not really. I know what you mean, though. I have to admit, looking at all the songs I've written that probably there's a little period in there that was my hottest period. 'Yesterday', 'Here, There, and Everywhere', a little bunch of stuff that just came all in a few years. I suppose it was because we were at our height and the novelty became a very important factor. What's happened with me over the past ten years is I've tended to assume that the critics were right. 'Yeah, you're right. I'm not as good as I used to be.' But in actual fact, recently I've started to think, 'Wait a minute, let's check this out. Is this really true?' And I don't think it actually is. For instance, a song called 'Mull of Kintyre', which sold more records than any other record in England, is from my 'bad period'. The song 'Band on the Run', that's also from my bad period. I think what happens if after such a success as the Beatles, everyone, including me, thinks there's no way we can follow that, so you just tend to assume it's not as good. I think, as a body of work, my ten years with the Beatles, I would say, is probably better than this stuff. I do tend to be a bit gullible and go along with whoever's criticising me and say, 'Yeah, you're right, I'm a jerk.'

Question: Do you feel as if you're competing with your past work?

Paul: Yeah, a little bit. I think this new song, 'No More Lonely Nights', I felt good about that. There are, I think, some decent things in there. It's not all rubbish. But I think it's a natural thing after the Beatles to assume he must be on a losing streak now. And I tend to go along with it. But I don't think it's really true.

Question: Do you just sit and wait for the songs to come to you?

Paul: No, I just tend to sit down and try and write a song, I think the best ones come of their own volition. 'Yesterday', I just fell out of bed and that was there. I had a piano by the side of my bed. I mean, that particular song I woke up and there was a tune in my head. And I thought, 'Well, I must have heard it last night or something.' And I spent about three weeks asking all the music people I knew, 'What is this song? Where have you heard this song before?' I just couldn't believe I had written it.

Paul with Julia Baird, London, 1986

Paul: Good morning and welcome to Radio Norwich. I have today with me Julia Baird who's . . .

Julia: Shut up!

Paul: . . . got some questions she's going to attempt to read in the first part of our 'Read A Question Telethon'!

Julia: Thank you. Well, Paul . . .

Paul: What, Julia?

Julia: Would you kindly tell me about your first meeting with John?

Paul: The first time I met your brother was at the Woolton village fete. I'd been invited there by Ivan Vaughan, who was our mutual mate.

Julia: Did you hear what's happened to him? Several years ago, Ivan Vaughan contracted Parkinson's Disease and is today a well-known advocate of research into the cause of this deadly neurological disorder.

Paul: Yeah. Actually I saw him last weekend, he came to our house. I know him quite well, still. He was born on exactly the same day as me, Ivan, 18 June 1942. So we've always had a lot in common as well as with John.

Julia: You mean to tell me you and John had mutual mates without ever knowing each other?

Paul: Well, John lived in Mendips and Ivan lived just a garden away or something. ['Mendips' was the name of John's boyhood home at 251 Menlove Avenue, Woolton, in suburban Liverpool.] So they were mates from where they lived. But Ivan was a mate of mine from school and so one day he said, 'Don't you want to come along to the Woolton village fete? A couple of the lads are going to be there and stuff and I'll take you.' I think at the time John was about sixteen so I might have been fourteen or fifteen . . . So anyway, I'd been invited by Ivan and he took me along. I remember coming into the fete and seeing all the sideshows.

Julia: Yes, the Scouts, Cubs and everything.

Paul: Right. And also hearing all this great music wafting in from this little Tannoy system. It was John and the band. Len Garry, Pete Shotton, Colin Hanton on drums, Griff on guitar and maybe Nigel Whalley who was their official manager. (He managed to get on stage!) Anyway, he was a good lad. I remember I was amazed and thought, 'Oh great, I'll listen to the band.' Because I was obviously into the music.

Julia: Hadn't you originally gone along to sing yourself?

Paul: No, no. I'd only come as a guest with Ivan. We were just in the audience watching. I remember John singing a song called 'Come Go With Me'. He'd heard it on the radio. It was a lovely song by the Del Vikings. John, however, didn't really know all the verses but he knew the chorus (*he sings*): 'Come, come, come go with me. Little darling, go with me.' The rest he just made up himself. Good bluesy lyrics like, 'Come go with me down to the penitentiary.' I remember at the time he was playing banjo chords on his guitar.

Julia: Our mum taught him to play the banjo. It was a big mother-of-pearl banjo she had.

Paul: Right, Julia taught him to play banjo chords but he'd got a guitar because it was more fashionable and modern than a banjo. He still played with banjo tuning though, and only had about four strings at the time. I just thought, 'Well, he looks good, he's singing well and he seems like a great lead singer to me.' Of course he had his glasses off so he really looked quite suave.

Julia: And his hair greased back. He must not have been able to really see too much with his glasses off.

Paul: Well, no, he wouldn't have been able to see. Are you short-sighted then, too?

Julia: Completely and utterly, I'm afraid.

Paul: I knew through friends at the art college there was this guy named Geoff who was even more short-sighted than your brother. So John used to often help him across the street. The blind leading the blind, I suppose!

Julia: That's right. Well, that's when he had the big, thick, black glasses, wasn't it?

Paul: The Buddy Holly look! You see, a rock'n'roll person we all liked wore those glasses, so it was great. Anyone who really needed to wear glasses could then come out of the closet, I suppose.

Julia: As long as that's all he was doing!

Paul: Until Buddy came along, any fellow with glasses always took them off to play. So anyway, getting back to meeting John. He was up there jiving away and after they finished their set I met them all in the church hall. They were having a beer, I think. It wasn't crazy drinking or anything, it was more just a bit of fun. You know, we all used to really think John was pretty cool. He was a bit older and would therefore do a little more greased-back hair and things than we were ever allowed. I just didn't do it. The way my dad was, really. But John looked a bit of a ted with his drake and all. He had nice, big sideboards as we called them. I remember him on this old guitar that was laying around. I knew a lot of the words and that was very good currency in those days. That was the big thing then. It was, 'How did you get the words to that, man?' 'Oh, I know a fellow who lives in Bootle and if you get a bus to his house, why, he'll teach you B 7th!' So we'd all pile on the bus to learn a chord . . . almost. Knowing the words to a song was the same, so it really was a big deal to actually know the full lyrics to 'Twenty Flight Rock', and I learned them all! It was one of the very first records I ever got. I bought it at Curry's in Liverpool.

Julia: I remember John and I slowing records down in order to try and learn the words.

Paul: That's right, we used to do that too. At the time I remember thinking John smelled a bit beery and was obviously a little older than I was used to. I was only still a kid when I met him and hadn't quite seen the grown-up world yet. Of course later, when George came around, he was even younger. He was my little mate, you see. Nonetheless, he could play guitar, particularly this piece called 'Raunchy', which we all used to love. You see, if anyone could do something like that then it was enough for them to get into the group. So what happened that first night with John and the lads, we all went to the pub for a couple of drinks and that. I had to try and kid the barman that I was really eighteen.

Julia: I was wondering how they let you in.

Paul: Well, you know, I had a sports coat on and I just tried to look like one of the boys. As I recall, there was a bit of a panic on because there was a big fight brewing and suddenly the word went round that we were all needed. Apparently there was a mob forming up the road getting ready to invade the pub! I just thought, 'Jesus, what have I got myself into here? I've only come for a day out and suddenly I'm with all these men who are about to begin hurling machetes at each other!' But somehow that all blew over and we ended up having a very nice evening. I think later the band went back over to the church hall for a jam but I had to get home and that. A couple of weeks later Pete Shotton came up on his bike and invited me to join the group. You know, one of the interesting things about John to me was that his people always had a bit of money. I was from the trading estate just like the rest of the Beatles and it was kind of like seeing another world from what I was used to. I remember being very impressed in Mendips seeing the complete works of Winston Churchill.

Julia: Yes.

Paul: And John had read them! I hadn't really met people like this before, so I was very impressed with that side of him, you know. I mean, with his going to art school and that kind of thing. Of course, I went to the school next to his so we met up there. I remember seeing him in the chippie one day, too. And you'd see him on the bus, you know. Actually, I saw him a few times before I met him. It was, 'Oh, he's that fellow! He's the ted who gets on the bus at the stop.' I always thought John was very hip. Then I was asked to join the group, probably on the strength of knowing 'Twenty Flight Rock'. I think I also sang 'Long Tall Sally' for him as well. That was my Little Richard thing, which I still do. The Eddie Cochran attraction to me was in the words, 'I've got a girl with a wrecking machine.' There's some great words in all those early rock'n'roll songs.

Julia: What did you think of the Quarrymen musically?

Paul: Well, I thought John was good. He was really the only outstanding member, all the rest kind of slipped away, you know? The drummer was pretty good actually, for what we knew then. One of the reasons I know they all liked Colin was because he had the record, 'Searchin'' and again, that was big currency. Sometimes you made a whole career with someone just because he had a particular record!

Julia: What sort of memories do you have of our mother?

Paul: Of Julia . . . Well, I always thought she was a very beautiful lady and a really nice woman, and of course, John absolutely adored her. Number one, obviously on the level that she was his mum, but also because she was a very spirited woman. As we were saying before, she taught him to play the banjo, and I mean, that's really very gay isn't it, in the old-fashioned sense of the word.

Julia: Full of life.

Paul: Full of life, yeah.

Julia: You know we used to get our fairy stories told to us with the banjo and sometimes even the piano.

Paul: Did you? I mean, our family was musical but there certainly wasn't a woman who could play the banjo, that was very unusual. It was always the men. Julia was very ahead of her time. Actually, you used to get quite a lot of that in the twenties or whatever that era was. I mean, that was one of the things I undoubtedly found very interesting about your family. I know my mother was a nurse and my dad a cotton salesman, so we always lived in the nurse's house on the estate. Nearly always it was the midwife's house we lived in. So to actually see this sort of middle-class thing was fascinating for me. Christ, I can even recall John getting one hundred quid for his birthday off your relatives in Edinburgh!

Julia: Yes, we all got it when we turned twenty-one.

Paul: One hundred quid! I mean, I still say I'd like it now. You know what I'm saying, isn't it true?

Julia: Just a minute, let me check my purse . . .

Paul: Someone just hands you a hundred quid, still feels good to me. And so I thought, 'This is amazing, I've never seen people like this!' I remember John talking about people the family knew from the BBC, friends that were dentists and uncles and aunts up in Scotland, so it was very exotic to me, all that. You know, we went to Paris on that money. It was supposed to be Spain, but we never got past Paris, we enjoyed it so much. We hitch-hiked but suddenly thought, 'We can't get to Spain on a hundred quid.' I don't really know if he was really fond of me or just into spending. And I would be there for the banana milkshake. I think actually I paid my own way, but you know, in those days it was much safer hitching than it obviously is now. We soon realised we needed a bit of a gimmick to get people to stop so we both wore bowler hats in addition to our leather jackets. We thought that might take the edge off the kind of hoody look or ruffian image we had then. I guess people would just think, 'Whoa, look, there's a couple of daft kids in bowler hats there. You know, they don't really look like a threat.' We got a bit drunk on the French beer. We had been drinking the British stuff so we thought we could handle it but this foreign stuff really went to our heads. It was all just so adventurous. I had never done anything like that. I'd hardly ever been out of Liverpool before. We'd been to Pwllheli, Skegness and Leamington Spa before, but that had been the whole of my travels. It was very exciting to get off on your own with a mate. John was a great guy because he was never boring. I don't actually think anyone in your family is boring. You're really a lively bunch. To be honest, John and I shared a lot of things, you know, cruel humour which we got into.

Julia: What's the first tune you ever wrote with John? Can you remember?

Paul: Yeah. I've got an exercise book at home somewhere with some numbers we started.

Julia: I wonder how many great things have been started in school exercise notebooks?

Paul: The first one I think might have been called 'Just Fun'. We actually wrote a few that never got published, looking back. They weren't put down anywhere so they only exist in my memory. Actually, it's something I want to do something with. I mean, they're pretty rough songs, but they're not bad rockabilly in a way. 'Just Fun' goes like (*he sings*):

'They said that our love was just fun
the day that our friendship begun'

It was really quite good but there were some terrible lyrics. That was one of the first. 'Love me do' was from that batch as well. 'Too Bad About Sorrows' was another one. I was very proud of them actually.

Julia: Would you ever consider actually writing a book yourself?

Paul: You know, I don't know. These possibilities are really starting to kind of come to the fore. To me John's passing has really made all this nostalgia, but for me I don't feel as though it's stopped yet.

Julia: No.

Paul: But, now that the twentieth anniversary of *Sgt Pepper* is rolling around it's beginning to dawn on me what a big nostalgic event it is. You know, I was talking to Neil Aspinall at Ringo's wedding, and we were remembering something that happened years ago and he said, 'Oh, I remember it exactly, it was in Piccadilly Circus, wasn't it?' I said, 'No, it was Savile Row.' We had exactly the same story but the background had somehow changed. So it suddenly made me think, 'Ding! Wait a minute, I'd better put this down because it ain't gonna get any better, the old memory.' Whether I'll write it all in longhand or whatever, I don't know. But you know, so much has gone on that to me I kind of want to try and play down the John and me thing. I've never really tried to say, 'Yeah, I'm the guy who wrote all the songs with him! I'm the guy who knew him best.'

Julia: But you are.

Paul: Well, I am, that's what I mean, it's suddenly dawning on me.

Julia: It was a partnership.

Paul: You know, ever since the days you're talking about at the Woolton village fete, we were always trying to write these little songs. Well, we eventually succeeded on a minor level, then on a huge mega level and now, here I am. When John went to New York I remember thinking that I might never see him again. Of course, there wasn't much I could do anyway because he was getting married. It's like a song we all used to do, 'Wedding Bells Are Breaking Up That Old Gang of Mine'. That was one of his songs, you know, I think your mum taught him that. I'll tell you another one she taught him, 'Ramona'.

Julia: Yeah, I remember. It's a lovely song.

Paul: To this day I remember those things. Actually, that's the kind of songs my music publishing business is into.

Julia: I love it. What was the other one?

Paul: (*he sings*) 'Girl of my dreams I love you, honest I do' and 'Little White Lies', 'The night that you told me those little white lies.' We actually used to try and write songs like those. For instance, in 'Here, There, and Everywhere' we'd put the little verse on the beginning because of our fondness for those old songs. (*He sings*) 'To lead a better life, I need my love to be here.' We just thought that was a great old tradition, they don't do that any more. A few of our songs did happily manage to bring that back. You know, a lot of John's musical influence has got to be traced back to Julia and, of course, mine would be my dad.

Julia: Paul, is it true that you didn't particularly want George in the group originally?

Paul: No, I got George in the group originally, he was my little mate. Obviously, it's so long ago now that all these little things become rumours. You see, I knew George when none of the others knew him. They were all from the Woolton set and we were the Allerton crowd. Originally, I lived in Speke (I was a neighbour of George's) and we both went to the Institute, so we caught the same bus to school. Occasionally, we'd sit together and chat. We even learned guitar from the same book, George and I. I was, in fact, the one who suggested George to the group. We were looking for a good guitar player and I said, 'I know this fellow who can play "Raunchy"' . . . They said, 'What, "Raunchy"? No one can play that!' So I said, 'Just wait till you hear him!'

Julia: So how old was he then?

Paul: George was a baby. You know, I have a string of memories from that time, but no idea what year or month things were. People have documented it all however, which I'm glad of actually, as I'm dotty about that stuff. Anyway, I'm more artistic, I'm creative, I don't need to be that specific. That's my excuse.

Julia: So what about George's audition?

Paul: That was on the top of the bus. Then about a week later we kinda went, 'Well, what do you think?' And they said, 'Yeah man, he'd be great.' Actually, the one I had problems with was Stuart and that is a regret now because he died, but you really can't help it if you run up against problems. The main problem there was, and it's been put down as millions of other things, was that he couldn't actually play his bass in the beginning. So that when we did photos and things it was a bit embarrassing. We had to ask him to turn away from the camera because if people saw where his fingers were he wasn't in the same key as the rest of the group. I was probably over-fussy at the time, but I thought, 'Well, this isn't really a good thing for an aspiring group, we have a weak link here.' He was really a lovely guy, you know, and a great painter, but he was the one I used to have all the ding-dongs with. Obviously, I wish now we hadn't because it all worked out okay and we eventually went to Hamburg with Stu as our bass player. I played guitar then but it got broken so I shifted over to piano. I was just learning how to do all this stuff as we went along. Eventually though, Stu wanted to stay in Hamburg because he fell in love with Astrid, so there was a kind of ceremonial handing over of the bass to me. Truthfully, we had our sticky moments, we even had a fight on stage one night. I assumed I'd win because he wasn't that big, but the maniac strength of love or something entered into him and he was no easy match at all. We were locked for about half an hour. 'I'll kill you. I'll bloody get you!' I think they had to pour water on us in the end.

Julia: What do you remember about your first visits to Mendips?

Paul: Well, the porch outside was always good (like the toilets) for guitars. We learned 'Blue Moon' in there. I remember Mimi as being a very forthright, middle-class woman. Most of the women I'd seen previously were off of the estate. Not to put them down, but they were rather common. Although my mum wasn't like that, she sort of aspired to talk less like the other ladies. In fact, one of the worst moments in my life was when I made fun of the way she talked, because she sounded slightly posh. I can just hear Mimi saying, 'John, your little friend is here to see you.' You know, that kind of thing when it's obvious she was belittling you. But when you looked at her like, 'Hey, wait a minute,' there was a twinkle in her eye, so you kind of knew she quite liked you really. Even though she often seemed to keep people at a bit of arm's length. I think she used to think that maybe I was one of John's nicer friends and was to be encouraged. Because obviously, there were a few that weren't to be encouraged. Inside the house, he'd be writing at the typewriter in his famous *In His Own Write* style. I never knew anyone who had a typewriter. If someone wanted to write it was like a pencil and a little pad. We used to play together in the garden in the summer, that was nice.

Julia: What do you think you'd have been if you hadn't become a musician?

Paul: I should have been a teacher because of the GCE thing I got. I doubt now whether I would have had the patience but I like kids okay. I enjoy passing on information.

Julia: What would you have taught?

Paul: I think the only thing I vaguely had was English. I got an A level in English literature because of this good teacher I had we called 'Dusty' Durband. He got me into things like Chaucer by telling us to read all the dirty bits. You know, the Miller's Tale and all that. He knew how to get our attention.

Julia: And what do you think John would have been? I would say a commercial artist. That's what he went to art college for.

Paul: I really don't know. I think John, in fact, had a great wanderlust, a great adventurous streak. I can imagine a scenario where from, say, eighteen, nineteen and twenty he might have worked as a commercial artist. Then from twenty-one, twenty-two and twenty-three maybe he'd have gone off on a boat somewhere. Because you know, he did have this rather colonial attitude. A lot of British, Liverpool and even Scottish people have this thing that they're going to colonise everywhere. We're gonna go and quell the natives or teach them a thing or two.

Julia: Okay, now for some quick impressions. Pete Best.

Paul: Pete? A good mate. His mum had a club where we played [the Casbah], you know. A good lad, he was our first real drummer.

Julia: Mal Evans.

Paul: Mal was a bouncer at the Cavern. A lovely, big, huggable, bear of a man, who used to always request, 'I Forgot to Remember to Forget', which was an Elvis song, because first and foremost he was a Presley freak. He took *Elvis Monthly* all the time. A lovely, lovely man. Terrible ending, but that's life or . . . death. [In 1977, Mal Evans was shot dead by Los Angeles police when they went to answer a domestic disturbance call].

Julia: George's parents.

Paul: Harry and Louise Harrison. Harry was a bus driver who was a great man, but forthright, and very straightforward. He would run over a dog with his bus rather than swerve and avoid it. Quite rightly, too, probably because he might kill people. I remember always being a little bit disturbed about that hardness in his character, however. Now, Louise was lovely, she was quite a hard lady but soft inside. I remember her pouring a pan of water on some fellow she didn't want to answer the door to. No, she'd tell you how she felt, Louise.

Julia: Cynthia Lennon.

Paul: Cyn was John's original girlfriend at art school. It was the time when you wanted to turn your girlfriend into Brigitte Bardot.

Julia: John adored Brigitte Bardot!

Paul: I know, we all did. We were all just at the age for a sex goddess to

139

be there taking her clothes off. At that age there's no contest with something as gorgeous as that. We were smitten, all of us. So all the girls, they had to be blonde, look rather like Brigitte, and pout a lot. John and I kind of had these secret talks where we intimated, without really saying it, that we wanted to try and turn our girlfriends into Liverpool's answer to Brigitte Bardot. So my girl was Dot and John was going out with Cynthia. I think we got them both to go blonde and wear miniskirts. Terrible isn't it, really? But that's the way it was.

Julia: Bob Wooler.

Paul: Bob was a lovely, lovely chap at the Cavern and everything. Strangest thing about him though was, late at night, we'd drop him off after a gig and he'd never let us in his house. I don't know to this day what he was hiding. We used to imagine all sorts of things. If you do another book we can go into what I imagined. You never got into his house. Other people, they'd invite you in for a cup of coffee, but with Bob it was, 'Well, goodnight, lads . . .'

Julia: Mimi.

Paul: Well, at first you might imagine she was a bit cantankerous, but she wasn't. She was forthright and I like that in women. I like them to stand up for themselves.

Julia: At the height of the Beatles' success it seemed as if John and George wanted to get off the road, whereas you might have liked to stay out a little bit longer. Is that accurate?

Paul: Kind of, yeah. No, what actually happened was that with John's 'bigger than Jesus' quote and all these Klansmen marching around protesting, we had kind of a rough tour. It wasn't really that much worse than any of the others. I mean, we sold out, we did great, the individual shows were great, but people were trying to knock us and stuff. I remember John and George getting pissed off at the whole thing and eventually we simply decided to give it up to work in the studio.

Julia: What can you say about Brian?

Paul: Eppie? There's a book that came out on me recently, *McCartney* by Chris Salewiecz, and although I only flicked through it, there's one bit where he quotes my dad as saying, 'Don't get in with Jew boys, son,' or something. That's exactly the opposite of what he actually said, which was, 'Get a good Jewish manager, they're very good at business.' It's a real Liverpool-working-class attitude. So we did eventually, and, of course, Brian came down to the Cavern and all that story. I think people know that bit. We liked him, we thought he was good. His gay bit never really entered into it as far as we were concerned.

Julia: It's something you didn't really hear about until he died.

Paul: Well, we knew about it from the off. He didn't make any secret of it. You'd have to be daft not to see the kind of people he was around. So you kind of knew he was gay but it never interfered, it was his world.

Julia: Well, I just remember him as being so polite and courteous.

Paul: He was a lovely man, a lovely man, Brian. I think one of his main faults, though, as I used to point out with a word he hated, was that he was a little bit 'green'. I think it was true, however. Some of the deals he struck, like the fact that Lennon and McCartney songs weren't our copyright, were very naive. He had some business acumen, it's true, but his real thing was the flair. Also, I would say he was good for the people he introduced us to. When we first came down to London we were meeting people like Larry Gelbart, who was the writer who created *MASH*. It was an artistic class of people that I don't think we would have got in with otherwise. I think probably Brian had lots of faults, but I liked him.

Julia: Are you a Beatle collector?

Paul: Yeah, odds and sods. I'm not a very thorough one though, because I haven't got all the records for instance, which is daft. I really ought to have all of them. I've got some great little things, however, like my Hofner bass with the gig list which is still taped to it. I've got my *Sgt Pepper* coat. I've got the first record we ever made, which is great . . . I have a bunch of stuff. Let's just leave it at that, shall we? I think we'll have to wrap up now, luv. So, goodnight everybody and remember, all the little birds and Daddy Bird say, 'See you!' So rock on, bye. Say bye bye, Julia . . .

Julia: Bye bye.

Paul, Auburn Hills, Michigan, 2 February 1990

Question: You made a comment last night about how you took a lot of your musical roots from this city. Were you referring to Motown or were there other things?

Paul: I mainly meant Motown, yeah. We were major fans of black American music, a lot of which came from this city, so . . .

Question: You've met a lot of the Motown people over the years; any particular favourites?

Paul: Oh, I love them all, you know. They kind of happened alongside us happening. The English people and the black Motown boom was great. So we were good mates, like Diana Ross and the Supremes. We were kind of contemporaries happening together.

Question: Did you think of having any Motown artists do a guest shot with you last night?

Paul: It's kind of difficult to work in guests. We've sort of got the show set now. Really the only person whose guested so far is Stevie [Wonder] in L.A., who is very much Motown, as you know. But that was easy because we do 'Ebony and Ivory' in the set. It's not too easy to open up the set when you get to this stage with the production.

Question: What made you decide to tour after thirteen years?

Paul: Maybe the fact that I got a good band. You know, I've been recording and doing solo stuff and little guest spots like Live Aid and shows like that but during the recording of the *Flowers in the Dirt* album the band felt really good. We've got a sense of humour in common and they're good musicians, too. So it was either a question of saying, 'Goodbye, see you next album,' or like 'Should we stay together, and if we stay together, what should we do?': 'Let's go on tour.'

Question: A lot of critics are quick to judge anything that you or any of the other Beatles do. How did you go into this LP mentally? Do you ever get to the point where you thought, 'To heck with them. I'm going to shove one down your throat'?

Paul: Yeah, I get to that point. I was not that pleased with the album before it, which is *Press to Play*. So I wanted to make this one better and shove it down a few people's throats. I'm quite happy with the album itself. It has some of my best songs on it.

Question: Has coming out on the road re-inspired you to go back in the studio a little earlier than you have in the past?

Paul: Not really, but it's good for you, getting on the road. It's a stimulating thing, actually seeing your fans instead of just getting letters from them. It really lifts you.

Question: In your programme last night, I noticed you said the best thing about touring is the audience. Was the audience last night as good as you expected?

Paul: It was a serious audience last night, really, because we've always been playing . . .

Question: What do you mean by that?

Paul: Seriously good, seriously fab. Seriously doody. We've just come from England and Wembley, which was a great series of concerts. We did eleven on the truck, I think, but the English are a little bit more reserved, you know. They get going, but it takes them like half an hour. This audience, it didn't take them but a second, and then screams.

Question: Paul, a lot of the people said your show was an emotional experience. Why did it take twenty years for you to come back out and finally play the classic Beatles songs?

Paul: When the Beatles broke up, it was a little difficult, it was a bit like a divorce and you didn't really want to do anything associated with the ex-wife. You didn't want to do *her* material. So all of us took that view independently and John stopped doing Beatles stuff, George, Ringo, we all did. Because it was just too painful for a while. But enough time's gone by now. On the last tour I did in 1976 with Wings, we avoided a lot of Beatles stuff because of that. So now it feels really kind of natural to now do those songs. It's a question of either getting back to those songs or ignoring them for the rest of my life. And, as I say, some of them I haven't actually done before and I didn't realise that until we were rehearsing with the band and I said, 'This feels great, "Sgt Pepper". I mean, why is this so great?' And someone reminded me, they said, 'You've never done it.' It's like a new song to me. It's just the right time to come back with that stuff.

Question: Will there be a time when you get together with George and Ringo? Not really a reunion without John but kind of a jam maybe?

Paul: I don't know. That's always on the cards but a reunion as such is out of the question because John's not with us. The only reunion would have been with John. But, like you say, we might easily get together. There's a couple of projects that are possible now that we've solved our business differences. I don't know, I haven't actually seen them. I've been living this whole thing through the press. People say to me, 'George said he won't do it.' I haven't even spoken to him yet.

Question: Why did it take so long to resolve your business differences?

Paul: Have you even been in a lawsuit? I was in one for the last twenty years. It just took forever. What happens is you get your advisers and they get theirs and then lawyers, I think, are trained to keep things like that going. The first rule in law school, you know, 'Keep it going.'

Question: Do you regret that the four ex-Beatles never got together again before John died?

Paul: Well, I regret it, you know, but I mean, this is life. It just didn't happen for a number of reasons. It would have been great, but John not dying would have been even better.

Question: What's going on in Eastern Europe?

Paul: I think it's very exciting. To me it seems like the sixties kicking in again. That's my point of view. It's all the stuff that was said in the sixties: peace, love, democracy, freedom, a better world and all that stuff. It's finally kicked in. The way I look at it, people like Gorbachev grew up with the sixties and I don't think you can be unaffected by it and I think it's all kicking in now. Look at those people who are coming across the border and a lot of them are wearing denim. It's *us* coming across that border. I think it's very exciting. I think China's next.

Question: Are you going to play any dates in Eastern Europe now that the Iron Curtain is history?

Paul: I'd like to, but we've got so many dates on this tour and they don't include Eastern Europe. I'd like to go to Russia, but the promoters say it's too cold, so we went to Italy.

Question: What are your plans after the tour?

Paul: I'll be writing after the tour. I've got a lot of writing I want to do. I'm doing a very interesting thing. It's a classical thing for an orchestra which is due to be performed by the Liverpool Philharmonic Orchestra in the Liverpool Cathedral in 1991 and that's like a serious work, so I've got a lot of writing to do.

Question: Why don't you write your memoirs?

Paul: I don't know, really. I always thought that you had to be like about seventy before you did.

Question: What new things are you listening to right now?

Paul: Um, I listen to everything. I listen to all sorts of things.

Question: James and Stella are travelling with you right now. Would you ever invite either of them on the stage?

Paul: Not really. It's too sort of showbizy, that kind of thing. I know a lot of people do that. If they really desperately wanted to do it then I'd help them, but it's got to come from them. I'm not going to push them on stage because it's a tough game.

Question: How do you compare the thrill of performing in the sixties with performing today?

Paul: It's very similar, actually. That crowd last night was strangely sixties. It's very good, you know.

Question: But now you can hear yourself.

Paul: With the new technology, yeah. I mean, you compare all this equipment here and you've got like Cape Canaveral. But when we started out it was like two guitars and a bass and one amp.

Question: There's a big controversy now over garbage, there's too many landfills and it's causing a lot of toxic . . .

Paul: I think they're basically just trying to address some of the more serious problems we got ourselves into. We're the only species of animals on Earth that fouls its own nest. Everybody else, all the other birds, they go over *there* to take a dump. But we don't; we do it *right here*, right where we live. We put all our toxic waste into our lakes and stuff. I mean, Britain's got this great business where we accept waste from, like, Japan and we put it in cans and put it under the sea. And they say, 'It'll be all right for a hundred years.' Well, I say, 'What about a hundred and one years, when it blows up? What's going to happen?' So, I mean, I think we've got to be clever. I think we're clever enough to address all of that, but it's going to take some doing.

Question: What was your inspiration for the film presentation before the concert? How did you go about putting the film footage together?

Paul: I talked to Richard Lester, who made *A Hard Day's Night* and *Help!* and we were thinking of having a support act before our act, but the promoters told me that was going to get difficult. So I suggested, 'Well, how about if we do a film?' So I rang Dick Lester and said to him, 'Could you do a film that says, "First there was the Beatles, then there was Wings and then there was now"?' He said, 'Let me think about it,' and he came back with the film, which I like. It's kind of uncompromising, it's a very grown-up film, gives people something to think about.

Question: Are you going to change the show when it comes to stadiums?

Paul: Yeah, we will magnify it a little bit. This style of show is fine in an arena like this, but when you get into a forty-thousand [seat] arena it starts to look a little small, so we'll just make it bigger. But basically keep the same show.

Question: There's been a flood of unreleased Beatles recordings, very high quality like the *Ultra Rare Trax* you probably heard about. What are your feelings on the release of those things and would you like to see EMI release them officially?

Paul: That's kind of a difficult question. It's like, as far as the Beatles were concerned we released all our good material, except for maybe one or two little things that at the time we didn't like. And there are one or two tracks I think are worth looking at. 'Leave my Kitten Alone',

John sings, which I think is very good. But in the main we released all our best material, so now you know, it's like memorabilia. People just like to hear the tracks that were the takes we didn't use or something. If people are interested it's fair enough. I mean, I don't get uptight about bootlegs. What are you going to do?

Question: I just wondered if you plan to tour again after this.

Paul: Yeah. It's funky because I think a lot of people come to the show and think, 'Well, it's the last time you'll see him.' I don't know why they think that, but, yes, the Stones and I, well, we're 'getting up there' kind of thing, but as far as I'm concerned I feel twenty-seven, not forty-seven.

Question: Will you rock and roll after you're fifty, do you think?

Paul: I think there probably is life after fifty, yeah.

Question: Paul, of all the songs you've written, what would be your favourite, if you still have one?

Paul: That's a very difficult question. I mean, musically, I might say 'Here, There, and Everywhere', but as far as success is concerned, it has to be 'Yesterday', because it's just done more than I could have ever hoped for.

Question: Does 'Yesterday' mean something different to you now that you're forty-seven?

Paul: Yes, it sure does. When I wrote it I was a twenty-year-old singing, 'I'm not half the man I used to be.' It's like, it's very presumptuous for a twenty-year-old. At forty-seven, however, it *means* something.

Question: At that time did you ever think you'd be rocking now?

Paul: I didn't think we'd be still rocking now. The great thing, as I say, is you look at what a lot of us have done recently and you look at people like Muddy Waters and you think, 'It didn't matter that he was seventy,' he'd still be singing the blues. Instead of a youth-orientated thing, it's become a music-orientated thing, so I think as long as you can still deliver . . . I mean, you look at the age of these audiences. I'm very surprised, the sort of young people, I thought it just would be my age group mainly, but there's a lot of young kids and they know this material.

Question: Are they simply looking for nostalgia?

Paul: I don't know, I'm always talking to my kids about that. You tell me. What songs are going to be remembered? It's going to be, I don't know, some rap song . . .

Question: Are you enjoying all of this, Paul?

Paul: Yes, it's great. I really am.

Question: How do you like your music today?

Paul: My music? I still like it.

Question: How do you feel when you look out into the crowds and you see parents holding their children to see you?

Paul: It's really beautiful because I've got four kids and the great thing about me and my kids is that there isn't this generation gap that I thought would be there.

Question: Do they listen to any music that bothers you?

Paul: No. But I know what you mean. I thought that they'd get into some odd punk music and I'd be saying, 'Well, the sixties was better,' but they're not. My son loves the Beach Boys. His big new turn-on album that I turned him on to is *Pet Sounds*. And he loves James Brown, Otis Redding, the Commodores, he's got some good taste.

Question: Are your children musically inclined?

Paul: Yeah, they are, but Linda and I have always said that we'd never push them because it's a tough game and unless they're really keen . . . But they're all very good, they're all very interested in music and they can all carry a tune and stuff.

Question: Are you surprised how many young people on this tour are responding to your music?

Paul: Well, kind of. But a couple of years ago I started to notice how kids like my nephews, who are eighteen now, but who I've known since they were two or whatever, started getting into the Grateful Dead. Now they're all Deadheads, it's incredible. I think maybe it is because modern music is a little bit synthetic and shallow that they're looking back to the sixties. And the great thing about a lot of that sixties stuff is that it does stand up still.

Paul, New York, 11 February 1993

Question: One of my favourite songs off your new album [*Off the Ground*] is actually 'Cosmically Conscious'. Does a longer version exist? I also heard that it was written quite a while ago, in India.

Paul: Yeah, it was. It's kind of on the end of the record, as one of those little snippets, almost as an afterthought. But there is a full-length version and it was written I think maybe twenty-five years ago, when we were with the Beatles in Rishikesh, with Maharishi, and he used to always say, 'Be cosmically conscious. It is a joy.' That's pretty much the entire lyrics of that song, which is why it's a snippet on the end.

Question: Does it bother you when people say you haven't been able to get rid of that wonderful soft image?

Paul: Not really, no. I mean, there's a lot of people who would like a soft image. I don't think I've particularly got a soft image actually, it depends if you know my work or not. Things like 'Helter Skelter' are certainly not soft, or 'I'm Down' or some of that stuff. Maybe I'm better known for songs like 'Yesterday'. But listen, I'm not knocking it, it's great to be known for both, anyway.

Question: Can you tell us anything about this potential project musically with George Harrison and Ringo Starr?

Paul: Yeah, well, normally when I'm asked this question, 'Will the Beatles ever get back together?' we've just sort of said, 'Well, no. It's absolutely impossible, and without John, it wouldn't be the Beatles.' That's kind of an easy answer and it's always been true. But at the moment they're making a ten-part series on the Beatles in England and it's going very well. We've got involved in it. It gives us a chance to give our own point of view, rather than everybody speaking for us. 'You know why he was walking across that crossing [on the *Abbey Road* LP] with no shoes on?' 'Because it was hot, man!' It was like a real hot day in London, I had sandals on and I kicked them off, big deal. But we're always answering stuff like that. In fact, I met a little kid who'd been to a Beatles summer camp and she was telling me all about how you turn the record backwards. And I was saying, 'No, no, no, I was there.' And she said, 'No, it's not true.' She wouldn't listen to me. So we're taking this opportunity with the series to try and put over our own point of view. What happened was, we were talking to the director and I said if there's a piece of film you've got, I was thinking in terms of maybe a montage of John material, him just looking great, nice memories of John. I thought, well, you'll need a piece of music to go with that, so we volunteered to do that. I kicked it around with the others and asked,

'Would you mind doing that? Would we hate to do that, is that a definite no-no?' George said, 'Well, that'll be good,' and Ringo said, 'That'll be great.' So we thought, that's a nice start, rather than trying to get the Beatles back together. We'll probably get together, maybe try and write or record something for this one piece of music and just see where that takes us. We're not looking for anything big, I don't think anyone really wants to re-form the Beatles. But just to get together as friends and make a piece of music would be nice.

Growing Apart

After Brian died, Apple was full of hustlers and spongers. The staff came and went as they pleased and were lavish with our money and hospitality. We have since discovered that two of Apple's cars completely disappeared and we owned a house which no one can remember buying.

People were robbing us and living on us to the tune of eighteen or twenty thousand pounds a week rolling out of Apple and nobody was doing anything about it. All our buddies that worked for us for fifty years were living, drinking and eating like fuckin' Rome. I suddenly realised it and said we're losing money at such a rate that we would soon have been broke, really broke. We didn't have anything in the bank really, none of us did. Paul and I could have probably floated, but we were sinking fast. It was just hell and it had to stop. (John, 1970)

We loved it like mad when we were first starting out because all we ever wanted was to go around Liverpool and be cute and popular, play our guitars and not have to work. But once it really became over the top we were forced to take a closer look. Was this what we really wanted? Shooting round the world locked in the backs of armoured cars and leaping about like performing fleas in baseball arenas? After a while the Beatles simply became an excuse for people to go around behaving like animals. (George)

'Wedding Bells' is what [the break-up] was: 'Wedding bells are breaking up that old gang of mine.' We used to sing that song . . . It was an old army song and the Beatles became the army. We always knew that one day 'Wedding Bells' would come true, and that was when it did. (Paul, 1986)

Don't you think the Beatles gave every sodding thing they got? That took our whole life . . . a whole section of our youth. When everybody else was just goofing off we were working twenty-four hours a day. (John, 1969)

There was a certain amount of relief after that Candlestick Park concert. Before one of the last numbers, we set up this camera, I think it had a very wide-angle lens. We set it up on the amplifier and Ringo came off the drums, and we stood with our backs to the audience and posed for a photograph, because we knew that was the last show.

There was a sense of relief after that, getting home. Then we spent what seemed like fifty years going in and out of each other's houses, writing tunes and going into the studio for *Sgt Pepper* and the White Album. But for me, I think for all of us, it was just too much. The novelty had worn off. Everybody was growing up, getting married and leaving home. I think it was inevitable, really. (George, 1987)

Yoko's taken a lot of shit, her and Linda; but the Beatles' break-up wasn't their fault. It was just that suddenly we were all thirty, married and changed. We couldn't carry on living that life any more. (Ringo, 1981)

By the time we got to *Let It Be* we couldn't play the game any more. We could see through each other and therefore we felt uncomfortable. Because up until then we really believed intensely in what we were doing. Suddenly, we didn't believe: it'd come to a point where it was no longer creating magic. (John, 1970)

One has to completely humiliate oneself to be what the Beatles were, and that's what I resent. I mean I did it, but I didn't know, I didn't foresee; it just happened bit by bit, until gradually this complete craziness is surrounding you and you're doing exactly what you don't want with people you can't stand, the people you hated when you were ten. Fuckin' big bastards, that's what the Beatles were. You have to be a bastard to make it, and that's a fact. And the Beatles were the biggest bastards on earth! (John, 1970)

Somebody said to me, 'But the Beatles were anti-materialistic.' That's a huge myth: John and I literally used to sit down and say, 'Now let's write a swimming pool.' We said it out of innocence. Out of normal fucking working-class glee that we were able to write a swimming pool. For the first time in our lives, we could actually do something and earn money. (Paul, 1990)

Someday they're gonna look back at the Beatles and the Stones and all those guys as relics. The days when bands were all just men will be on the newsreels, you know. They will be showing pictures of the guy with lipstick wriggling his arse and the four guys with the evil black make-up on their eyes trying to look raunchy. That's gonna be the in-joke of the future. It's tribal, it's gang and it's fine. But when it continues and you're still doing it when you're forty, that means you're still only sixteen in the head. (John, 1980)

I could be singing 'Yesterday' and wondering what we were going to have for dinner. It's like driving, that thing when you almost fall asleep at the wheel for a second. That can happen when you're performing. (Paul, 1990)

After the Beatles' last tour, which was the one where the Ku Klux Klan was burning Beatle records and I was held up as a Satanist or something . . . we decided no more touring . . . So I said yes to Dick Lester that I would make this movie with him. (John, 1970)

Message from George Harrison

Everybody is looking for Krishna.

Some don't realise that they are, but they are.

Krishna is *God*, the Source of all that exists, the Cause of all that is, was or ever will be.

As God is unlimited, *He* has many Names. Allah – Buddah – Jehova – Rama: All are Krishna, all are *One*.

God is not abstract, he has both the impersonal and the personal aspects to his personality which is *Supreme, Eternal, Blissful*, and full of knowledge. As a single drop of water has the same qualities as an ocean of water, so has our consciousness the qualities of *God's* consciousness ... but through our identification and attachment with material energy (physical body, sense pleasures, material possessions, ego, etc.) our true *Transcendental Consciousness* has been polluted, and like a dirty mirror it is unable to reflect a pure image. With many lives our association with the temporary has grown. This impermanent body, a bag of bones and flesh, is mistaken for our true self, and we have accepted this temporary condition to be final.

Through all ages, great saints have remained as living proof that this non-temporary, permanent state of *God-Consciousness* can be revived in all living souls. Each soul is potentially Divine.

Krishna says in Bhagavad-Gita, 'Steady in the Self, being freed from all material contamination, the yogi achieves the highest perfectional stage of happiness in touch with the Supreme Consciousness. Yoga (a scientific method of *God – Self –* realisation) is the process by which we purify our consciousness, stop further pollution and arrive at the state of Perfection, full *Knowledge*, full *Bliss*.

If there is a God, I want to see him. It's pointless to believe in something without proof, and Krishna-Consciousness and meditation are methods where you can actually obtain *God* perception. You can actually see *God*, and hear him, play with *Him*. It might sound crazy but *He* is actually there, actually with you.

There are many yogic paths, Raja, Jnana, Hatha, Kriya, Karma, Bhakti, which are all acclaimed by the *Masters* of each method.

Swami Bhaktivedanta is, as his title says, a *Bhakti* yogi following the path of *Devotion*. By serving *God* through each thought, word, and deed and by chanting of his holy names, the devotee quickly develops God-Consciousness. By chanting:

> Hare Krishna, Hare Krishna
> Krishna Krishna, Hare Hare
> Hare Rama, Hare Rama
> Rama Rama, Hare Hare

one inevitably arrives at *Krishna*-Consciousness. (The proof of the pudding is in the eating!)

Give peace a chance.

All you need is love (Krishna) Hari Bol

GEORGE HARRISON 31/3/70

Apple Corps, Ltd
3 Savile Row
London, W1
Tel: 01–734 8232

Radha Krishna Temple
7 Bury Place
London, WC1
Tel: 01–242 0394

George, Los Angeles, 1974

Question: Why did you decide to return to America?

George: I've been back here many times. This is the first time I've been back to work, but it's the first time I've had an H-1 visa since 1971.

Question: What was the reason for not having the H-1?

George: I had the same problem as John Lennon. I was busted for marijuana way back in 1967 by Sgt Pilcher who was in jail for six years for planting dope on people.

Question: Looking back, what do you consider so far the crowning glory of your career as a musician?

George: As a musician, I don't think I've got that yet. As an individual, just being able to sit here today, and be relatively sane. That's probably my biggest accomplishment to date.

Question: What is the possibility that you and the rest of the Beatles will join together and become the Beatles again?

George: It's a very slim possibility at the moment, everybody's enjoying being individuals, we were boxed together for ten years. And personally, I'm enjoying playing with this band.

Question: You said in your bio in 1964 that meeting the Beatles was one of the biggest breaks in your musical life, in '74 leaving the Beatles.

George: The biggest break in 1963 was meeting the Beatles, the biggest break since then, I mean in retrospect, was getting out of them.

Question: Are you getting divorced?

George: No, I mean that's as silly as marriage.

Question: Allen Klein is suing the Beatles. How is that affecting you? Do you have to sell more albums now?

George: No. No. To tell you the truth, there's a whole lot of money which is in receivership since Paul McCartney sued us and actually it's fortunate that he did sue us, because the money's in receivership so at least nobody can spend it. There's a lot of millions of dollars from the Beatles partnership and we either give it to the lawyers or we give it to the Revenue.

Question: What's your relationship now with John and Paul?

George: It's very good, actually.

Question: Do you see them often?

George: I haven't seen John because he's been in the States, although I've spoken to him quite a lot on the telephone and he sounds to me like he's in great shape. It's as if we've gone right round the cycle and we're back at the beginning again. I just met Paul recently and he's . . . everybody's really very, very friendly. But it doesn't really mean we're going to form a band.

Question: Do you pay much attention to what the critics say?

George: Oh, I cancelled all my newspapers five years ago, to tell you the truth, so I don't really know what people say. If I do see a review of an album I'll read it although it doesn't really make too much difference what they say because I am what I am whether they like it or not.

Question: Are you ever amazed by how much the Beatles still mean to people?

George: Not really. I mean, I realise the Beatles did fill a space in the sixties, but all the people the Beatles meant something to are all grown up now. It's like anything you grow up with, you get attached to it. I mean, that's one of the problems in our lives, becoming attached to things. I can understand the Beatles, in many ways, did nice things and it's appreciated that people still like them. The problem comes when they want to live in the past and hold onto something. People are afraid of change.

Question: Are you involved in any serious negotiations to get the Beatles back together for one night?

George: No, no, you've been reading *Rolling Stone*. I thought the fifty million for one shot . . . after reading that I was a bit disappointed at Bill Graham saying he could make us four million, especially as Crosby, Stills, Nash and Young made eight. I mean, sure, we could make more than that. The point is, it's all a fantasy, the idea of putting the Beatles together again. If we ever do that, I'll tell you, the reason will be that everybody's broke. And even then, to play with the Beatles, I'd rather have Willy Weeks on bass than Paul McCartney. That's the truth, with all respect to Paul. The Beatles was like being in a box, it's taken years to get to play with other musicians because we were so isolated together. It became very difficult playing the same old tunes day in, day out. Since I made *All Things Must Pass*, it was so nice for me to be able to play with other musicians; I don't think the Beatles are that good. I mean, they're fine, fine. Ringo's got the best backbeat I've ever heard and he'll play a great backbeat twenty-four hours a day. He hated drum solos. Paul is a fine bass player, he's a little overpowering at times, and John has gone through his scene, but it feels to me like he's come around. I mean, to tell you the truth, I'd join a band with John Lennon any day, but I couldn't join a band with Paul McCartney, but that's nothing personal. It's just from a musical point of view.

Question: What do you think of Lennon's solo material?

George: His new record I think is lovely.

Question: Is it conceivable you could get together the Beatles to generate some money for charity?

George: Well, if you're a promoter I'd say no. I wouldn't rule anything out in life. People think we plan, but we don't plan anything. It's all at the mercy of the Lord and I'm sorry to keep talking about the 'Lord' to y'all, but He's there, I have experienced something in my life, and I know He's there . . .

George, Brazil, 1979

Question: Do you think there ever will be any group which will rival the Beatles?

George: Well, there may be groups that can sell as many records. But the Beatles were unique because of the four particular personalities. The Beatles were bigger than the four people separately. There is always someone like Sinatra, Elvis or the Beatles and maybe somewhere down the line there will be something bigger, but certainly not now. Not like the Bee Gees: they make good records but they don't have whatever it was the Beatles had.

Question: Are there any unreleased tracks by the Beatles?

George: 'Not Guilty' is on my new album, actually. I wrote that for the White Album in 1967 and forgot all about it. I remembered it last year and we re-recorded it and it's really nice, sort of jazzy.

Question: Which one of your songs do you like best?

George: I don't know, whichever you like best is best for me. 'Something' was very good for me, because it had about a hundred and fifty cover versions. It is nice if other people make recordings of your songs. But there are other songs that are better. There is one on the last album [*Thirty-Three and a Third*] I think was as good as 'Something', 'Learning How to Love You'. And there is a song on the new LP [entitled *George Harrison*], 'Your Love is Forever', which I think is as good as 'Something'. But it might not be as popular because it was the Beatles who made 'Something'.

Question: What about punk music?

George: Rubbish, total rubbish. Listen to the early Beatles records, they were simple too, but they still had much more depth and meaning. It was innocent or even trivial, but it still had more meaning than punk which is deliberately destructive and aggressive.

Question: Have you had any more problems with 'My Sweet Lord' lately?

George: Well, in America it's all become a complete joke, because the man who wrote the song 'He's So Fine' (they were suing me about) died years ago and the company was taken over by his accountants, who were suing me for all this money. When we were going to court the judge said there was no way that I copied that song, but 'Because of the similarity we must talk about compensation.' Then the mother of the songwriter started suing her own company who was suing me! Then, Allen Klein, who used to be the Beatles' manager (Klein had been suing us for years and then we made a settlement) was unhappy having no lawsuits against the Beatles. So when the composer died, he brought the case. So now it's Klein against me. But Klein was the one who was promoting 'My Sweet Lord' so it is a very funny position and the judge doesn't like it. Ten years ago Klein did interviews saying 'My Sweet Lord' had nothing to do with this other song. And now it's the other way round just to get some money off me. So it's just a joke, but for a few years it made me depressed. Having to go to court and do these things, it's terrible, it's a pain in the arse.

George with Madonna, Press Conference for *Shanghai Surprise*, London, 6 March 1986

George: Good afternoon. On behalf of us both and HandMade Films, welcome. I'd like to ask for maybe a bit of order. Whoever wants to ask a question, maybe you could say your name, what newspaper you're from, and also your intentions at the next general election.

Question: Madonna, what kind of boss is George Harrison and were you a Beatlemaniac?

Madonna: I wasn't a Beatlemaniac. I don't think I really appreciated their songs until I was much older. I was too young to really get caught up in the craze. But he's a great boss, very understanding and sympathetic.

Question: What sort of advice has he given you?

Madonna: I think he's given me more advice on how to deal with the press than how to work in the movie.

Question: Is it fun working with your husband, Sean Penn?

Madonna: Of course it is. He's a pro. He's worked on several films and his experience has helped me.

Question: Has it caused any personal problems off set, do you argue at all?

George: Do you row with your wife?

Question: George, is it true you are playing a cameo role in the film?

George: Well, yes and no, really. There is one scene in a nightclub with a band playing in the background, and because I'm writing the music to the film I decided it would be easier if I was the singer in the band.

Question: Mr Harrison, are you confident that this film is going to be as successful?

George: I think so, yeah.

Question: It seems as though it's a more ambitious film than *A Private Function*.

George: Well, it is certainly a larger budget film than *A Private Function*, but it's totally different to any of the previous films we've made. It's a sort of adventure film, slightly humorous. I think it's actually a very good-looking film. This will be the thing in the end because there has been so much written in the papers that has absolutely nothing to do with what the film is about, and these two people have spent the last couple of months working on this thing.

Question: George, when you hired Mr Penn, did you think that there would be . . . let's face it, this film is surrounded by a lot of hype . . .

George: Well, you're the people who create the hype, let's not get that wrong.

Question: What I'm saying is, did you expect the sort of coverage you're getting?

George: I did expect a certain amount of commotion from the press, but I must admit I overestimated your intelligence.

Question: George, there's been a lot of reports that you've had to personally separate the warring factions on the set. Do you think this will affect the film adversely, and would you work with Sean Penn again?

George: Sure. I happen to like Sean very much because I don't see him like you. I see him as an actor who we hired and the role that he plays, and has played in the past – which is one of the reasons we chose him – is of a feisty young guy. That said, he's actually a human being who's very nice, and he's a talented actor. You just have to separate the two things, his job and his ability to do it and the sensationalism because he happened to marry Madonna.

Question: Why isn't Mr Penn here at this conference?

George: Because he's busy working.

Madonna: He's in more scenes than I am.

Question: Would some of the commotion have been cut down a bit if the original press conference hadn't been cancelled? Isn't this just one of the old Hollywood ways of getting publicity?

George: The press conference was postponed because after we returned from Hong Kong the schedule had to be reorganised and, let's face it, we're here to make a film, not hold press conferences.

Question: One of the people from HandMade told me that the reason they cancelled it was that after the scene at the airport they didn't feel like giving the press an even break. Is that true?

George; Well, maybe that's true as well. I can't speak for whoever said that, you'll have to ask them. The purpose of this is to try and clarify some situation. I can see the attitude written all over your face. There's no actual point in you asking anything because you've already predetermined what it is you're going to say. I'd like to ask if there's anybody who is actually honest. That's what we want, a bit of honesty. Because if you want the truth, you'll get it. But I don't suppose that some people here are actually capable of recognising it when they see it.

Question: George, what do you think of the so-called British film revival? Did you see *Letter to Brezhnev* and do you have any plans to film in Liverpool?

George: Well, actually, *Letter to Brezhnev* resurrected my original belief in the character of the Liverpool people. It's a fantastic example of how someone with no money and no hope can actually get through that. I think it's fabulous. I've not spent a great deal of time in

Liverpool over the years, but I'm happy to say the film has revitalised my image of Liverpool people. I think the British Film Year was a good idea, just to try and stimulate more interest from the public. I think to a degree it helped a lot.

Question: Madonna, will you be singing on the soundtrack at all?

Madonna: I'm not really thinking about the musical aspects of the movie, I'm just trying to concentrate on the acting.

George: At this point I'm doing the music. If she wants to she's welcome, but she wasn't hired as a musician.

Question: Madonna, I wonder if either you or your husband would like to apologise for incidents which have involved bad behaviour on your behalf?

Madonna: I have nothing to apologise for.

George: I would add to that. Everything that's been written in the papers has been started by someone in the press, either the photographer that sat on the hood of the car or the woman from the radio station who broke in and also the appalling behaviour of the journalist who actually stole photographs from the continuity woman. So there's nothing to apologise for. I think certain elements of the press should apologise and at the same time I hope that all of them who do have intelligence will recognise that they're not the ones who have made us angry.

Question: Do you think that situation has been antagonised by the enormous amount of security that's being used?

Madonna: We don't have an enormous amount of security.

Question: There is today.

George: Yes, today. If you had been with us in the car trying to get in here, you'd realise it's like a bunch of animals. Absolute animals. Do you just want us to get torn apart and beaten up? Because that's really what those people are like.

Question: You must have realised what the British press are like. Do you regret shooting the last few weeks here rather than in the States?

George: It's a British film. You know, if you like we'll all go to Australia and make our movies there in the future. We'd like to make them in England. We'd like to be reasonable and we'd like you to be reasonable because it doesn't do anyone . . . I think in a way certain of the press have actually got in the way. You would have achieved more if you had a different attitude.

Question: But big stars come over here and make films perfectly well.

George: You know it's *you*, the press, who decide how big you want the stars to be. Let's face it, stars are actually people, human beings who have become famous for one thing or another and that is usually encouraged by the press to the point where the only thing left to do is to knock them. It's a historical fact and it's unfortunate that she [Madonna] happens to be going through that at this time.

Question: Surely it was worse in the sixties?

George: It was worse because it was a new experience to me. But now I don't give a damn what you say about me, because I know who I am and I know what I feel and I know you can't get me any more. The press can't get me. You can write your snide little things about me, but ultimately I'm all right. I know I'm all right. I don't care about those kind of snide remarks. I care about the truth.

Question: You depend on the media for publicity. Without the publicity no one would go to your films. So what are you standing there saying we're wrong to be here for?

George: I didn't say you were wrong to be here. I was just making a point: he asked, 'Is it any different from the sixties?' and I said, 'Well, in the sixties it was a new experience for me, but now I've been through so much I've learnt how to deal with it.' I didn't say anything about what you said.

Question: We have had loads of film stars over here, but have never had these sort of fights.

Madonna: When Robert De Niro comes to the airport, are there twenty photographers that sit on his limousine and don't allow him to leave the airport?

George: Those people, let's face it, are big stars but they're not news.

Question: But I've never seen scenes like this.

George: Yes, but it's been created by the press. All those photographers are out there to get as many pictures as they can because they sell them to everybody. They make money out of it and because she's hot they're trying to make as much money as they can.

Question: But that's why you hired her.

George: Yes, but we expected non-animals. You're all quite nice now, aren't you?

Question: Talking of animals, is it true that Sean Penn has been on the set giving orders . . .

George: What kind of introduction is that? That doesn't even deserve an answer.

Question: What about the incident at the airport?

George: That was the press jumping all over the car.

Question: It wasn't the press that were at fault, there were two other people who got involved who were plain clothes detectives and they shouldn't have been involved.

George: But nevertheless he was trying to jump on the front of the car as it drove away. What do you expect? Whatever the facts, it is still something which doesn't really justify the amount of attention it's been given.

Question: How do the naked scenes fit into the film?

George: It's not that kind of movie.

Madonna: There are no naked women in the movie.

George: Lots of naked men, though!

Question: Madonna, do you care what's said about you in the press?

Madonna: I think what George meant was he doesn't feel it any more when bad things are written about him.

George: I don't particularly want you to say more nasty things, but I've learnt not to read them. It's just water off a duck's back. Otherwise we would all be ulcerated, wouldn't we? The sad thing is that people have got brains in their heads and maybe we should just try and use some of the other cells in our brains rather than the ones that are just to do with all this sensational stuff.

Question: What's your favourite scene in the movie?

George: I like it when she kills the monster from outer space!

Question: What state of production are the other current HandMade titles in?

George: We've got a number of films in the making, because we've been able to break even, or have been able to come up with the funding for certain films. Some of them are scripts that are being worked on. Others are in the casting stage. For instance, there's a film called *Travelling Men*, which has been in pre-production for a number of years.

Question: When did you first become aware of Madonna?

George: I don't know. A couple of years ago . . .

Madonna: When he wrote 'Lady Madonna'!

Question: Were you aware of her records?

George: Sure, I was aware of her with all the TV, videos and stuff. The first time I heard her was on the radio when I heard her singing something about 'Living in the Material World'!

Question: Madonna, I hear your management contract is up for sale. And George, would you like to buy it?

Madonna: You're a little troublemaker, aren't you!

Question: Was this film written for Madonna and Sean Penn?

George: It wasn't. It was taken from a book called *Farraday's Flowers* and the producer wrote the screenplay. We talked about various possibilities for casting and someone suggested Madonna. Apart from the fact that everyone knew she was a famous singer, if you saw *Desperately Seeking Susan* you know even Barry Norman agrees that there was some potential there. She got the screenplay, and Sean Penn, who had also worked with John Combs, the producer, on a couple of other films, read the screenplay and said that he would do it too. It was quite a coincidental thing. It wasn't any sort of huge plot to get these newlywed people; I don't think they had even got married then. In a commercial sense, it was obviously good to have her in it because it's better than having someone nobody has ever heard of. But the rest of it was just luck. But I mean, lots of our films do have people no one's ever heard of. It's not any policy.

Question: How many actresses had you seen for the part?

George: I'm not too sure of that. I wasn't in the country at the time. There were obviously other considerations, I know there were for Sean's part. But there's no point in me giving you a list of people who I thought would play the part well.

Question: What are your responsibilities as Executive Producer?

George: Well, really, the part I've played in the past was to provide the film unit with the money, and apart from that, if there's any comment I would like to make on the screenplay or the casting. It varies from film to film. Some films I have very little to do with and others, like this one, I have a lot to do with. But there's no other way around it on this one because originally I was just going to do the music, but I got dragged in much more than I would have normally. Usually I tend to like a low-profile existence and it's been years since I got involved in the newspapers like this.

Question: George, are you happy with the progress of the film despite any difficulties you've had?

George: Whatever difficulties there have been are all behind us. I hope this press conference will help us to calm things down a little. I'm very pleased with what I'm seeing on the screen, which is the main thing. That's all I want, to get them to be able to complete shooting with the least problems.

Question: Is it true that there have been problems between director Jim Godard and Sean Penn?

Madonna: No, it's not true.

George: No more than in any other film, you know. Every film has discussions and debates as to how it should proceed.

Question: Do you tell the director to change camera angles?

Madonna: I don't tell anyone anything and neither does Sean.

George: I think most people look through the camera, because when you're on the other side it's handy to know what is actually in and out of shot.

Question: Did you say it's been a great many years since you held a press conference?

George: Me personally, yeah. I think 1974 was the last time I did anything like this. I just do gardening, you know. I like a nice quiet life!

Question: Despite it all, Madonna, are you happy?

Madonna: I am.

George: That's about it, thank you.

Madonna: We're not such a bad bunch of people, are we? Bye.

George with Eric Clapton, Tokyo, 29 November 1991

George: Short message, hello! Very nice to be here after such a long time.

Eric Clapton: Yes, it's nice to be back in Japan, this time with a friend. I love to come to this country. I come as often as I can and will continue to do so. I hope this will be a success and hope you will enjoy it.

Question: What attracts you to each other?

George: Well, it's very difficult; it's simple, but difficult, because something mutual that you like . . . you can say it's the way he bends the strings or the way he says 'Hello'. It's difficult to say. It's just an attraction we have, an attraction in our lives and it's also the way he bends the notes. Was that good enough?

Eric: Well, George is senior to me by, what, I don't know, a year?

George: I'm about thirty. How old are you?

Eric: Seventy-nine. But I've always thought that he's a great songwriter, a great musician, a very unique man; and he gave up smoking, I have to respect him for that. I think he's very brave to come here because he hasn't worked on the stage for a long time and it can be a very frightening experience, but I think it will be rewarding. But I always thought of George as being a little like the elder brother I never had, so I respect his judgement and his values and I think he's a wonderful man. I like the way he bends the strings, too. He's a great slide player, most of all he's a fantastic slide player.

Question: What do you think about Prime Minister Major?

Eric: Very anonymous. He seems to be okay, but he just seems to be rather bland.

George: I've not met him. I've only seen him a couple of times on TV, because I also gave up watching television as well as smoking and I also gave up reading newspapers. So I don't really know much about him, but I still think he's better than Mrs Thatcher.

Question: How did the idea of a tour come about and why did you come to Japan?

George: Well, the reason that I came to Japan was because Eric suggested to me that this time of year would be good if I wanted to do a concert tour. He was not working and he and his band were available to become my band. That was one reason why I thought about working, because Eric asked me. And the reason we came to Japan was, he likes Japan and he suggested that we come here. That was the first question. To convey to the fans, really, just whatever the meaning of the songs are, if they have some meaning for the fans of Japan. I've had a lot of mail over twenty-five years from Japan. Very nice letters from the Japanese people and they seem to like – or the ones who write, anyway – seem to like my records. So I just hope they like the live music as much as they like the records.

Question: How were the songs chosen?

George: They were chosen by either the fact that they were hit singles or that it had a feeling for me that it would be good to put on – like the song, 'Taxman' – it's a song that goes regardless of if it's the sixties, seventies, eighties, nineties. There's always a taxman, so if the song seems to fit . . . Just what I felt would be reminiscent, like, 'If I Needed Someone' I sang at the Budokan twenty-six years ago, maybe, so might as well sing it at the Dome twenty-six years later. The rest were mainly singles or a selection from different albums going right from 1965 until last year.

Question: Will you play 'Roll Over, Beethoven'?

George: Yes. It's very popular in Japan.

Question: What would you like to do in Japan?

George: Well, I'd like to see all the bits I didn't see last time. That's maybe from the hotel to the Tokyo Dome and back. I'd like to go to Kyoto and see some temples and some gardens although it's not the best time of the year to see the gardens. But still, I may not come back for another twenty-six years so I better go now. And maybe go to the electric shop and buy an electric toothbrush or something.

Question: Why is your song 'Tears of the World' not included in your book, *Songs by George Harrison*?

George: It fell out on the way to Japan. I don't know, really. You should write to the publisher and ask him. Or, you'll have to buy volume two. The publisher of the book is coming to the Tokyo Dome, so I'll tell him.

Question: Will the Beatles reunite?

George: No. It can't be possible because the Beatles don't exist especially now that John Lennon is not alive. It just happens, every time Paul needs some publicity he announces to the press we're getting back together again. I wouldn't pay much attention to that.

Question: Eric, what are your plans?

Eric: When this is finished, I go back for Christmas and then I'll start a world tour next year. I don't know what George will do. Maybe he will start a world tour on his own, I don't know.

George: Who knows, we'll have to wait and see.

Question: December ninth, the anniversary of John's death, takes place during your tour. Do you plan to do anything special on that day?

George: I'd have to look at the itinerary. We'd have to be doing a concert or if not we'll be travelling to a concert. But we won't be doing anything other than singing songs. We won't be doing anything special. No, the day doesn't have any special meaning to me.

Eric: I think the fact that George will be playing is tribute enough.

George: It's not that I don't respect the day John Lennon got killed or anything, I'm just not into days. I don't remember my own birthday, I don't remember anniversaries or anything. I'm just not into remembering days.

Question: What changes have you experienced since you were last in Japan?

George: Everything has changed over twenty-five years. First of all, I'm much younger now than I used to be. I think I can sing better, I can play better and I can be a happier person. Everything's changed.

Question: Are you planning to play 'Layla'?

Eric: I don't think so, unless there's some kind of riot or public outcry and we have to play it. I've played it at nearly every show for the past twenty so it doesn't bother me not to play it now and then. And George has only given me a very limited space (*laughter*) so I'm going to try and do a couple of new songs. But, it's all negotiable, don't worry.

George: I don't mind if he does it.

Eric: We'll see, we'll see.

George: Thank you all very much, it's nice to be here.

Eric Clapton, on First Meeting George

I was in the Yardbirds, and we were playing a thing called the Beatles Christmas Show at the Hammersmith Odeon, in London. The Yardbirds were on the bottom of the bill, but all of the acts in between Beatles were sort of music-hall, English rock 'n'roll groups. And the Yardbirds were an R&B band, or even a blues band, so there was a bit of, like, 'What's this all about?' George was checking me out, and I was checking him out to see if he was a real guitar player. And I realised he was. But we come from different sides of the tracks, I grew up loving black music, and he grew up with the Carl Perkins side of things, so it was blues versus rockability. That rockabilly style always attracted me, but I never wanted to take it up. And I think it's the same for him. The blues scene attracted him, but it evades him somehow. He's much more comfortable with the finger-picking style of guitar.

Ringo, London, 1984

It's very hard to cross over, for a musician to be accepted as an actor. It's also the same in reverse. When an actor or actress makes an album, we tend to ho-hum it. I know because I'm in the music game. Very few actors have made a good record and very few recording artists have made good movies. I'd like to change that.

I've played with Paul plenty of times since the Beatles. But it is typecasting, yeah. I wanted to play the baddie [in the film *Give My Regards to Broad Street*], but the part was already taken. Paul says people don't think of me as a bad guy anyway. I say they haven't talked to my kids. I say, 'Go to bed,' and they think I'm an ogre. Come to think of it, that's what I thought when my mum said, 'Go to bed,' to me.

People call me a comedian, but I don't tell jokes. I am good at quips. I can do that sort of humour because it's part of English tradition, nothing set, just get off some fast quips and carry on. That's the difference between British and American humour. American humour is more worked out in advance.

I was totally amazed at the younger generation's reaction to [the film] *Caveman* because in the San Fernando Valley and places like that they started speaking *Caveman* language. I've never seen the finished movie myself. The producers were kind enough to give us a copy, but Barbara and I never got all the way through it. We kept getting hungry!

You know, you make a film and people say to you, 'Oh, I guess you're not drumming any more.' It's not true. At least they can't say that about *Broad Street* because I'm acting *and* drumming at the same time.

Beatles on Beatles

Even if I'm friends with Paul again, I'd never write with him. There's no point. I was living with Paul then, so I wrote with him. It's whoever you're living with. He writes with Linda, he's living with her, you know. So it's just natural. (John)

You're constantly trying to remember if you're okay or not. I hate justifying myself. I remember asking George Martin once, 'George, are we really going to have to keep justifying ourselves?' He said, 'Yeah. Forever . . .' (Paul)

I have a great fear of this so-called 'normal' thing. You know, the ones that passed their exams, the ones who went to their jobs, the ones that didn't become rock'n'rollers, the ones that settled for it. Settled for 'the deal'. That's what I'm trying to avoid. But I'm sick of avoiding it through my own self-destruction.
   I've decided now that I want to live. I'd actually decided it long before but I didn't really know what it meant until now. It's taken me however many years to get this far and I'm not about to give it up. I want to have a real go at it this time. (John)

The Beatles didn't really come up with anything new. They just heralded the change in consciousness that was happening in the sixties. (George)

I've never claimed divinity. I've never claimed purity of soul. I've never claimed to have the answer to life. I only put out songs and answer questions as honestly as I can, no more, no less. I cannot live up to other people's expectations of me because they're illusionary. And the people who want more than I am, or than Bob Dylan is, or Mick Jagger is . . . Whatever wind was blowing at the time [the sixties] moved the Beatles, too. I'm not saying we weren't flags on the top of a ship; but the whole boat was moving. Maybe the Beatles were in the crow's nest, shouting, 'Land ho,' or something like that, but we were all in the same damn boat. (John)

They are my brothers, you see. I'm an only child, and they're my brothers. I've always said that if I ever spend all my bread, I can just go and live with one of them, and vice versa, because we all love to spend it. (Ringo)

I've withdrawn many times, part of me is a monk and part a perform-ing flea! The fear in the music business is that you don't exist if you're not at Xenon with Andy Warhol. As I found out, life doesn't end when you stop subscribing to *Billboard*. (John)

There was a definite strained relationship right from the White Album. There was a lot of alienation between us and him. Well, there was alienation amongst all of us. It was particularly strained because having been in a band from being kids, then suddenly we're all grown up and we've all got these other wives. That didn't exactly help. All the wives at that time really drove wedges between us. And then, after the years, when I saw John in New York, it was almost like he was crying out to me to tell me certain things or to renew things, relationships, but he wasn't able to, because of the situation he was in. (George)

Whatever made the Beatles the Beatles also made the sixties and anybody who thinks that if John and Paul got together now with George and Ringo, 'the Beatles' would exist, is out of their skulls. (John)

I sometimes hear myself in interviews going, 'Well, I'm just a sort of ordinary guy.' And I think, what will they go away thinking? 'Did he really say he was an ordinary guy?' Because there's quite a lot of evi-dence to the contrary. (Paul)

I was getting into that established, fat, professional-pop-star-can-do-no-wrong, worker genius, a record every few months and that's all right. A few Hare Krishnas here and there and I've done my social bit. (John)

I didn't like her [Yoko] because she was taking my friend away. (Ringo)

You can't tell George anything. He's very trendy and has the right clothes and all that. But he's very narrow-minded and doesn't really have a broad view. One time I said something to George and he said, 'I'm as intelligent as you, you know.' (John)

We [the Beatles] have been having dinner together. We are friends now; it's the first time we have been this close for a long time. But it doesn't mean to say we are going to make another group or anything.

You know, I could go out and try to become a superstar, and I tell you, if I went to any agent and a manager and checked myself out and practised a bit, I could do it. But I don't really want to do that. That's being a kamikaze pop star, the tours and everything. I don't have to prove anything. I don't want to be in the business full-time because I'm a gardener: I plant flowers and watch them grow. (George)

Some people discovered a new reality and really do feel confident about the future. Everybody's talking about the way it's going, with all the decadence and the rest of it. But nobody's really noting all the good that came out of the last few years. Look at the vast gathering of people at Woodstock. It was the biggest mass of people ever gathered for anything other than war! Nobody ever had that big an army without killing somebody. Even Beatles concerts were more violent than that, and they were only fifty thousand. (John)

The Beatles saved the world from boredom. (George)

Talking is the slowest form of communicating, anyway. Music is much better. We're communicating to the outside world through our music. The office in America says the folks there listen to *Sgt Pepper* over and over so they know what we're thinking in London. (John)

That was a songwriting partnership. We were very special. I could feel it was a special kind of thing because it was dead easy to write. Talk about sitting around for days trying to write songs; in a matter of hours we'd feel we'd been at it too long. John and I were perfect, really, for each other. I could do stuff he might not be in the mood for, egg him in a certain direction he might not want to go in. And he could do the same with me. If I'd go in a certain direction he didn't like, he'd just stop it like that. (Paul)

I have a problem, I must admit, when people try to get the Beatles together. They're still suggesting it, even though John is dead. They still say, 'Why don't the Beatles get together?' I suppose the three of us could, but it was such a struggle to find our individual identities after the Beatles. (George)

Starvation in India doesn't worry me one bit. Not one iota, it doesn't, man. And it doesn't worry you, if you're honest. You just pose. You don't even know it exists. You've just seen the charity ads. You can't pretend to me that an ad reaches down into the depths of your soul and actually makes you feel more for these people than, for instance, you feel about getting a new car. (Paul)

Yeah, well, how about just a cup of tea [instead of a reunion] together? Even that, you see, to get them together; get these four people together and just put them in a room to have tea. Satellite it all around the world at twenty dollars each just to watch it and we could make a fortune. We could just sit there and say, 'Well, John, what have you been doing?' But it would be difficult even to do that because everybody's left home and they're living their own lives. I haven't even seen John for two or three years. (George)

Having reached the end of space, you look across the wall and there's more space. (Paul)

Names are far out. Ray Cooper, for instance. A 'cooper' is a barrel maker. Larry Smith. Well, a smith's a blacksmith. George Harrison. You know what that means, don't you? Son of Hari! (George)

We were a band who made it very big, that's all. Our best work was never recorded. (John)

We always make our mistakes in public. (Paul)

We would rather be rich than famous. That is, more rich and slightly less famous. (John)

We're just a bunch of crummy musicians, really. (George)

I Write the Songs . . .

'If someday I came across some kids singing it, that will be it,' so it had to be very easy, there isn't a single big word. Kids will understand it much easier than adults. 'In the town where I was born/lived a man who sailed to sea/And he told us of his life/in the land of submarines.' That's really the beginning of a kids' story.

There's some stuff in Greece like icing sugar, you eat it. It's a sweet you drop into water. It's called submarine; we had it on holiday. (Paul, 'Yellow Submarine')

It just came to me. Everybody was going on about karma, especially in the sixties. But it occurred to me that karma is instant as well as it influences your past life or your future life. There really is a reaction to what you do now. That's what people ought to be concerned about. Also, I'm fascinated by commercials and promotion as an art form. I enjoy them. So the idea of instant karma was like the idea of instant coffee: presenting something in a new form. I just liked it. (John, 'Instant Karma')

Klaus Voorman had a harmonium in his house, which I hadn't played before. I was doodling on it, just playing to amuse myself, when 'Within You' started to come. The tune came first, then I got the first sentence. It came out of what we'd been discussing that evening. (George, 'Within You, Without You')

Often the backing I think of early on never quite comes off. With 'Tomorrow Never Knows' I'd imagined in my head that in the background you would hear thousands of monks chanting. That was impractical, of course, so we did something different. I should have tried to get nearer my original idea, the monks singing. I realise now that was what it wanted. (John, 'Tomorrow Never Knows')

It sounds like Elvis, doesn't it? No – no, it doesn't sound like Elvis. It is Elvis – even those bits where he goes very high. (Ringo, 'Lady Madonna')

George Martin always has something to do with our tunes, but sometimes more than others. For instance, he wrote the end of 'All You Need Is Love' and got into trouble because the 'In the Mood' bit was copyrighted. It was a rather hurried session and we didn't mind giving him that to do, saying, 'There's the end, we want it to go on and on.' Actually, what he wrote was much more disjointed, so when we put all the bits together we said, 'Could we have "Greensleeves" right on top of that little Bach thing?' And on top of that we had 'In the Mood' bit. (Paul, 'All You Need Is Love')

Act Three

The Inner Circle: Family and Friends

John's Aunt Mimi Smith, Bournemouth, 1970

Question: What do you really think of the Beatles?

Mimi Smith: The boys had talent, yes, but they also had a lot of luck as well. When they first played me 'Love Me Do', I didn't think much of it.

Question: How do you view the many troubles the Beatles have been going through these last few years?

Mimi: I don't know what all this business between John and Paul is about and I don't dare ask John. I did ring Paul about it, and he told me things would straighten up. The boys have been friends so long. I remember them coming home from school together on their bikes, begging biscuits. I'm sure they'll get back together again. This is just a phase they're passing through.

Question: These days your nephew is very involved in a variety of social, political and avant-garde causes. How do you feel about all that?

Mimi: I've just stopped reading the papers these days. Apple sends me his records, but I won't play them. And I've asked my friends not to tell me about them. That shameful album cover [*Two Virgins*, on which John and Yoko appeared nude] and that [erotic] art show of his. He's been naughty and the public doesn't like it, and he's sorry for it. Now he wants sympathy. That's why he's come out with all these fantastic stories about an unhappy childhood. It's true that his mother wasn't there and there was no father around, but my husband and I gave him a wonderful home. John didn't buy me these furnishings, my husband did. John, Paul and George wrote many songs together sitting on the sofa you're sitting on now, long before you'd ever heard of the Beatles. Why, John even had a pony when he was a little boy! He certainly didn't come from a slum! None of the boys did. The Harrisons weren't as well-off as the other families, perhaps, but George wasn't from a slum, either, the way the press had it. And that's why you never saw photographs of John's boyhood home. We certainly weren't impoverished, the way John's talking now!

Question: What do you think changed John so much from his early days as a carefree kid?

Mimi: She's responsible for all this, Yoko. She changed him, and I'm sure she and Linda are behind this split with John and Paul. Cynthia was such a nice girl. When she and John were at art college, she'd come to my house and say, 'Oh, Mimi, what am I going to do about John?' She'd sit there until he came home. Cynthia really pursued him. He'd walk up the road and back until she got tired of waiting and went home. I think he was afraid of her, actually.

Question: You realise of course that to many people John is something of a political leader with such songs as 'Power to the People', for example . . .

Mimi: Don't talk to me of such things! I know that boy. He doesn't know what he's saying! It's all an act. If there were a revolution, John would be first in the queue to run! Why, he's scared to death of things like that! That's Yoko talking, not John! Yoko is not exactly right in the head. Every time John does something bad and gets his picture in the papers he rings up to smooth me over. See that new colour television? It was a Christmas present, but he had it delivered early. A big present arrives every time he's been naughty. I usually have a large photograph of John hanging in the lounge. When he's a good boy, it'll go back up again!

Aunt Mimi, Bournemouth, 1983

Question: How do you remember your nephew?

Mimi Smith: John liked to run along the sands. Sometimes I imagine I see him. Is it him? I like to think it is . . .

Question: Why is it that you raised John instead of your sister, Julia?

Mimi: Do you believe in fate? Because I knew the moment I saw John in that hospital that I was the one to be his mother and not Julia. Does that sound awful? It isn't really, because Julia accepted it as something perfectly natural. She used to say, 'You're his real mother. All I did was give birth . . .' I brought him up from a few weeks old until he was twenty-one. My husband George adored John just as though he were his own son. And like all dads, he spoiled him. Sometimes when John had done something wrong and I sent him up to his room, I'd find George creeping upstairs with the *Beano*, John's favourite comic, and a bar of chocolate.

Question: Did John ever have it tough as a child?

Mimi: All this talk about John's hard upbringing in a Liverpool slum is a fantasy. He wasn't pampered but he had the best of everything we could provide.

Question: To what do you attribute his early interest in music?

Mimi: I couldn't understand it. Here was a nicely-spoken boy attending church three times on Sunday of his own free will in the church choir, suddenly taking to twanging a guitar. I told him it was awful and that it was distracting him from his studies as an art student. Nothing would have convinced me that John would make his fortune with that boy at the front door [Paul McCartney]. But in the end I had to concede that music was far more important to him than the career as an artist and illustrator I had mapped out for him.

Question: Didn't John's half-sister Jacqui live with you for quite some time?

Mimi: Yes, but one day she didn't turn up for work so I looked in her room to find her clothes had gone. No note, nothing to say where she'd gone. After weeks of worry she turned up on the doorstep crying bitterly, 'I'm pregnant.' After that she stayed for a while but eventually vanished again. I only heard from her when she got herself pregnant yet again and wanted more money.

Question: And what did you think of Yoko?

Mimi: I have to admit Yoko was a good wife and mother and, thank goodness, I told John so long before. Sean is a darling, he's the living

183

image of John. He has his mannerisms and his sense of adventure. We are very good friends. He tells me what he's been up to and I tell him all about his dad, he's very interested and can't discover enough. When he's twenty-five he'll be a very rich man, but for now he needs a good education. Yoko is a sensible girl and is seeing to that.

Question: And your other grand-nephew, Julian?

Mimi: I think Julian ought to get a real job. I've heard him sing and it's not my cup of tea. Julian doesn't keep in touch, not that it worries me too much.

Question: How did John and Cynthia come to be married in the first place?

Mimi: One day I came home to find John moping around with a long face – he would have been about nineteen. 'It's to do with Cynthia,' he said at last. 'She's coming round to see you. She's got something to say.' Then he went up to his room. I knew Cynthia had been keen on John ever since they studied together at college, I knew she was making a play for him but I didn't know exactly what was going on. When she arrived I let her in and called upstairs for John. He came down crying his heart out. 'Whatever is the matter, John?' I said. Then, clinging to me just like he did as a child, he blurted out, 'Cynthia wants us to get married. Please, I don't want to get married.' I asked Cynthia if it was true and she nodded. Cynthia said she'd called round to ask my permission because John wasn't yet twenty-one. I got John on his own and asked him outright if he loved her. He shook his head, saying he wasn't sure. That settled it. I went to Cynthia and looking straight into her eyes I said I would not give my consent. I said when he's twenty-one he can do what he likes but until then I was still responsible for him. Of course she got him in the end, although she had to wait another three years.

Mary 'Aunt Mimi' Smith was John Lennon's maternal aunt who raised him as a boy. She and her husband George lived in the Mendips at Woolton.

John: My Mum

It's very important to me for people to know that I actually had a mother. She just happened to have a husband who ran away to sea when the war was on and so she had it very rough for a while.

I wasn't an orphan by any means, though. My mum was very much alive and well and living only a fifteen-minute walk from my auntie's. I always saw her off and on. I just didn't live with her full-time, that's all. (John)

Julia Baird, Chester, 14 September 1986 (interview by Geoffrey Giuliano)

Question: Tell me the social worker's story, if you would.

Julia Baird: When John was three or four, Mimi was to have said to my mother, 'You're not fit to have him.' That would have been just after Victoria's birth. I suppose Mimi's concern was for John though, wasn't it? John could have greater stability with her. My mother, of course, desperately wanted him. As far as I know, Mimi had to go away the first time she tried to take him. My father said, 'It's her child and if she wants him then that's it. It's her son.' Anyway, Mimi returned with a social worker and said, 'I don't want them to have him, they're not married.' The worker then said, 'Well, I'm sorry, Mrs Smith, but John's her son. Come, show me where he sleeps.' They were then shown the room where John was sleeping with my mother and father. John was given to Mimi at that point. And the social worker said, 'When you have somewhere for John to sleep, then he comes back.'

Question: Later your mother presumably became convinced that it was better for John to live with Mimi.

Julia: My mother probably thought he'd been backwards and forwards enough. The only reason she handed him over was for his own good.

Question: What does Mimi say about Julia? Does she ever imply she might have been derelict in her duty, to have given John up?

Julia: All of my family say that my mother was a most wonderful person and I remember it to be so. I think she was a bit eccentric though.

Question: What about this idea that your mother was of loose morals?

Julia: Obviously it's not something I want to confront. But I know now that first there was John and then there was another child, Victoria, before me, which I didn't know until about two or three years ago.

Question: Would the other sisters have lit into her for that?

Julia: I'm sure. She already had John, didn't she? There was no money coming from his father and Pop [Julia Lennon's father] was helping keep them. From what I gather, between my grandfather and Mimi the pressure was on to have the baby adopted. Mummy didn't go into Sefton General to have Victoria where John, Jacqui and I were born. She went into a nursing home where they arranged the adoption. Mum had the baby and it was adopted by a Norwegian sea captain as far as I know.

Question: This Victoria would be forty-two now, with virtually no knowledge of her background.

Julia: Apparently Norwegian law says you don't have to tell the child anything. Now here, if you're adopted you get your birth certificate and you see immediately if you've been adopted.

Question: I suppose it's very difficult to give us your first memory of John because, as you've said, he always seemed to be there.

Julia: I never realised he was a half-brother because you don't realise such things, do you? Unless the family's going to make it clear, which they didn't.

Question: Until when?

Julia: I was about sixteen. I overheard two aunts talking.

Question: But surely you knew his last name was Lennon?

Julia: It didn't mean a thing to me. They were always talking about Freddy Lennon and it began to wash over me when I was about fourteen but I completely put it to one side until I heard the two aunts discussing it. We'd never been brought up as 'this is your half-brother, this is your half-sister'.

Question: From what I can gather, your family was close, to the extent that the whole clan became an extended family. John might live with Mimi, you could stay with one aunt and another aunt could take care of the other kids for a while. That's very different.

Julia: Yes, we cousins were together when we were growing up. Leila, Stanley and John were close and David, Jacqui, Michael and I are like a second family within the children's generation. We're all still called 'the children', however. We did visit a lot because all the sisters were really very, very close.

Question: What kind of big brother was John?

Julia: Obviously he didn't live with us full-time. You look back now and think, 'Why didn't we think it was odd?' But we didn't, it was just the way it was. He'd come over weekends, we'd get up and John would be there. The older we got the more he came round with his mates until he was there almost nightly and at lunch. When he was younger he used to take us to the park. My mother would say, 'Take the girls to the swings please, John.' He'd take us out while he played football with his friends and we had a go on the swings. He used to take us to the pictures under duress. We went to see the Elvis film, *Love Me Tender*, which we saw twice because we were abandoned there. He'd watch it once with us and then run off. I don't know where he went, probably to see his friends or something. Then he'd pick us up after the second show.

Question: Tell me about John's bedroom at Mendips.

Julia: Well, he had this small front room which you could just about get you and the cat in. You'd open the door and he'd have skeletons and things flying about with their arms all going in the air. John made them himself. The lights went on and off and these puppets jiggled around when you opened the door.

Question: Tell me something about John as a boy.

Julia: Happy as a lark, whimsical, always dancing up and down, very good with us girls. Really just a lovable big brother hanging around the house. We were all great friends.

Question: People say that he was rather aggressive, though.

Julia: He wasn't within the family. He was always a very family-oriented person.

Question: What about his relationship with Mimi? It was rather tempestuous, wasn't it?

Julia: Not always. I think as a teenager he was certainly a rebel. He rebelled against school as he didn't really like the uniformity. He also rebelled against art school by not working when he finally got there. I don't really know what he would have done if he hadn't broken into music so successfully.

Question: Tell me about John singing to you girls.

Julia: He'd sing to all of us, not just Jacqui and me. He'd perform for all the children in the road. My mother would do exactly the same.

Question: What did he sing?

Julia: Very simple stuff on the piano. And later Elvis songs, just banging away.

Question: Did John and Mimi argue much?

Julia: They started having great rows about John's clothes and things. Mimi was doing the bread and butter and looking after us. My mother was the fun girl. It must have been a difficult position for Mimi to be in.

Question: You've commented that your mother and John had a great thing going, humour-wise.

Julia: They both had a fantastic sense of humour. There was a terrific rapport between them. There was a lot of wit flying backwards and forwards.

Question: You've said it really wasn't like a mother–son relationship at all. It was more of a friendship.

Julia: Well, I mean this is how it is when you got older, isn't it? She would still do the washing for him, though.

Question: Did he always call her Mummy?

Julia: Always.

Question: Do you remember John's first girlfriend?

Julia: The girls always liked John. This one girl, Barbara Baker, appeared a lot. She lived up in Woolton near Mimi. John was coming down more and more so she used to show up as well. We would all be playing and there she was. I remember once she asked us to go and fetch John. We did and my mother came out and shouted, 'What do you want from him?' The next thing I know, John was walking down the road with her. They would cuddle together in the grass.

Question: I've heard that Mimi once wanted John to accept a job as a bus conductor.

Julia: It must be very worrying to see somebody you're responsible for living in a dream when their whole life is stretching out in front of them.

Question: Did you ever go to the Cavern to see the Beatles?

Julia: Everybody went to the Cavern. I didn't go as much as I might have as we lived quite a long way out of town. The last bus back was ridiculously early so we couldn't really stay out very late.

Question: How did it affect your life when the Beatles became very successful in Liverpool before they went to America?

Julia: At school it was nice. We spent quite a few double A level lessons sitting and chatting about the Beatles. Still, the school, like me, had grown up with it and we were all a little blasé about the whole thing. I went down to London on shopping trips and it was all very exciting. Kenwood [John's mansion in Weybridge] was just being renovated.

Question: Do you remember when the Beatles went to the States for the first time?

Julia: Oh yes. That's when John really departed from our lives.

Question: Didn't Mimi go on one of those trips?

Julia: Mimi went on a world tour. She went to Hong Kong and brought us all back watches and things. We have family in New Zealand and she went to stay for about six months, but that wasn't a Beatle thing. She went to see her family and stopped off in Hong Kong on the way and brought us all stuff back.

Question: Do you remember what it was like at Mendips when the fans were going nuts in the garden?

Julia: Oh yes. That was awful. Poor Mimi. I really felt sorry for her. She was beleaguered by people camping in the garden.

Question: How did John change when he got money?

Julia: He was still very family-minded.

Question: People have told me he never really cared that much about money.

Julia: I think anyone who asked for it, got it. Which prevented a lot of people who maybe would have liked to have done, from asking. John was very family-minded and lovable. The Beatles were doing shows at the same time. He did a gig once and we all went to watch it. We were in the dressing room and Mick Jagger was there. People would come in to wish them well and everyone was drinking Cokes. Jacqui and I were put in the front row. We wanted to go out front so we could see the show. When it got a bit raucous John said, 'Get the girls,' and we were hauled onto the stage and watched from the wings because we didn't realise everyone was raging forward.

Question: You must have felt very special going up on stage when all the other girls were clambering about.

Julia: No, it wasn't as glamorous as that. We were just hauled up belly-wise into the wings to get out of the way.

Question: Where did John and Cynthia stay when they first got married?

Julia: I was there chatting with Mimi in the morning and she said, 'John wants to see me this afternoon. I know what he wants, he wants to move in and I'm going to let him.' I said, 'What are you going to do, Mimi?' She said, 'I'm going to live upstairs,' and that's exactly what she did. John's bedroom was converted into her kitchen. Just a tiny little cooker where John's bed was and she made the front bedroom her sitting room.

Question: How long did they live there?

Julia: I don't know. A couple of months or something. Then I don't know where they went. I remember them moving in, though.

Question: How did Mimi react to John's initial success?

Julia: At that stage you couldn't really argue with it, could you?

Question: When he first got money, what did he do? Did he run out and buy a big car?

Julia: He couldn't drive until he lived at Kenwood. He didn't have a licence so he didn't buy a car. I don't know when he bought his Mini, but I know that Harrie [John's Aunt Harriet] borrowed it for a time because John couldn't yet drive.

Question: Do you recall hearing the Beatles on the radio very early on?

Julia: We'd come home from school and John was always there to inform us when the Beatles would be on the radio. At that time they did a big concert in Liverpool and we all had front-row seats. That was our first experience of the wildness of Beatlemania. We were locked in the dressing room, unable to get out. I think that's when it really hit me. I thought, 'What is going on?'

Question: Tell me about these wild shopping sprees John and Cynthia took you on.

Julia: We had whatever we wanted. Jacqui got a pair of beautiful leather trousers. It was just clothes beyond what you would have normally been able to afford. Expensive jumpers, records and things.
Question: What about your visit to George Harrison's house?
Julia: We went to Esher not long after George moved in. John said, 'We're just going across for a visit.' Cynthia drove. It was John, Cynthia, Julian, Jacqui and me.
Question: Was he married to Pattie Boyd at the time?
Julia: I don't know. All I could think was that she was the Smith's Crisps Girl and she had a lisp. The house was very bare, but nice. There were cushions on all the floors. I think it was the last time I've ever personally seen George. We'd seen Pattie once before at Woolworth's in Liverpool promoting Smith's Crisps.
Question: How did you and John get back together again after all those years?
Julia: Mater [John and Julia's Aunt Elizabeth] rang one night just after John had gone back with Yoko in 1976. He told Mater, 'Get in touch with the girls.' He said that he wanted to see us. He told her that he had been thinking about Mother a lot and wanted to make it up to us. He said he could set Allan up in a business and if we needed anything we were only to ask. Probably, if he hadn't been such a mega-bucker we'd have been in touch before. If he had emigrated to Australia and become a sheep farmer I would have gone and stayed, but his financial position put him out of touch with just about everyone. Allan was saying, 'Are you going to ring him?' 'I need time,' I said, 'I need to think about it.'
Question: Did Allan want you to call?
Julia: Yes, but he wasn't a money-grubbing idiot. The first time I phoned I didn't know what to expect. A woman answered and said she'd been expecting my call for some time. She asked all kinds of questions, my maiden name, who had given me the number, my father's middle name. After a few minutes I said, 'Forget it, just forget it, it's all wrong.' As I put the phone down I heard John shout, 'Hang on, don't hang up! I'm sorry about that, but you have no idea how many sisters, cousins and aunties I've got.' Then we had a long, long chat. Mostly he was going on about, 'Do you recall laughing with Mummy and do you remember her spotted dress?' He said he had a new baby and asked about ours and Jacqui's and wondered if ours looked Irish. He wanted to know if my daughter Nicki had red hair like Mummy's. We didn't talk about being famous at all.
Question: Were there any tears?
Julia: Oh yes, he cried and I cried. We spent a lot of money crying! John

said, 'I've thought a lot about you over the years. Really and truly I have.' We were talking about how he felt about Mummy and how he felt now that he had a baby. He said he'd screwed things up with Julian, completely. 'I've been looking for a family and now I realise I've had one all along,' he told me. I said, 'Yes, you have, but we're here and you're there.' Then we talked about his green card and how the US government was trying to boot him out of the country. There was so much he wanted to do in America and if he left they wouldn't let him back in. 'You'll have to come over,' he said. But nothing ever materialised. Ironically, it was John who said, 'We'd better get off this call. Next time, call collect.' 'You mean reverse the charges?' I said. 'Speak to me in English, you've gone American on us!'

Question: Didn't John ask you to send him some family photographs?

Julia: He asked if I had any of Mummy and I said yes. There was one in particular where she was pregnant with Jacqui and I had this big, furry hat on. Leila, Stan and John were also in it. Allan did a twenty-by-sixty black and white print of it, but with only Mummy and John. I eventually snipped John off it because I only wanted a photograph of my mother. John said, 'Send it to me, please. Send it to me.' I said, 'You must be joking. You must have far more photographs than I. You should send me what you've got!' He said, 'The stupid reporters took them all and I never got any of them back. I haven't a single one of Mummy.' The next day we packed up loads of photographs and sent them over.

Question: How long did that first call last?

Julia: Two and a half hours. Allan paid the bill. It was enormous. After that, I called collect.

Question: Was it difficult getting through to John on the phone?

Julia: Sometimes I got through to John, sometimes his secretary and sometimes to Yoko. Initially it was all, 'Yes, I'll go get John and yes, here he is.' Sometimes, however, Yoko just broke in on a phone call. That was fine. We never said anything she wouldn't have already known, I'm sure. In the first phone call when John said, 'You should have come to see me. I have thought about you and Jacqui. Recently in the last year I've thought about you more than ever. I wanted a family and now I realise I've had one all along. You should have come to find me,' I really think he was right. I should have made more of an effort. The onus was more on me than him. I mean, John could have rung, there's no doubt about that. I thought, we'll get in touch and just see what's happening. The next thing I heard was that he was coming over in January of 1980. It was on the family grapevine.

Question: Tell me about the letter you got from Yoko.

Julia: In the midst of John writing me letters, after I sent some photographs over, Yoko wrote to me. It was just headed, 'Summer of '75, New York City.' It was just a chatty letter saying that Jacqui looks like John when he's in good condition, chatting about Sean and what they did together. I was quite surprised though to see that it was from Yoko and not John.

Question: What did John tell you he'd been up to during all those years he spent away from the music business?

Julia: I asked him what he did with himself and he said he was a house-husband. He looked after Sean. He was going to give him the years he hadn't given Julian, which he always regretted. He was steeped in things like changing the baby and seeing to his needs. He also learned how to bake bread and was always asking me how to cook. He asked me how hard my loaves were and how soggy bread was supposed to be in the middle. He said he always wanted to look at them when he knew he shouldn't open the oven. 'Wasn't it lovely eating it straight out of the oven,' and things like that. As children, none of us cooked. We always came in from school to a full delicious meal every night. We never had to do anything. So we left home not knowing how to boil an egg. Now John was learning on his own. He told me that at first his bread was rock-hard and couldn't be eaten. Then he talked about cooking meat. His favourite must have been lamb. When he came home to Harrie's with Yoko in 1969 she cooked him a leg of lamb when he was all macrobiotic and he loved it. When Cynthia and he were entertaining at Kenwood he particularly wanted her to cook a leg of lamb. Then he asked me, 'How do you cook lamb?' And I was saying, 'I just roast it, I don't do anything particular.' 'Do you put it in baking foil or not?' It was like two old women exchanging kitchen news. He was making me laugh, saying, 'You've no idea how exhausting it is looking after a baby.' I said, 'I'm on my second one now, of course I know.' He seemed to be thoroughly enjoying life. He said he loved going to the park with Sean and Yoko, pushing the baby.

Julia Baird is John Lennon's younger half-sister. Holding several degrees, she is today a French teacher and lives outside Liverpool. Julia has three children.

Dr Leila Harvey and Julia Baird, Manchester, 1986 (interview by Geoffrey Giuliano)

Question: Tell me a bit about John's mum.

Leila Harvey: John was Julia's only son and his pictures were put up all around the kitchen. He was never, ever separated from his mother. It was an extended family of five sisters and seven children. We could be in anybody's house and so could John. His mother lived only about ten minutes away from Mimi so we could always go and spend the weekend with Judy [Julia].

Question: Although Julia was untrained, could she sing?

Leila: Yes. She played the banjo and sang beautifully. Me being prejudiced, I would say she was even more gifted than John. Judy had personality, she was a little darling. She was offered professional work by Mater's [John and Julia's Aunt Elizabeth] husband but she refused. She was too lighthearted. Judy wasn't serious enough to sing or be an entertainer but she could catch anyone's heart.

Question: Julia [Baird] says that had she lived, Judy would have been right up there on stage with the Beatles.

Leila: She would. Right up front and everybody would have loved her. I guarantee you won't find one person who would say a bad word against Judy, apart from people writing silly books who don't know anything about her. She was lovely to everybody. Anybody who stopped by would have a cup of tea. The main thing about her was that she was always very, very witty.

Question: Do you remember anything particularly charming about John's childhood?

Leila: At about fourteen or fifteen John could pick up any instrument and play it, the mouth organ, the accordion. He was very affectionate and sweet natured. We'd sit watching television and he'd always put his head on my lap.

Question: There's another view of John, you know, that he was a bit of a neighbourhood bully.

Leila: Aren't all fifteen-year-olds trying to be a bit macho? He was very sweet and soft. And quite serious about things, what's right and wrong. John would often talk to me about what he should do. He was a very serious little lad sometimes. Still, I only knew him until the age of fifteen.

Question: What are your first memories of the Beatles? Did you go and see them when they were in Germany?

Leila: I didn't, no. I was working day and night. I did buy their first four records and then I thought, 'Well, four, that's enough. He's going to go on doing this forever so I'm going to buy a bit of classical music now.'

Question: Did John ever ring you, or anything?

Leila: I had no contact with him. The next time we connected was when the Beatles were beginning to break up in 1969. The family said he was on this terrible diet and looked very ill. When I saw him I was shocked. It was at Apple and he looked a hundred. He was eating his three lentils and two grains of rice a day. He looked really ill. I visited him once at Weybridge. There was no security, I just walked right into his office. I visited him there because that was the last time I could see him as I was back at work and had my three children to look after.

Question: Life does goes on, doesn't it?

Leila: Families do separate to that extent, yes. I was with John totally from the age of two to fifteen. Our whole childhood, all our Christmases, Easters, all our summers were spent together. After that, hardly at all.

Question: What did you think when you saw John in this condition?

Leila: I was very upset at the state of his health and worried about him.

Question: Did you say that to him?

Leila: It wasn't easy to get a word in edgeways with the lady there [Yoko]. We had a good old chat at Weybridge though. At that point John was very separated from his family.

Question: We've been talking around it, but obviously, you weren't very impressed by Yoko. Do you think she had a positive influence over him?

Leila: No, I wouldn't say that. I think Yoko provided John with what he needed at the time. I think his life would have been more in balance if he hadn't gone so far out. We didn't like the vulgarity. It's not our style and really, it's not John's style. John was a healthy, normal male. We didn't like the exhibitionism.

Question: Are you referring to their *Two Virgins* nude album cover?

Leila: The nude photographs, yes.

Julia Baird: All of that sort of nonsense.

Question: Why do you think he did it?

Leila: John was not really an exhibitionist. John had a musical talent. His body was nothing to write home about. As Mimi said at Apple, 'It would have been all right John, but you're both so ugly. Why don't you get somebody attractive on the cover, if you've got to have somebody naked?' It was just silly. It was childish exhibitionism. It's like, 'We've done everything else, now what can we do? Take our clothes off!' That's what children do at the beach. I've had a recent argument with

Yoko concerning the sale of my letters from John. She was rather rude on the phone, telling me off about it. And I don't consider that she is in any position to criticise my morals. I said, 'Look here, you were only married to John, but he was our blood.' That really annoyed her. She said a rude word, which I'm not going to repeat because that would be bitchy. She stopped sending her little Christmas gifts after that, so she's obviously annoyed. She rang my brother David and thought I would apologise. She has no right to ring me up and criticise my morals. If I wish to sell John's letters, and I didn't actually, I wanted to wait until I was dead.

Question: No one ever made any more money off John Lennon than Yoko Ono!

Leila: Well, I certainly haven't made any, but my daughter did. I could have had anything I wanted from John when he was alive but it would have hurt him if I asked, so I didn't. I've never been short of money. But my daughter is just starting off in life and she wanted something. So she sold them and she got the money. She shared it with her brothers and I never touched it. I think Yoko feels that the family might try and take away a bit of her fun. But we're not interested in publicity. We have our normal lives and our families. That's her life. She thinks we're muscling in on her turf, but we're not. She was afraid that my daughter selling those letters might somehow affect the attendance at her concerts.

Question: The only thing that affected her concerts was her complete, innate inability to sing on key and people not wanting to buy tickets to hear her crucify John's songs.

Leila: I was never rude to her. The only thing I said which really annoyed her was, 'Look, Yoko, John was our blood, you were only married to him,' which I think is fair comment.

Dr Leila Harvey is Lennon's first cousin on his mother's side. As children, she and John were exceptionally close.

Ken Brown, London, 1965

Question: How does it feel to have left the Beatles just before they really made it big?

Ken Brown: Sometimes I could kick myself – hard! I could still be one of the Beatles, earning thousands of pounds a week, instead of living in a caravan. I was with John, Paul and George the first time they played together at the Casbah. I knew John's wife Cynthia – in fact, I saw their romance blossom. I knew George's first girlfriend, Ruth Morrison. We shared everything – our music, and the three pounds a night we used to earn in those far-off days of August, 1958. Now, my old ten-watt amplifier lies in a corner of my caravan. The Hofner guitar I played hangs on the wall, but I still play for my wife, Marcia. These are my only souvenirs, and I often think if it hadn't been for a row over a paltry fifteen bob, I might still be with them.

Question: What do you remember best about those days?

Ken: The memories flood back . . . I was with the Beatles the day they were formed – quite by accident. It was summer 1958 and Harrison and I were playing in the Les Stewart Quartet with a chap called Skinner. We spent hours practising in the Lowlands Club, Heyman's Green. We would probably have gone on playing at clubs but for George's girlfriend, Ruth. George had never been really too keen on girls. He was only sixteen and at the Liverpool Institute with Paul McCartney. Later, he suddenly seemed to go head-over-heels for Ruth, who eventually moved to Birmingham to become a nurse. One evening the three of us were sitting in the Lowlands drinking coffee, moaning about the fact that we had nowhere regular to play, when Ruth suggested we see Mrs Best at the Casbah. She promised that the Les Stewart Quartet would play at the club when it opened. On the Saturday we were due to open so I went round to Stewart's house. George was sitting in the lounge, his Hofner across his lap, idly plucking at the strings. The atmosphere seemed a bit tense. 'What's up?' I asked. George looked down at his guitar, and said nothing. So I turned to Les. He looked daggers, saying, 'You've been missing practice.' 'I know,' I replied, 'but only so's we can have somewhere to play; I've spent hours working at the club.' 'You've been getting paid for it,' challenged Les. 'No, I haven't.' 'Well, I'm not going to play there,' said Stewart, as our argument got steadily more heated. I turned to George. 'Look,' I said, 'the club opens tonight. We've spent months waiting for this; you're not backing out, too?' George thought for a moment. Then he said he would go on with me, so we left Les at his house. As we were walking down the road, I turned to George and said, 'We can't let Mrs Best down now. Let's try and get a group together ourselves. Do you know anyone?' 'There's two mates I sometimes play with out at Speke,' ventured George. 'Okay, let's ask them,' I said, and George went off on the bus, joining me two hours later at the Casbah with his two mates – John Lennon and Paul McCartney.

Question: Did you have any idea who his two mysterious mates were?

Ken: No, not at all. This was the first time I'd ever met them. Paul was fifteen, still at school and had a schoolboyish haircut. But John was already a bit of a beatnik, with his hair hanging over his collar, dressed in a check suit coat and old jeans. I told them we would each be paid fifteen bob a night. They seemed glad about that; in those days most groups played just for experience.

Question: What were you called at this point?

Ken: We talked over various names to call ourselves, and finally settled on the Quarrymen, a name John had used once or twice before for skiffle groups he had formed since leaving Quarry Bank Grammar School. So, that night the Beatles were born and the Casbah opened after all. We went down great, particularly when Paul sang 'Long Tall Sally'. Our most popular numbers were John and Paul's vocals (I was the rhythm guitarist). John's pet solo was 'Three Cool Cats', which he used to growl into the mike.

Question: What are your thoughts these days on John?

Ken: John was always very quiet. He was a lonely youngster, seldom talking about his family, maybe because his father had deserted him in childhood, and then his mother had been killed. John seemed in need of affection, and depended on Cynthia.

Question: How did your days with the band finally end?

Ken: One night, just as we were due to start a Saturday session, I felt a crippling pain in my leg. I could barely stand, but insisted on doing something, so Mrs Best asked me to take the money at the door and, for the first time, John, Paul and George played without me. Just as everyone was going home I was in the club when Paul came back down the steps. 'Hey, Ken, what's all this?' he said. 'What?' I asked him. 'Mrs Best says she's paying you, even though you didn't play with us tonight.' 'That's up to her,' I replied, as Paul bounded back up the stairs, still arguing with Mrs Best. They all came downstairs to me. 'We think your fifteen bob should be divided between us, as you didn't play tonight,' said Paul. So of course I didn't agree. 'All right, that's it then!' shouted McCartney, and they stormed off down the drive towards West Derby village, shouting that they would never play the Casbah again. But that wasn't the last time I saw them – nor the last time they played the Casbah – though we didn't play together again. The last time I saw the Beatles was on 16 March 1963. I had moved to London and married Marcia. The telephone rang and it was Neil Aspinall, their road manager. He told me the boys were in a bit of a jam; they had run out of money; the next night they were due to appear in Sheffield; unless someone helped them out they would have to sleep in the van. Neil wondered if I would lend them twenty quid. Eventually, I agreed, and they all turned up at our flat. Neil came to the door, then Marcia and I went down to the van to see the boys. I handed over the money, which they repaid six weeks later. I told them we were moving into a caravan. 'Great,' said Paul. 'We'll all drop in to see you some time.' And with that they drove off into the night.

13 September 1965

Ken Brown played with the Quarrymen during their final days together.

Rock at Neston Institute

A Liverpool rhythm group, the Beatles, made their debut at Neston Institute on Thursday night when north-west promoter, Mr Les Dodd, presented three and a half hours of rock'n'roll.

The five-strong group, which has been pulling in capacity houses on Merseyside, comprises three guitars, bass and drums.

John Lennon, the leader, plays one of the three rhythm guitars, the other guitarists being Paul Ramon and Carl Harrison. Stuart Da Stael plays the bass and the drummer is Thomas Moore. They all sing, either together, or as soloists.

Recently they returned from a Scottish tour, starring Johnny Gentle, and are looking forward to a return visit in a month's time.

Among the theatres they have played at are the Hippodrome, Manchester; the Empire, Liverpool; and Pavilion, Aintree.

11 June 1960

Pete Best, New York, 1965

Question: Could you tell me a little about your early life?

Pete Best: I was born in Madras, India. I came to Liverpool when I was four years old. The transportation was a troop steamer. On board were dozens and dozens of wounded soldiers. During the war my father was involved in the Great Bombay Explosion. More than thirteen hundred tons of raw explosives went up that day, turning the ship they were stored in (plus twelve others) into a useless pile of scrap metal. The tragedy claimed hundreds of lives and flattened three hundred acres of the Bombay Docks. A tidal wave caused by it was so gigantic it lifted a four-thousand-ton ship nearly fifty feet into the air and literally threw the vessel onto the roof of a nearby shed. My father was one of many men who helped rescue the wounded and those buried under mountains of debris.

Question: What were your first impressions of your new home?

Pete: When we arrived at Liverpool, the first thing I remember is seeing snow. Of course, there was never any snow in India and to me, picking up a handful and playing with it was quite an experience! The next few years were uneventful. I did well in athletics, judo, boxing, etc., representing my class in active competition with other schools.

Question: How did you come to be associated with the Beatles?

Pete: The first time I met John, Paul and George was when my mother was opening a club called the Casbah in the cellar of our home. I was seventeen years old. We had booked the Les Stewart Quartet and the day the Casbah was scheduled to open, Les broke up with the other guys. John and Paul approached us at about the same time and Mum got hold of George Harrison who was playing in another club two hundred yards down the street. They rehearsed for two and a half hours and Mum liked them very much. They signed on under the name the Quarrymen and played the club for several months. Then they went to Scotland for another engagement. By that time, I had formed my own group and we took over the spotlight in Mum's club. Eventually, all of us broke up and went our separate ways.

Question: What about actually signing up as a full-fledged Beatle?

Pete: One day, unexpectedly, I received a phone call from Paul. The group had an offer to go to Germany but they needed a drummer and he was wondering if I could help them out. Paul said that he and the others had talked over the matter and they wanted me to audition for them. Stu Sutcliffe had joined them on bass with George on lead and John and Paul on rhythm guitar. I auditioned and they kicked things around. Within thirty-six hours we were on the way to Hamburg, to play the Indra Club. At that time, we were all pretty young and reckless, really living it up. We were staying at the back of the club and the surroundings weren't, shall we say, very elaborate. But the kids were beginning to dig us. Later, we moved down the street into a bigger club. We were performing for a solid eight hours every night.

Question: Didn't you continue to play your mother's club after returning from Germany?

Pete: Sure. Our first date was in December, just before Christmas. More than five hundred kids were there and they gave us a great home-coming reception. The news of our Hamburg success apparently spread throughout Liverpool. Virtually overnight, we were the number one group. We stayed there for about eight months and then returned to Hamburg for a period of ninety days or so. Of course, Paul and I had earlier been deported from Germany, in August of 1960. George was also sent home because he was considered too young to get proper working papers. Paul and I had a big argument with the club owner over several matters, most important being the fact that he'd paid for five musicians in the group and wanted to reduce our pay after George left. It turned into a fight. We weren't about to pay any fine, so we got the boot. But our deportation came later. There were no electric lights where we'd been living and we couldn't see a damn thing to pack. Finally, though, we managed to get our things together. We went out to buy some cigarettes, John and I. By the time we'd returned, the living quarters were ablaze. Paul had accidentally knocked over a candle which set some torn pieces of tapestry ablaze. Both he and Stu were arrested. The manager claimed we had tried to burn down his club in order to get back at him. So we were deported!

Question: How did you feel after being ousted from the Beatles?

Pete: I'm much too quiet. I don't like to fight or argue. I was raised to be well-mannered and respectful and never to lose my temper. So I just stayed in my room at home and didn't come out. I thought I was really finished. I would stare into space and do nothing, not eat or drink or anything. Pretty soon, the incident got around and my friends came and tried to make me snap out of my depression. Girls were sleeping in our back garden, waiting for me to pass by a window so they could shout how they still liked me despite the fact that I was no longer with the Beatles. I became a hermit, literally living alone and sealed off from the world around me. I was living in a world of my own. Then my parents got hold of me and told me how foolish I was acting. They urged me to go out and be with people. After ten days, I managed to bring myself back to reality.

Pete Best was the Beatles' first real drummer, playing with the group from 1960 to 1962. He was ultimately sacked on the eve of the group's phenomenal success.

Pete Out, Ringo In

Regarding the sacking of Pete Best, he was, frankly, too conventional and didn't fit well as either a drummer or a man. His beat was too slow, or George thought so. I liked him, though he could be moody. He was friendly with John and Paul, but George didn't like him. They all liked Ringo although I thought he was rather loud. Anyway, the Beatles finally said, 'We want Pete out and Ringo in.' I had to tell him and I didn't sleep that night. I hate sackings. A session man has never been put in. At the time Ringo was in Skegness, at Butlins. Pete took it very badly. That night he failed to turn up in Chester and Nel, with whom he lived, didn't arrive either. Pete never played with the Beatles again. Matthew Street [outside the Cavern] became dangerous. Fans were roaming the streets singing, 'We want Pete! Pete forever, Ringo never!' I asked Ray McFall for protection and he gave me Paddy Delaney as my bodyguard. It was very dangerous. Rory Storm was annoyed too that we had taken his drummer. So was his mother, for Rory now had no drummer. It was all very difficult. I remember John said, 'Get rid of your beard, Ringo. Keep your sidies.'

So Ringo became a Beatle and started to grow his hair. They had £40 suits from Benidorm in Birkenhead. I chose them with them. They only pay £30 now.

Ringo did seem to complete a visual pattern with the Beatles. Pete was a conventionally good-looking lad. But I wasn't too happy about Ringo. I didn't want him but then, as now, I trusted the boys' instincts.

Brian Epstein

Mona Best and Pete Best, Liverpool, 28 August 1985

Question: Mrs Best, what inspired you to open a club on the outskirts of town?

Mona Best: I used to have them coming in and out of my house as if it were a railway station, so I thought to myself, we've got a nice cellar, maybe the gang would all like to go down there? The boys said, 'What are we going to do down here? There's nothing going on, let's make it into a little club.' That little club ended up with nearly three thousand members. Every night it used to be jam-packed solid. We use to light the fire even if it wasn't a hot night so they'd buy more Coke. They'd say, 'It's hot, another Coke please, Rory.' The people would be enjoying themselves chock-a-block. I've never seen a club with such atmosphere. It was all volunteers that helped get the club together. They put in a lot of hours.

Question: This was really before the Cavern Club, wasn't it?

Mona: Yes. Later, when I spoke to [Cavern owner] Ray McFall, he was doing jazz in his club. I believe he said, 'You've opened up a little rock'n'roll club. Why don't you come down to the Cavern?' I said, 'I can't, I'm too busy with my own place. But there's a very good rock group over here called the Beatles. Why don't you put them on?' He said, 'I'm thinking of changing over to rock. Maybe I'll do it.' And that's how the boys eventually went on to play the Cavern.

Question: Could you give us some idea what it was like at the club?

Mona: Everybody used to call each other by their Christian names. My mother, who was very ill at the time, was 'Gran' to everybody, though she seldom came out of her room. It was an unusual place, with a fantastic atmosphere, very friendly. We had a jukebox, in fact, one of the guys used to play records for us. So from a little acorn a very big oak tree grew. I remember the day the Quarrymen first showed their faces, the four of them: John, George, Paul and Ken Brown. We didn't allow any ale in the club, or any other drinks for that matter. Sometimes though, the kids use to smuggle them in and we had to pitch them out when they got drunk.

Question: How much was a membership?

Mona: Half a crown. And threepence for a bottle of Coke. In fact, a lot of club owners in town would say, 'Hey, you're spoiling it for us, at least raise the price to nine.'

Question: Pete, how did you become involved with the Beatles?

Pete Best: My first recollection of meeting them was just before the club opened. We needed a group to open on the Saturday. Well, I knew

George because there was another club down the road called the Low-lands and he used to play there with Ken Brown and their skiffle group. When you talk about skiffle, you're talking very small amplifiers. Anyway, Ken said the group had broken up, but George turned around and said, 'I know a couple of guys who say they've played in a band before. If they're interested in coming down, would you let them open?' Mum said, 'Yes, let me see them.' Well, it turned out to be John and Paul. But there was no drummer. It was John, George, Paul, Ken Brown, and they decided to play under the name The Quarrymen. On that fateful night the Casbah opened, the Quarrymen took the stage as a foursome (without a drummer) and history began.

Question: So the night the Casbah opened, the first group to play there was the Quarrymen.

Pete: Yes, and I believe they didn't do too badly subsequently.

Question: What was your first impression of the group?

Mona: The Quarrymen were never a very smart lot. Whenever you saw them they looked scruffy, just as scruffy and untidy as when they went on stage. Out of them all, Ken was the cleanest. The rest had ruffled heads, dirty clothes and filthy jeans. But they were a happy lot.

Pete: At the time John was still at art college so he was a typical Bohemian. He'd come in with his black jacket, white cape, and chukka boots. He never used to wear his glasses. I remember he was helping out at the club and painted several murals on the ceiling. He painted his usual pot bellies and caricatures, but the Casbah had to be dark so one day he said, 'I'll just paint the ceiling black,' and they all went. Paul was a little more sedate, he'd wear jeans, an off-white shirt and a cashmere jacket. That's the way they knocked around. They were very relaxed in what they did. They were always laughing and joking. There was nothing serious about them. Somebody would crack a joke and they wouldn't work for two hours. They were scruffy, but don't get the impression they were tramps or anything.

Question: Did you think these guys really had something special?

Pete: Remember, they were a group without a drummer and very different in as much as their material was not the run-of-the-mill stuff. They weren't interested in the Top Twenty, they were playing Chuck Berry, Carl Perkins and Gene Vincent. They were all harmonies and saying what they liked, it's as simple as that. They also had great charisma on stage. There was something about them. The way they stood, the things they did, which made them stand out from the rest of the groups. Stu Sutcliffe use to come down and watch the Quarrymen. He was very much a Beatles man.

Question: How did you personally become involved with the Beatles?
Pete: They played the Casbah for nearly twelve months and one particular night Ken Brown wasn't too well and they played as a trio. At the
end of the evening the princely sum of fifteen shillings was kept back by
Mum. There was a bit of a disagreement as they wanted that split up
amongst them. Which, by the way, would have only bought them
another beer in the pub or something.
Mona: They were always like that where money was concerned.
Pete: After that, they disappeared and Stu joined them. By that time they
had changed their name to the Silver Beatles. At the end of their first tour
of Scotland, a guy called Tommy Moore was drumming for them and he
told me, 'The tour was a complete flop, it didn't go anywhere.' When the
Quarrymen changed to the Silver Beatles there was another group in the
wings, which was my own funky outfit. I formed a band with Ken Brown
called the Blackjacks and took on another couple of guys, Chas Nugan
and Bill Low. We played skiffle at school as I knew some guitar stuff, but
later on I switched to drums and got a kit. I started off with a thirty-six-
inch bass, a ten-inch snare, one cymbal, a pair of brushes and eventually
got a drum kit which happened to be blue. After Tommy Moore disappeared, of course, the boys never managed to find another drummer. I
got a call from Paul one night, saying they were booked to go to Germany. Allan Williams [the Beatles' manager at the time] closed the deal
and he wondered if I would be interested in joining. I told him my group
really wasn't professional, we were just doing it for kicks. Anyway, the
offer was there so I just said okay.
Mona: He gave up school to go, you know, he was going in for lan-
guages. He said, 'Can I finish school to go off to Germany?' I said, 'If
that's what you want.' He said, 'I want to go into show business, that's
where my heart is.' 'Do what you want,' I told him, and off he went.
Pete: So I auditioned and as the story goes: Two days later we were on
our way to Hamburg.
Question: After becoming a Beatle, did you think you were on your
way to superstardom?
Pete: Joining a band which was fully professional was one thing, and
joining a bunch of guys with no real experience quite another. Still, we
were friends. No, I didn't think we were going anywhere, but it was a
chance to break into show business. I mean the German audiences were
going wild and that's when the charisma really started to grow. I don't
think that they, in their wisdom, thought they'd ever become megastars
either. I think we knew we were going to get in the charts and that was
the first stepping stone; in fact, that was the ultimate at the time.

Question: I once saw a movie which portrayed the early Beatles and it had John saying, 'Lads, where're we going? Straight to the top!' Is that true?

Pete: Yes. When we were on stage and things were going well, he'd shout, 'Where're we going, guys?' And the reply was, 'To the toppermost of the poppermost!' Which meant we were going to get there. He'd call that out even if we were in the middle of a number.

Question: Who actually made the decision to retire you from the band?

Pete: I don't really know, because of the manner I received it.

Question: It seems they got Eppie to do their dirty work.

Mona: The Beatles never really had the courage to speak their minds unless it was something to their advantage. If there was any dirty work to be done Brian had to do it.

Pete: As far as I'm concerned, there was no build-up to it even though the conspiracy was obviously going on. It would have been nice if I'd been in the position to defend myself or ask the reasons why. In fact, while Brian was actually dismissing me, there was a call from Paul asking whether the deed had been done. It would have been nice to have had them there and actually ask the reasons why.

Question: What was John's reaction to Stu's death?

Pete: For the first time I actually saw him physically break down and shed tears. The rest of us, too, had tears in our eyes. John respected Stu as an artist. I think it hurt him a lot more than us.

Question: Professionally speaking, if you had one thing to change, what would it be?

Pete: Well, since I was once a Beatle I'd like to have found out what it was really like to be on top with the group.

Question: What were your feelings when you learned of John's death?

Pete: My wife, Cathy, actually heard it first. She called me upstairs while I was getting ready for work, saying, 'Pete, John's dead, he's been murdered.' Due to the fact that I hadn't seen any of the Beatles for many years or even spoken to them, the name John didn't mean anything, but when Cathy said, 'It's John Lennon,' it was a sick feeling. I had known the guy personally, he'd come to the house, I'd befriended him, he spent time in the Casbah raiding the Cokes.

Question: How often did he stop by?

Pete: Very often. After the venues, John would be the guy running through the Casbah, raiding the stores, putting his head down for the night and listening to records.

Question: Were the Beatles very different to the rest of the bands in Britain after you came back from Germany?

Pete: Oh yeah, without a doubt. The bands which were playing in Liverpool at the time were mostly *Top of the Pops* type groups. You know, smart stage suits, doing cute little walks and dance routines, very prim and proper. We came back playing the music we liked the way we wanted to play it. When Brian took us over, though, the image really started to change. It may have been good management from his point of view, but at the time every group in Liverpool was copying our performance, mannerisms and the material we were playing. Everyone was trying to outdo one another and all of a sudden Eppie comes along and says, 'Okay, you've got to tidy the act up. I'm going to put you in suits and you're going to have to play the same repertoire every night.'

Question: Do you think Lennon actually sold out to make it?

Pete: I don't think 'sell out' is really the right word. I think they realised that to keep on the bandwagon they'd have to emphasise material the public wanted. They may have been reluctant to do it, but I think it was a matter of necessity.

Question: Do you think it affected the music?

Pete: Sure. They started to play their own material as opposed to before. If you look at the material John wrote, there's quite a lot of freedom lyric-wise. He couldn't actually portray the original sound we created as the Beatles so he went more into the lyrics. If you listen to John's lyrics, that's where his true feelings were.

Question: Mrs Best, have you ever thought of writing a book?

Mona: If I put my true feelings in a book I think someone would shoot me! There would be an awful lot of bitterness because I do feel bitter and sometimes find it very, very difficult to answer certain questions. Especially when people ask, 'How do you feel towards the Beatles?' My feelings towards the Beatles are nil. I can't possibly feel anything for them, although I do admire their music, don't get me wrong. They're good musicians, but as people, for what they did to Peter, I could never forgive them. I'm sure I will be bitter to the day I die because you can't see somebody hurt as badly as Peter and not take a certain attitude against them.

Question: Someone once said that you probably played more hours with the Beatles than Ringo, when you add it all up. Do you think that's an accurate statement?

Pete: Most definitely, because for an awful long time we were playing eight hours a night, and that mounts up compared with the tours they later played with only forty-five minutes on stage.

Pete Best's mother Mona ran the Casbah Club in the basement of her home in Liverpool from 1958 to 1962.

The Homely Drummer

The story goes that around the time Pete Best was tossed out of the band, Paul went around Liverpool trying to find the ugliest drummer he could that happened to have his own kit. In those days it was very tough finding someone with a full kit, you know. Anyway, along came Ringo, so there they were with a homely drummer and a great kit to boot! Now to be honest, between Pete and Ringo, technically I find Pete to be a somewhat better drummer but he probably lacked the overall appeal Ringo had. The point I'm trying to make here is that according to Pete, it was jealousy that started the whole thing, not musicianship. After I took Pete on as an artist I saw first-hand just how upset he was about being let go practically on the eve of the Beatles' great success. Whenever they came on television he wouldn't do anything but kind of hang his head and look the other way. He often tried to change the subject or ignore the situation, but deep inside I knew it was eating him up.

(Bob Gallo, Pete Best's mentor and producer following Best's split from the Beatles.)

Paddy Delaney, Liverpool, 1984 (interview by Geoffrey
Giuliano)

Question: Paddy, you were the bouncer at the Cavern Club when the
Beatles were around, correct?
Paddy Delaney: I was.
Question: Is there a bouncer at the newly restored Cavern Club?
Paddy: No, not quite, but I'm involved with going down there occasionally and chatting with people about the old days.
Question: What is your first remembrance of the Beatles?
Paddy: Well, their first appearance on the scene occurred on 21 March
1961. The first one I ever saw was George Harrison. In those days,
hairstyles were very strict and tidy, but George's hair was down to his
collar. He was very scruffy and hungry-looking. I remember him
ambling down the middle of the street and for a minute I didn't think he
was coming into the Cavern. I stopped him at the door and asked him if
he was a member. Of course I knew he wasn't, and he said no, he was
with the Beatles. Now we'd heard a lot about the Beatles over the previous weeks and I knew they were on that particular night, so I let him
in even though he was wearing blue jeans (jeans were strictly banned
from the club). About fifteen minutes later, Paul McCartney tumbled
down the street with John Lennon in close pursuit. Paul was carrying
his bass guitar and John had his hands dug deep into his pockets. I had
an idea they were with George because they all had the same sort of
hairstyle. It wasn't quite a Beatle haircut then, but it was still well past
their collars. A little while after they strolled in, a taxi pulled up in front
of the club and out came their drummer, Pete Best. He was carrying the
Beatles' first sound system which consisted of two cheap chipboard
speakers and a beat-up looking amplifier. He also had a set of drums
which he unloaded and took down the stairs. This is how the Beatles
first arrived at the Cavern.
Question: What was their attitude in those days?
Paddy: They had a certain animal magnetism and a raw vibrancy to
their music. There was an air about them that seemed to say, if you
didn't like them, too bad, they couldn't care less.
Question: The Beatles ultimately became one of Liverpool's top
groups. How affected were they by their early success?
Paddy: Well, shortly after they recorded 'Please Please Me' Brian
Epstein was giving them a weekly salary of only eight pounds. Onc
night, Paul went over to the snack bar to buy himself a Coke and a
cheese sandwich. Now, he had enough for the Coke but not for the

sandwich, so he asked me for a loan, and I said, 'Yeah, sure, but don't forget me when you're at the top.' Well, he winked at me and said, 'Don't worry, Pat, I won't forget.'

Question: Do you have a quick John Lennon story?

Paddy: Well, the Beatles were on one of their first major tours of the country, they were starting out in the south with Brian Epstein or 'Eppie' as we called him, and working their way up north. Their last engagement on the tour was to be the Cavern. Brian worked it out in such a way that they ended up at the Cavern on a Saturday night, so on the Thursday night I went to the Blue Angel to have something to eat. By this time I was fully aware of most of the Beatles' activities, everybody was, especially the media, of course. Anyway, at the Blue Angel I saw the back of a man sitting on a stool at the bar, he had on a light blue mohair suit, had very well-groomed hair down to his collar, and I thought, 'It can't be, but it looks very much like our John.' As I drew a bit closer to him and saw his famous profile, dear, it was John Lennon at the bar and he had a large Scotch in front of him. Now, I remember when the Beatles were sharing two pints between the four of them. They would each take a sip out of the glass and pass it around! Now, a large Scotch cost a hell of a lot, I certainly couldn't afford to buy Scotch! I said, 'Hello, John, what are you doing here?' 'Having a drink, Pat.' A typical Lennon answer. He said, 'My mate here will have a double Scotch, please, barman,' even though that's not what I ordered. I said, 'Now wait a minute, John, I'm having my supper and then I'm going straight home.' So anyway, we finished the Scotch and one thing led to another, of course; he was paying for the drinks so we drank a bit more and little by little we both got very, very drunk. Now, when I entered the Blue Angel it was about 12.30 a.m. (we used to close the Cavern at 12.15) and at 4.30 a.m. on a bright summer's morning I was practically thrown out of a taxi outside my front door by a very pissed-up John Winston Lennon! You see, I had to go to work at eight o'clock that morning and I would have had a full night's sleep but he got me pissed as a rat. He was giggling all over the place, falling about in the cab. As it turned out, on Saturday they were all laughing and joking about what had happened.

Question: Did you ever see any of them after they got very famous in the sixties?

Paddy: I've seen Paul, he came down to the Cavern in 1969. He was with Linda and the children. I haven't seen George in years, but I've seen Pete Best around and he's still the same as ever.

Question: Is he bitter about what happened?

Paddy: Pete can take it but the people around him can't, his mother and his wife especially. He's been very badly done to. He's a very good-looking fellow, you know, he looks a little bit like Jeff Chandler.

Question: Some people say that he was sacked because the girls liked him better than Paul, so Paul went around Liverpool looking for the ugliest drummer he could possibly find.

Paddy: He also wouldn't conform to the style that Brian Epstein wanted for them. He didn't believe in a lot of the things the boys were into at that time, I think. But I loved them all and I think about them often. Those days were magic and they, my friend, were four incredible magicians.

Paddy Delaney worked as the Cavern's big-hearted bouncer from 1959 onwards.

Gerry Marsden, Liverpool, 1986 (interview by Geoffrey Giuliano)

Question: Tell me about your first meeting with the Beatles.

Gerry Marsden: I was thirteen. They were called the Quarrymen and I was with the Gerry Marsden Skiffle Group. We played a show together, I think I was fourteen or fifteen. The nice thing was, we got on well then and we're still basically getting on well together.

Question: You used to gig with them?

Gerry: Yes, in fact, one time at the Liverpool Town Hall we formed a big band. It was the Beatles and ourselves. It was good fun.

Question: When the Beatles got very psychedelic, you didn't follow along, did you?

Gerry: No. Basically, I never liked the Beatles' psychedelic situation at all. Their ideas were correct, it just wasn't the Beatles to me.

Question: When you think of the Fabs you think of 'She Loves You', 'Twist and Shout', 'I Want to Hold Your Hand' . . .

Gerry: 'Please, Please Me'. Yeah, that to me is the Beatles. It's what John was doing before he was killed. John was going back to his roots. To me the psychedelic period and the transcendental meditation crap was a joke.

Question: So did you see them during these days and ask them what they were doing?

Gerry: Sure I did. Silly boys.

Question: And what did they say?

Gerry: They said it was a new field, it's what's happening. I could see it was a fad, just crap.

Question: Would you see them during the Apple days?

Gerry: Certainly, but that was a different thing. They became businessmen and they couldn't be businessmen.

Question: Is that why they broke up? Did they lose their sense of humour?

Gerry: When bands have been together for twelve or fifteen years there's no having conversations together. You know everything about everybody else and it just gets very boring. The break-up was inevitable. They would have broken up at some time in their career. I don't think it was because of Apple. They were only a band. They were only kids playing and it got very heavy.

Question: There were so many groups back then, why did the Beatles click so much more?

Gerry: They had talent and that's all it is. You're talking about three guys (forget Ringo), John, Paul and George, and there's this great charisma and talent they shared. When I was a kid every street had a pub filled with music and it was the seamen home from the States and all over the world playing music. We grew music in the pubs, as did Glasgow, Newcastle and Southampton, but in Liverpool we stayed with rock. When I say 'rock' I mean more 'rhythm and blues', until we found Fats Domino, Chuck Berry, Ray Charles, the greatest rock in the world and the greatest jazz musicians in the world. We never did songs by Cliff, Billy Fury or Adam Faith. We always stayed with rock.

Question: That must have taken a lot of courage. The Shadows were doing these tight little dance steps in their silk suits, but you guys said, 'We want to do rock'n'roll.' That must have been very tough, going against the market.

Gerry: The point you're missing, we never thought of making records. We were playing to enjoy what we were doing. The only time we thought of records was when Brian Epstein came on the scene because Eppie would say, 'Why are you asking for these obscure records?' We'd say, 'Because we play this music.' Then Brian came down to the Cavern one last time, Paul and I got him down, and I've never seen a man find his forte so quickly. He went, 'Wow, this is where I should be.' Here was a very gentle, lovable man whose father had been selling furniture, who didn't know music and just fell in love with the whole idea and saw the potential. We didn't. We always wanted to play music wherever we were. Like I did on the railways. I worked for Woolie's, just to get a new guitar. Brian said, 'Hang on, you've got a thing here I can sell.' We said, 'Brian, what do you know about bleedin' records?' He said, 'I'll go to London.' And Brian went to London and it happened. Even when we had the first hit record we were still basically a nothing commodity. We'd done Hamburg, we played there for three years, seven hours a night, playing all types of music. So when we did a live show we had so many numbers to play and out of that came this thing called the Mersey Beat. It was just American gear, not our gear, and through that the Mersey Beat evolved. Of course, 'the Mersey Sound' is a stupid phrase because nobody actually sounds like each other. But the Mersey Beat came from that.

Gerry Marsden, the genial lead singer of Gerry and the Pacemakers, has been friends with the Beatles from the very beginning.

Mike McCartney, Liverpool, July 1984 (interview by Geoffrey Giuliano)

Question: What was your name again, McGear or McCartney?

Mike McCartney: McGertney. Establish where we are. Go on.

Question: We're in a delightful restaurant in a wonderful old baronial home in Liverpool.

Mike: It was our first home, you know, but they kicked us out because we couldn't afford the bloody rates!

Question: I went by your old home today, actually.

Mike: You know, they once offered me £20,000 to do an exclusive Beatle tour of Liverpool for all the executive Japanese, Americans, and Torontonians. For the Garden Festival. Can you imagine, £20,000 reward to do my own private . . .? Get off! . . . This is the sound of my wife, Rowena, and I fighting over the Peking Duck.

Question: So really, what's your name these days?

Mike: Mike McCartney. That's my name now. I've changed it from McFab to McCartney.

Question: Your brother's not Paul McGear now, is he?

Mike: Who's he? Oh, you mean Linda McGear's wife?

Question: How intimidating was it to get into show business with your group, the Scaffold, with Paul McCartney being your brother?

Mike: Actually, it was no problem at all. The only way to survive was to choose a theatrical comedy concept. If I had chosen pop music I'd be dead by now.

Question: Would you have liked to go into straight pop music but thought you couldn't because of Paul?

Mike: Look, Brian Epstein once said to me at the height of the Beatles' success, 'Michael, would you like to be a pop singer? Please, come and join our organisation.' This was when they were just getting Gerry and Cilla organised. I said, 'Brian, you must be jokin'. We've got one up there already who is doin' rather well, thank you.' To try and emulate that, to try and put myself up there and draw on Paul as a comparison would be a pretty dumb thing to do. I'm as good as he is. He's a natural singer and a natural player of instruments, but I'm a natural singer too, though I've never been relaxed enough to really let anybody hear it.

Question: Did the Scaffold ever play on the same bill with the Beatles?

Mike: No. We played the Cavern, though, but we didn't go down too well because they were used to pop groups, and we'd come on spoutin' poetry and bloody comedy.

Question: Well, the Beatles were always edging towards comedy.

Mike: John was a great comedian all right, a natural.

Question: Paul was no slouch either.

Mike: No, no, but John was the heavy one, and Paul was a very good feed. Two good comedians. But then again, Ringo's a very funny guy as well.

Question: George came out with a few zingers too, you know.

Mike: Oh yeah. Well, you've been to Liverpool now, and all the people reading your book will understand that when they come to Liverpool, they might actually see why the Beatles are so big. Liverpool life is the best apprenticeship in the world, because our families are virtual gold mines of upbringing. Without that grounding I doubt very much whether the Beatles would have stayed on top for so long or kept their sanity when all about them so many died. Of course an enormous contribution to that longevity was their sense of humour. They always say in Liverpool: 'You've got to have a sense of humour to survive.'

Question: I went around to their boyhood homes today, and I can see where you'd have to keep a sense of humour, because it all seemed so harsh.

Mike: Hold on. There's two ways of looking at it. Ringo's neighbourhood was heavy. Now I don't particularly know what George's was really like, as he was in Speke, and I only vaguely remember going up to his house. Paul would have known George in Speke when we lived in Harwood Grove. George lived about three streets parallel to us. I remember walking up the back alleyway with some fireworks under my arm, going to George's one night. I can't remember George as a kid, particularly. He lived very close to us, and from there we moved to Forthlin Road.

Question: Which is very near John's.

Mike: Oh, very near, just down the road. So the point you were making was about all this poverty we were brought up in. The reality was quite different! We were actually lower working-middle-class. My dad was a cotton salesman, which was a good job, very well respected. He was earning good money. And my mother was a midwife: again, a highly respected position. Look at John's place on Menlove Avenue. It's bloody posh.

Question: I've met Paul and Linda, and they're the nicest people you would ever want to meet. How can you take a guy, give him everything and have him end up so cool?

Rowena McCartney: The Beatles weren't particularly star-struck though, you know what I mean? A lot of groups today seem to be. The Beatles still got around, I mean, they went on every chat show. They did almost everything they were asked instead of saying, 'No, we're far too big for that.' They realised that being amiable was much better. I can imagine your father taking the piss out of Paul if he ever got too big for his boots.

Mike: Yes, that's right. But again that can only come from your upbringing. And that's why you don't get thrown when you're at the top, when the pressure's really on. Paul was always in contact with his relatives. Families tend to cut one down to size, so suddenly it isn't that big a deal being rich and famous as in Paul's case. I know family life is more important to him. And when you get too big for the family then that's very uncool.

Question: Was it the same for the rest of the Beatles? Did they have strong family roots as well?

Mike: Yes. You just said to me in the car what a magical, amazing place Liverpool is.

Question: So what you're telling me is that one of the most significant factors in the Beatles' success was simply being from Liverpool?

Mike: Yeah.

Question: Do you ever see many people from the old days?

Mike: I saw John's mate, Pete Shotton, in Liverpool when Queenie Epstein opened up Beatle City. I didn't meet him though, but I did meet Pete Best.

Question: You did? What was that like?

Mike: Very good. I thought he was very much like he always was, quiet, dignified, and shy.

Question: They say he got canned from the Beatles because he was too good-looking and Paul didn't dig it, so he said, 'Let's find the ugliest drummer we can who's got a cool drum kit.'

Mike: Nonsense. It was just fate that decreed he should go. It's like they said, 'Something's got to happen. Somebody's got to go, and it's not us.' It could have been any one of them fate chose. George could have been the one, you know. None of them was that strong. But when they all got together, that's when the magic happened. The other three were very quick, but Pete was moody, magnificent, and good-looking. The girls screamed for him, and that was an asset. They wouldn't have sacked the sod for that! Think about it: that would have been much bigger, a good-looking drummer with Paul, John, and George fronting him. It was basically down to his drumming ability in the end. There were quite a few drummers around Liverpool, and I used to go home and tell Paul about Ringo. I often saw him play with Rory Storm. We didn't think about how ugly he might have been or even about the little white streak in his hair. It was just that this guy with Rory was a very inventive drummer. He goes around the drums like crazy. He doesn't just hit them, he invents sounds.

Question: So why's it taking Paul so long to do his Rupert cartoon?

Mike: Oh? We were brought up on Rupert. A lady who is now a Beatle Guide phoned me a while back and said, 'I've got you and Paul's first Rupert annual which I found in my attic.' And I said, 'That's nice.' 'What should we do with it, Mike?' You see, this girl's mum was a midwife, as was me mum, so I said, 'Well, I have no idea. You could sell it at Sotheby's and make a fortune. Or what would be a nice idea, why don't you give it to Paul from you as a Christmas present or something? It would be beautiful.' I left it with her and the next thing I knew it was in the Walker Art Gallery.

Mike McCartney, formerly Mike McGear, is Paul's talented younger brother.

The German Connection

We were asked, or I was asked, by a young boy, for a record by the Beatles. It always had been our policy to look after whatever request was made. So I followed up this enquiry. I didn't know anything about it and after a week or two he told me that they were, in fact, a Liverpool group. I assumed, for some reason, that they were from Germany. Anyway, he told me they had just returned from Germany and were playing in a club called the Cavern, about one hundred yards away from my office. I arranged to go down there and I saw them one midday session.

Brian Epstein

Alistair Taylor, New York, September 1984 (interview by
Geoffrey Giuliano)

Question: How did you first come in contact with Brian Epstein and
the Beatles?

Alistair Taylor: Well, I had a very boring job in an office when I saw an
advertisement for a record shop assistant at NEMS which I applied for,
had an interview with Brian and he offered me a job as his personal
assistant. Which I took. That was long before the Beatles. Then this guy
Raymond Jones came in and asked us to find this record called 'My
Bonnie', from Germany.

Question: Were you there when he came in?

Alistair: I was there every day. We got a box of twenty-five, then
another twenty-five and they just kept selling as fast as we could import
them. Then a few weeks later we went down to meet this group at the
Cavern. So we just took it from there.

Question: So what was your initial reaction to the personalities of the
Beatles? Did they seem very ordinary?

Alistair: No, no. They were sensational. I hated pop music at the time, I
was into jazz and the classics. I still am, really, but they were just so
fantastic. Not necessarily musically, as a matter of fact they were
bloody awful then.

Question: So we couldn't have gone to Woolton back then and found
four other guys who had the same buzz?

Alistair: Liverpool was full of guys like that at the time but the Beatles
just had something else. Charisma, I call it 'Ingredient', I don't know
what it is but they certainly had it!

Question: Was Brian very enthusiastic about his discovery of the
Beatles? Playing at managing a pop group was a total departure for
Brian, I would think.

Alistair: Yes, there's a lot been said about how he went round saying
they were going to be bigger than Elvis. But I don't remember it being
as blatant as that. I mean, we were enthusiastic. As a matter of fact,
when we went for lunch that same day we talked about what we should
do. But I think that he'd actually signed them, you know. It was just
something new and fun.

Question: Now, what about when the Beatles changed their public persona from lovable moptops to psychedelic lords of London? What do
you think changed these guys? Was it their fame? Did they need a
release or were they looking for God or something through acid?

Alistair: Look, if you weren't there, you can't begin to understand the pressure and their way of life. I don't give a damn how many books you've read or how many people you interview, I can't convey to you what it was like. I mean, I was close to them and even I was under pressure, and I was not remotely in their league, you know? It was unbearable and they just had to do something. Imagine, you can't walk down the street, you can't go out in a car, you can't do anything without being torn to shreds, day in, day out, night in, night out. In the early days I know they were on pills, but that was just youngsters experimenting. We've all done it. But the real development, I think, came as an escape. It was fun, they could afford it and they mixed with people that said, 'Hey, try this.' I mean, Lennon spent weeks trying to persuade me to go on a trip but I never did. I had nothing to do with drugs. I tried a joint about twice, you know, and I decided it was an idiot's game, quite frankly. Who needs it? But John and Derek would spend hours trying to persuade me. 'We'll be with you, it's great.' It was all done in fun, really. Certain people have come out with that statement that John Lennon was high every single day of the sixties! Well, when in the hell did he find time to write songs, make movies, go on tour, do interviews, television shows and write books?

Question: You were involved at Apple from the beginning. There are all sorts of stories about the financial mess it was in; someone was certainly fiddling the till at Apple.

Alistair: The Boys. They were stupid, you know. I mean we were all accused of ripping them off and, of course, there was stupidity. I tried to tell them this and it was my idea that they eventually got Klein in. I suggested Klein. I'm the guy who actually said to them one day, 'Look, this is stupid. We cannot manage this business, you know.'

Question: They put John's old friend Pete Shotton in and gave him a big position.

Alistair: Let me tell you something. One Sunday we were sitting in Hilly House, Brian's private office, having an Apple meeting. It was just the Boys, myself and Neil, and suddenly they just picked up the phone, there on a Sunday morning, and said, 'Hey, let's get hold of Derek.' And they rang Derek Taylor – it was when he was with the Beach Boys – and they said, 'Pack your bags and just come on over.' Well, I said, 'What's he going to do?' 'Oh, ah, we don't know. We'll find something.' Later, when Derek arrived, he said, 'Okay, let's set some kind of business up.' There was talk about doing one of these dispatch express rider delivery things . . .

Question: A Beatles courier service?

Alistair: Yeah. This literally happened. Now, who were we going to have to run publishing? So Derek said, 'Hey, there's this marvellous guy in the States.' 'Well, get him on the phone. Bring him here!' They were just pulling people in and saying, 'Oh shit, what are we going to do with them?' 'Oh, it doesn't matter. We'll think of something.' So is it any wonder that money was flying out?

Question: John once said, 'Apple was like playing Monopoly with real money.'

Alistair: That's right. But you know, they've accused everybody else of ripping them off but they gave *carte blanche* to anyone. People were buying genuine antique desks for their offices, I mean, really. Ron Kass had this incredible all-white office which cost the earth, I mean it was unbelievable! Peter Asher had real Old Master paintings on the wall of his office. I mean, it was marvellous. 'The Beatles have plenty of money so let's spend,' you know? And we had this crazy idea of the *cordon bleu* chefs in residence. The idea was great, I went along with it very much. I think it was probably my idea because here we were entertaining people, spending a lot of money in restaurants, and I said, 'Look, this is much more sensible. Here we've got this beautiful house on Savile Row, let's have our own cooks.' They were two girls out of the Cordon Bleu school but it was never used for that. We still took people out to lunch and the only people that ever dined at Apple were Peter Brown and Neil Aspinall, who were having eight-course lunches with Mouton Rothschild wine. There was this huge metal cabinet full of vintage wine and champagne. It was unbelievable. You'd go in and there they were, just them, no visitors. Yeah, oh yeah, great stuff.

Question: So what about this wonderful idea the Beatles had about saving the world with Apple and giving all the young artists a break? What happened when you started getting billions of audition tapes by post?

Alistair: They collected dust in the corner. I mean we just couldn't cope.

Question: Did you try?

Alistair: Yes, we tried. Obviously we got hold of a few people – Billy Preston, James Taylor, Mary Hopkin, my darling Mary. The kids were sending tapes and sheet music in. Yeah, you'd come in in the morning and switch on the answering machine and get some guy auditioning on the tape. We used to send a lot of them around to the Grade organisation.

Question: Was there a time when they said, 'Hey, I guess we're not going to save the world with Apple after all'?

Alistair: It was never meant to save the world! Let's put Apple into perspective, right? A lot of bullshit has been talked about Apple. Apple was set up purely and simply as a tax-saving project. Instead of paying nineteen and six in the pound, we only paid sixteen shillings. In the beginning, when there was an executive board at Apple, the Boys and Brian didn't want to know. It was Clive Epstein, myself, Geoffrey Ellis, a solicitor and an accountant, and the idea was that we would just quietly announce to the tax authorities that we would be opening a string of shops. That was the original idea and when the Boys heard about this they decided this could be boring, they didn't really want their name above a string of shops. The original idea was greetings cards. Imagine Beatles greetings card shops! They didn't like that at all. Gradually they started drifting in on meetings and Apple Corp really evolved from there. Later it turned into this silly philosophy, admittedly – even then it was not designed to save the world, all it really was was to get rid of the hassle of big business. I mean, why couldn't business be fun and pleasurable? So that's what it was all about.

Question: Why do you think the Beatles broke up?

Alistair: They broke up long after I'd gone. But come on, they were breaking up from about day one. I mean, more than once in the very early days I had to go and find George; he'd just say, 'I'm not doing this,' and he'd piss off, you know. So it was nothing new. I think the pressures got so bad toward the end I'm astonished they stayed together as long as they did!

Alistair Taylor was working as Brian Epstein's personal assistant when he first met the Beatles. He later worked as part of the Apple management team for several years.

Yoko Ono, New York, January 1983 (interview by Geoffrey Giuliano)

Question: John always said it's the Englishman's inalienable right to live any damn place he wants to.

Yoko: Well, God is an Englishman, I understand.

Question: Or an English woman!

Yoko: No, it's said God is an Englishman. It's a book I saw when we browsed through a shop. I spotted it, 'Well, we'd better get this for you, John.' That was the attitude, I suppose, for a long time.

Question: Did you like England?

Yoko: Oh yes, until – even after I met John, until after a very long courtship we were finally together. People are very nice there.

* * *

Yoko: John encouraged me to be independent so we can have a dialogue. Then after John died, somehow, when people called me Mrs Lennon I felt good about it. People write to me, saying, 'We grieved over John's death, and just wanted to know how his widow was doing.' That would have maybe made me feel a bit strange two years ago, but now I'm grateful people are writing because they love John and are concerned about his family. Whenever I do something now I feel my first concern is: 'Do you think John is liking this?' I don't want to do anything that would shame his name or embarrass him. When I'm doing something and I know John would have approved, I feel better. Let's say all this has mellowed me in a way. As Yoko Ono, I am very mellowed to the point that yes, it's all right I am Mrs Lennon . . . I was a kind of cynic in a way, part of me. When I'm making music I didn't really care so much about how people were going to take it. This time around it was really in my mind I was carrying on what John and I did together. So, I didn't have a partner who was taking care of the mass media side. In those days I thought, 'Okay, he can take care of that side and I'll just do my own thing, thank you.' But it wasn't like that this time. I was really talking to his fans as well. Because they were the ones who were really concerned about us and sent us their love and prayers, which really helped us get through the hard times. That's another new discovery, I didn't really think that would happen.

Question: You showed a lot of people, my wife and I, for example, that I can be yin sometimes and she can be yang, and we can go back and forth like that. That's a very nice thing that John and Yoko gave to a lot of people growing up around you.

Yoko: It has a lot to do with John, too; I mean, if he didn't have the material, I couldn't have worked on it, you know? As I said before, John was an Englishman, and you can imagine an English couple, the strong-headed woman, independent, but caring . . .

Question: Like Auntie Mimi, right?

Yoko: Yes, you know, saying 'It's time to get some milk for the cats, dear,' or whatever, and the men tending the garden. That's how it was in a way, and that's all right. John had that side of him. Making tea was very natural for him to do, so he'll make the tea for me – it was very nice . . .

Question: And bake the bread!

Yoko: Yes. So there was nothing new about that, really. But we were trying to state that, yes, we can do that too if we want to. He had a very vulnerable side, and I had the tough side, I suppose, as well – just as much as the vulnerable side. So we can all exchange roles once in a while and that was very natural for us.

Question: 'Walking on Thin Ice' too had a bite to it.

Yoko: Maybe because of how I dealt with the situation after John died it lets people think I'm a very strong woman and therefore I am different; so when they say, 'It's all right for you, you're especially strong,' no, nothing like that. I consider myself just normal. If somebody says something nasty about me I get hurt and think about it for the whole day. And the way I coped with the situation was almost a miracle! Part of me was . . . well, part of me is still in shock . . . and the other side of me was like a little baby. I felt like I was five years old, saying, 'Oh, why did this happen?' And, 'I need a big teddy bear,' or whatever. So when I look back on what I did last year – the videos, or the album, and the announcements, that's when I think, 'Wow, how did I do that?' So, there are several people in me, and they somehow organised it, you know? That put me in a situation and I just coped with it; if you were in that situation you would've done the same, or maybe even better, I don't know . . .

Question: I got a bootleg the other day of 'What a Shame Mary Jane Had a Pain at the Party'. It's the funniest thing I've ever heard, and you're in there. I heard Magic Alex [head of Apple Electronics] was at that session and John wanted to release the song on Apple.

Yoko: Yes.

Question: Is it the same as 'It's The New Mary Jane'?

Yoko: Yes. I don't know how to tell you, it was just one of those . . .

Question: Do you remember who was there?

Yoko: The usual crowd; I don't think Paul was there, I think probably George was . . . I don't particularly remember that. I do remember we did it, but I don't particularly remember it as a very great time.

Question: I heard that you and John were going to a march with Cesar Chavez near that terrible time in 1980, weren't you?

Yoko: The plan was we were going to go to San Francisco that Thursday to join a march the next day for equal pay for Oriental people in San Francisco. It was announced, we sent a statement there, and John was very happy to do this, because John had a son who was half Oriental. So he was envisioning carrying Sean, and saying 'Here's . . .'

Question: Living proof of the harmony.

Yoko: Yes . . . that was one of the things we were going to do. And that probably indicated we were going to do a few things in that direction.

Question: I was reading in some book that you and John actually lived with the founder of the Hare Krishna movement, Swami Prabhupada.

Yoko: Yes, he was with us.

Question: Tell me about that.

Yoko: He was in one of the cottages we had at Tittenhurst.

Question: How did you find him? Because everyone says, 'They're a cult, they're going to rob you and take your mind, zombies' – but they didn't seem . . . they were at your 'Give Peace a Chance' Bed-In, they banged the drum and all that.

Yoko: Well, I think each person has his or her own karma. So I'm not the one to say which one is which. People gather where it's naturally important for themselves. In my view, all religion is the same, in a way. If somebody understands it this way better, then they should go there, you know?

Question: Elliot Mintz said that in John's famous 'God', which, by the way, is a great song . . .

Yoko: I was just saying that this morning! Somebody was saying, 'What songs do you like of John's?' and of course I said that 'Imagine' is probably one of the most important songs he put out, but 'God' is one that I like very much.

Question: John said, 'I don't believe in Jesus, Krishna, Gita, etc.,' but Elliot said John did believe in all that. Because when he went with you to Japan, he visited the temples of Buddha . . .

Yoko: Oh sure. He believed in all that because it's just a variation. All this is just another way of expressing the same thing. He believed in the 'root', which is the big power, and any expression of that he had respect for. I do too. But what he did in 'God', that very powerful song, is like a declaration of independence. 'Let me be me now, and let's start from here!'

Question: No more daddies.

Yoko: Yeah, right, so it was a beautiful statement – I really like that song. Also, the myth is 'The Beatles – and Yoko' or whatever. I'd like to say that until I met John I didn't really know what the Beatles were about; I suppose I heard about them like most people in those days, not as fans, but as a social phenomenon. Elvis Presley was another phenomenon I wasn't involved with, but just sort of knew about. Since I got involved with Paul I now know what he has done . . . and it's a beautiful thing he did. After all, he's one of the Beatles and that's what John did as well, and John being Sean's father, etc., so I'm part of it! I feel a family pride in what they did; it's beautiful, as opposed to – not to knock them or anything, but certain groups making their career out of only saying negative things. What the Beatles were about was just simple love and – I want to hold your hand, that's the gist of it. It's a beautiful thing and no wonder it was so popular. It changed the whole world. Working class was something to be ashamed of before that, especially in Britain. But now, even the shopkeepers know that if a young guy comes in, who's speaking with an accent, you're not supposed to be impolite to them just because they're young and not from an aristocratic family. It changed everybody's consciousness. If you can make it when you're young, that's fine. Being young and rich doesn't mean that you were born into a good family.

Question: You performed with the Beatles on 'Bungalow Bill'. Actually you're on a few Beatle cuts . . .

Yoko: But that doesn't mean anything, it just could've been some girls outside. When they needed a chorus they used to say, 'Let's get some girls in here.' So it doesn't mean anything, but I would say I was definitely there when John and I started to do our thing. A lot of things we did together were not a waste – it was something that spoke and will probably speak much later, too.

Question: Can you say anything about the night John died?

Yoko: I was still shaking in bed, so to speak, and the bedroom was the old one that John and I used to sleep in, which is on the 72nd Street side. All night these people were chanting, or playing John's records, so that I heard John's voice, which at the time was a bit too much. What I learned was that I don't have much control over my destiny or fate or anything. Seems like it's all out there, somehow, and certain things I'm not supposed to know. John and I thought we knew all about enlightenment, so there was that arrogant side of us. And this was like a big hammer from above, saying, 'Well just remember you don't know it all, there's a lot more to learn.'

*   *   *

Yoko: Piano has been my security blanket all my life, and whenever I'm nervous or something I tend to go to the piano. I was playing 'Moonlight Sonata' and John said, 'Oh it's beautiful – could we just hear the chords and play it from this end, backwards,' and he used a chord progression from the back on, and it worked. In classical music, chords are nothing, really . . . well, we know all the chords, let's put it that way – but in rock, knowing a chord progression means a lot. So that's what I learned – 'You mean you don't know all the chords?!' It's very interesting, John knew a lot. When I did *Double Fantasy* with him, I had to realise yet again how much he knew. He was like a living dictionary about all the little licks and this and that, just everything. It was amazing. I feel that now John is helping me through Sean.

Question: Same birthday.

Yoko: Mmmm. You could ask his statement, because the last time some British radio people came in they said, 'Could we ask Sean to make a statement?' I was sort of worried, then thought, 'Look, these guys are very nice guys, they'll edit whatever. So don't worry about it, it's for the girls and boys in Britain.' He was thinking so long I thought, 'He's stuck, he's stuck, oh, it's not gonna work,' and he just said, 'Keep having fun, because it's worth it.' I thought that was like John. John used to tell me about his salmon fishing. One of his aunties lived in Scotland and she had married a Scottish man, so whenever John visited them he went salmon fishing. This man really liked fishing and he did it by himself usually, but sometimes John was allowed to join him. Salmon was a big thing to him. John used to say, 'Scottish salmon, there's nothing like it.' When I visited this auntie with him I did get to eat the salmon and it was very fresh. Here, we used to get smoked salmon, but most of it that I get here is sort of salty and the salmon we got in Scotland were really good. I don't know why they don't export that one. Salmon was one of the things we enjoyed eating.

Question: How profound!

Yoko: Yeah, right!

Remembering the Music

This was one of the first songs I ever finished. I was only about eighteen and we gave it to the Fourmost. I think it was the first song of my own I ever attempted with the group. (John, 'Hello, Little Girl')

'Love You To' was one of the first tunes I wrote for sitar. 'Norwegian Wood' was an accident as far as the sitar part was concerned, but this was the first song where I consciously tried to use the sitar and tabla on the basic track: I over-dubbed the guitars and vocal later. (George, 'Love You To')

I used to wish I could write songs like the others – and I've tried, but I just can't. I can get the words all right, but whenever I think of a tune and sing it to them they always say, 'Yeah, it sounds like such-a-thing,' and when they point it out I see what they mean. But I did get a part credit as a composer on 'What Goes On'. (Ringo, 'What Goes On')

That's me again, with the first backwards tape on any record any-where. Before Hendrix, before the Who, before any fucker. Maybe there was that record about 'They're coming to take me away, haha': maybe that came out before 'Rain', but it's not the same thing. (John, 'Rain')

'All Too Much' was written in a childlike manner from realisations that appeared during and after some LSD experiences and which were later confirmed in meditation. (George, 'All Too Much')

That's me, 'cos of the *Yellow Submarine* people, who were gross animals apart from the guy who drew the paintings for the movie. They lifted all the ideas for the movie out of our heads and didn't give us any credit. We had nothing to do with that movie and we sort of resented them. It was the third movie that we owed United Artists. Brian set it up and we had nothing to do with it. But I liked the movie, the artwork. They wanted another song, so I knocked off 'Hey, Bulldog'. It's a good-sounding record that means nothing. (John, 'Hey, Bulldog')

Oh, that was written about a guy in Maharishi's meditation camp who took a short break to go shoot a few poor tigers, and then came back to commune with God. There used to be a character called Jungle Jim and I combined him with Buffalo Bill. It's a sort of teenage social-comment song and a bit of a joke. Yoko's on that one, I believe, singing along. (John, 'The Continuing Story of Bungalow Bill')

George Martin's contribution was quite a big one, actually. The first time he really ever showed he could see beyond what we were offering him was 'Please Please Me'. It was originally conceived as a Roy Orbison-type thing, you know. George Martin said, 'Well, we'll put the tempo up.' He lifted the tempo and we all thought that was much better and it became a big hit. (Paul, 'Please Please Me')

I often sit at the piano, working at songs, with the telly on low in the background. If I'm a bit down and not getting much done then the words on the telly come through. That's when I heard, 'Good morning, good morning.' It was a cornflakes advertisement. (John, 'Good Morning, Good Morning')

That was a piece of unfinished music that I turned into a comedy record with Paul. I was waiting for him in his house and I saw the phone book was on the piano with the words, 'You know the name, look up the number.' That was like a logo and I just changed it. It was going to be a Four Tops kind of song – the chord changes are like that – but it never developed and we made a joke of it. Brian Jones is playing saxophone on it. (John, 'You Know My Name (Look Up My Number)')

'The Inner Light' came really from 'Within You, Without You'. There was a David Frost show on television about meditation, Maharishi Mahesh Yogi was interviewed on tape with John Lennon and myself live, and amongst many others in the audience was Juan Mascaro who is the Sanskrit teacher at Cambridge University. He wrote me a letter later, saying, '. . . a few days ago two friends from abroad gave me the recording of your song 'Within You, Without You'. I am very happy, it is a moving song and may it move the souls of millions; and there is more to come, as you are only beginning on the great journey.' (George, 'The Inner Light')

I was trying to write about an affair without letting me wife know I was writing about an affair, so it was very gobbledegook. I was sort of composing from my experiences, girls' flats, things like that.

I wrote it at Kenwood. George had just got the sitar and I said, 'Could you play this piece?' We went through many different versions of the song, but it was never right and I was getting very angry about it, it wasn't coming out like I wanted. Finally I said, 'Well, I just want to do it like this.' So they let me go and I played the guitar very loudly into the mike and sang it at the same time. Then George had the sitar and I asked him if could he play the piece I'd written but he wasn't sure because he hadn't done much on the sitar but was willing to have a go. I think we did it in sections. (John, 'Norwegian Wood')

Everybody thinks Paul wrote it, but actually John wrote it for me. He's got a lot of soul has John, you know. (Ringo, 'Strawberry Fields')

'Cold Turkey' is self-explanatory. It was banned again all over the American radio, so it never got off the ground. They were thinking I was promoting heroin. They're so stupid about drugs! They're always arresting smugglers or kids with a few joints in their pocket. They never face the reality. They're not looking at the cause of the drug problem. Why is everybody taking drugs? To escape from what? Is life so terrible? Do we live in such a terrible situation that we can't do anything about it without reinforcement from alcohol or tobacco or sleeping pills? A drug is a drug, you know. Why we take them is important, not who's selling it to whom on the corner. (John, 'Cold Turkey')

I think this is my favourite on The Beatles album. (Paul, 'Happiness Is a Warm Gun')

This was about my dream girl. When Paul and I wrote lyrics in the old days we used to laugh about it like the Tin Pan Alley people would. And it was only later on we tried to match the lyrics to the tune. I especially like this one. It was one of my best. (John, 'Girl')

George [Martin] is quite a sage. Sometimes he works with us, sometimes against us, but he's always looked after us. I don't think he does as much as some people think, though. He sometimes does all the arrangements and we just change them. (Paul, 'All You Need Is Love')

Derek Taylor got held up one evening in LA and rang to say he'd be late. I told him on the phone that the house was in Blue Jay Way. He said he could find it okay, he could always ask a cop. Hence the song. (George, 'Blue Jay Way')

This song is about a hole in the road where the rain gets in; a good old analogy, the hole in your make-up which lets the rain in and stops your mind from going where it will. It's you interfering with things; as when someone walks up to you and says, 'I am the Son of God.' And you say, 'No you're not; I'll crucify you,' and you crucify him. Well that's life, but it is not fixing a hole.

It's about fans too: 'See the people standing there/who disagree and never win/Wonder why they don't get in my door.' If they only knew that the best way to get in is not to do that. Because obviously anyone who is going to be straight and a real friend, a real person, is going to get in; but they simply stand there and give off, 'We are fans, don't let us in.'

Sometimes I invite them in, but it's not really cool, because I let one in and the next day she was in the *Daily Mirror* with her mother, saying we were going to get married. So now we tell the fans, 'Forget it.'

If you're a junkie sitting in a room fixing a hole then that's what it will mean to you, but when I wrote it I meant if there's a crack or the room is uncolourful, then I'll paint it. (Paul, 'Fixing a Hole')

This was just a fragment of an instrumental which we weren't too sure about, but Pattie liked it very much so we decided to leave it on the album. (Paul, 'Wild Honey Pie')

Well, Dr Robert is a joke. There's some fellow in New York, and we'd hear people say, 'You can get everything off him; any pills you want.' It was a big racket, but a joke too, about this fellow who cured everyone of everything with all these pills, tranquillisers and injections for this and that. He just kept New York high. That's what 'Dr Robert' is all about, just a pill doctor who sees you all right. It was a joke between ourselves, but they go in in-jokes and come out out-jokes because everyone listens and puts their own thing on it, which is great . . . You put your own meaning at your own level to our songs and that's what's terrific about them. (Paul, 'Dr Robert')

George wrote this. Forget the Indian music and listen to the melody. Don't you think it's beautiful? It's really lovely. (Paul, 'The Inner Light')

I was having a laugh because there'd been so much gobbledegook about *Pepper*: play it backwards while standing on your head and all that. Even now, I saw Mel Torme on TV the other day saying that 'Lucy' was written to promote drugs and so was 'A Little Help From My Friends', and none of them were at all. 'A Little Help From My

Friends' only says 'get high' in it, it's really about a little help from my friends, it's a sincere message. Paul had the line about 'little help from my friends'. I'm not sure, but I think he had some kind of structure for it. We wrote it pretty well 50–50 but it was certainly based on his original idea. (John, 'Glass Onion')

This was one of my favourite songs, but it's been issued in so many forms that it missed it as a record. I first gave it to the World Wildlife Fund, but they didn't do much with it, and then later we put it on the *Let It Be* album. (John, 'Across the Universe')

'Not Guilty' was written in 1968 although it appeared for the first time on the 1979 *George Harrison* album. I wrote it before *The Beatles* White Album and it seems to be about that period: Paul, John, Apple, Rishikesh, Indian friends, etc. (George, 'Not Guilty')

This forms part of a medley of songs which is about fifteen minutes long on *Abbey Road*. We did it this way because both John and I had a number of songs which were potentially great but which we'd never finished. (Paul, 'She Came In Through the Bathroom Window')

That's about the Maharishi, yes. I copped out and I wouldn't write 'Maharishi, what have you done, you made a fool of everyone,' but now it can be told, Fab Listeners. (John, 'Sexy Sadie')

George Martin, London, 1987

Question: Why is Ringo performing the vocals on 'A Little Help From My Friends'?

George Martin: Well, that song was especially written for him. That was the standard practice, we would always have one Ringo vehicle on every album. And Paul had the idea of writing this song which fitted in well with the *Sgt Pepper* idea. With creating the Billy Shears character, Ringo became Billy Shears, in the same way that all the Beatles became Sgt Pepper. It was a jolly good song and suited his voice very well and was supported nicely by backing vocals from the group. So it was custom-built.

Question: Why do you feel so strongly that 'Penny Lane' and 'Strawberry Fields' should have been on *Sgt Pepper*?

George: It was actually designed that way. I mean, we went into the studios in December 1966 in order to start the new album. It wasn't a question of recording 'Strawberry Fields' and 'Penny Lane', it was a question of beginning work on a new album and those were the titles we started with. That and 'When I'm Sixty-Four'. The only reason they didn't become part of the album was that Brian Epstein came to me and said we badly need a single because the Beatles were slipping a bit and he didn't want that to happen, quite rightly. So we rushed out a single which was the best coupling ever, I think. It was so good that it didn't make number one the first week for the first time. It was kept out of the English charts by Engelbert Humperdinck with 'Release Me'. So that's justice for you. And in those days we liked to give as much value for the money as we could to the public and, wrongly, we decided to keep our singles separate from our albums. Nowadays, of course, you must have a single off the album. If we weren't so high-minded then, 'Strawberry Fields' and 'Penny Lane' would have been part of *Sgt Pepper*.

Question: Would you have liked to have put them on the CD?

George: I was sorely tempted to. But then it would have unbalanced everything. I mean, even on the CD there is a little explanation which says we were tinkering around with the order and if you wanted to hear the original running order you could programme your CD player. So it would have been quite wrong to put on 'Strawberry Fields' and 'Penny Lane'. It would have destroyed history, wouldn't it?

Question: I think people feel that things were done in the making of *Sgt Pepper* that had a profound effect on the way albums were produced and engineered from then on.

George: They may have affected other people, but it didn't affect me because I just went on making records the same way I had been doing for ages. As far as technology is concerned, there was no great revolution. *Sgt Pepper* was done on a four-track, as was *Beatles for Sale*. *Abbey Road* was only the beginning of eight-track, so there wasn't a great deal of difference there. Technology didn't evolve that rapidly. As far as the techniques involved, the kind of musical collage, the use of orchestras and overdubbing was the beginning of something.

Question: So, by the time *Sgt Pepper* was made, using many overdubs even on as few as four tracks, was a technique with which you were well acquainted.

George: We overdubbed as much as we could with the techniques and the facilities available. We couldn't overdub too much on two-track, obviously, but we did. Sometimes we would just put down a backing on one side and add the vocals or replace them on the other. We generally did things live. It was quite interesting when I was listening to the tracks for 'Yesterday' – it was a four-track, of course, and two tracks were used for the initial performance of Paul with his voice and guitar simultaneously. A third track was the string quartet overdubbed and the fourth track was a first attempt by me to get a better vocal performance. In fact, it wasn't used except for one little part where you hear a double track voice, so that was obviously an overdubbing technique in the fairly early days of four-track. With *Pepper*, it was a question of going beyond one four-track and on to another because we did run out of tracks. Obviously, if we had had twenty-four tracks available, we would have used them, but we didn't. So I had to go from one four-track machine to another mixing four tracks down to maybe two over a stereo pair, and then filling up another two tracks.

Question: So it was bouncing down rather than syncing two machines?

George: Absolutely. Syncing didn't exist, therefore we didn't have any sync unit which enabled two machines to run together. It was hit or miss. Even when we overdubbed the orchestra in Number 1 Studio for 'A Day in the Life,' we just ran the machines in sync by hand. In other words, they weren't in sync and you can hear that. If you listen, you can hear the ragged ensemble of the orchestra because there are several orchestras coming in slightly at a distance from each other.

Question: Did your role as producer on *Pepper* change from the way it had been before? When you started with the Beatles on the early albums, they were quite rightly totally subordinate to yourself as the experienced person. They were new to their craft, certainly in a recording studio. By the time you got to *Pepper*, which is a great leap in inventiveness all round, how much greater part were they taking in the building of the album, musically?

George: Oh, very much so. Obviously, Paul and John were the prime movers of *Sgt Pepper*, Paul probably more so than John. But their inspiration, their creation of the original ideas, was absolutely paramount, it was fundamental to the whole thing. I was merely serving them in trying to get those ideas down. So my role had become that of an interpreter, particularly in John's case, who was not all that articulate. His ideas were not very concise so I had to try and realise what he wanted and how to effect it. I would do it either by means of orchestras, sound effects or a combination of both. The songs in the early days were very simple and straightforward, you couldn't play around with them too much. But here we were building sound pictures, and my role was to interpret those and realise how to put them down on tape, which we eventually did.

Question: It's been reported that since the band had stopped touring about six months before recording *Sgt Pepper*, this was their most prolific period as recording artists and writers. In the case of John and Paul, did you notice any change in attitude or ability regarding songwriting and performance?

George: Well, yes, because the last track we recorded on *Revolver*, in fact, pointed the way to the future, and that was 'Tomorrow Never Knows'. Which was a very imaginative track, you could say almost psychedelic, because it was John's idea. The song was based on the Book of the Dead and it was very wordy material, pretty far-out stuff. John actually said that he wanted his voice to sound as if he were the Dalai Lama singing from a hilltop, but what could we do to give him that effect? What I did was I chose to put his voice through a Leslie speaker for the first time, but then the rest of the track was also pretty far-out. There was a tamboura and Ringo's very insistent drumming. The thing that made it, of course, were all the little tape loops the Beatles themselves had prepared at home on their Grundig recorders. They were into experimenting and they always wanted to try different things. It was Paul who hit upon the idea of removing the erase head on his tape recorder, then playing some stuff, maybe just a guitar phrase, into the microphone, and if he made a loop of tape that would go around and around, the effect was of saturation so that the tape would absorb no more. He would then have a piece of concrete music. They would bring these tapes for me to listen to. In the case of 'Tomorrow Never Knows', they brought over thirty tapes and I played them at different speeds, backwards and forwards. I selected some, and they became the input of that particular track. This kind of work, this building up of sounds and collages, was exciting. I enjoyed it and they thought it was great fun and part of discovering life for them. That really pointed the way to *Pepper*, which became an experiment in itself.

Question: Is it true that there were three songs which were recorded, but never included and indeed, have never been released in any form? Harrison's 'Pink Litmus Paper Shirt'; Lennon's 'Colliding Circles'; and 'Peace of Mind', do any of those ring bells with you?

George: I haven't any recollection of them at all. Quite often they would do busking things and they would put down something, a little bit of nonsense. A lot of the songs didn't have titles when we recorded them, so it is quite possible that someone, at a later date, has found this and said, 'Oh, that's "Peace Of Mind".' But I have absolutely no recollection of anything like that. They couldn't have been very good.

Question: Was the laughing at the end of 'Within You, Without You' George Harrison's idea and, if not, did he like it? Bearing in mind it was his only song on the album.

George: It was George's idea and I think he just wanted to relieve the tedium a bit. George was slightly embarrassed and defensive about his work. I was always conscious that perhaps I didn't devote as much attention to George as I had the other two. I actually think that 'Within You, Without You' would have benefited a bit by being shorter, but it was a very interesting song. I find it more interesting now than I did then. I think it really stands up extremely well.

Question: Going on to orchestration and arrangement: this was entirely your responsibility and, considering it was done on four-track, did that present a problem?

George: Well, no, because it was just a question of recording in stereo on whatever we did. So on 'A Day in the Life,' for example, I didn't use the whole four tracks or even the four-track machine. Incidentally, when we had the orchestra in the Number 1 Studio, we would be playing to a guide track, which was an existing rhythm track, of 'A Day in the Life' on one four-track machine, but we were not recording on it. We were recording on another machine, which was wild. At a later stage I just laced the thing together, so that I used a four-track machine, but I wouldn't be recording the whole orchestra because I'd probably only be using two of them in a stereo effect.

Question: So you were using a sort of matched pair of stereo microphones for the entire orchestra.

George: That was what I invariably did for most of the orchestras I recorded. Later on we started dividing up the orchestra into more segments, but if you get the balance right, you have to come down to stereo in the end, so you might as well do it then.

Question: Is *Sgt Pepper* your favourite album of all the Beatles' albums?

George: It's not really my favourite, but I do like it very much. I'm very happy I was involved in it, but I have a sneaking regard for *Abbey Road* as being a better album. Don't ask me why, except I think it's such a nice contrast between one side and another. And there's some great writing on it too.

Question: What are some of the particular tricks you played on tape? Two things that constantly come up are the famous run-out groove, and the organ music on 'For the Benefit of Mr Kite'.

George: The run-out groove was just a giggle, a silly schoolboy prank. I think it was probably Paul who said, 'When you have an automatic record player, the record lifts before you reach the run-out groove on the end.' But in the old days before you had an automatic, the needle would get stuck in that groove and go round and round forever. Paul said, 'It's just a terrible hissing noise, why don't we put some music in that? So if people don't have the modern machines, they will hear something a lot less sing-song.' So we said, 'All right, let's do it.' They just went down into the studio and I said, 'Sing the first thing that comes into your head when I put the red light on.' And they did that. They hadn't got any prior warning, all four of them sang something quite ridiculous, and I lopped off about two seconds of it at random and then stuck it round in a circle and laid that in the groove. We also put in a fifteen-kilohertz note for dogs. Again, a stupid prank, but it was fun. Later on, I believe the vinyl discs had that removed, so that now, quite a few discs don't have it. And, of course, the problem came when I put it over to CDs. CDs don't have run-out grooves. What we thought would be nice was to go back and have that again, so we just gave the sound as though it were a run-out groove. We had several revolutions going on and it gradually fades at the end. Giving an idea to people what it was all about.

Question: And the 'Mr Kite' thing was basically the same operation, but for a different reason.

George: Well, yes, 'Mr Kite' was an attempt to create an atmosphere. John wanted a circus fairground atmosphere for this song. He said he wanted to hear the sawdust on the floor, so I had to provide that. And apart from providing this sort of organ sound, I wanted a backwash of sound, as tin on metal is a sound. You know, when you go into a fairground and shut your eyes and listen, you hear everything; you hear rifle shots and hurdy-gurdy noises and people shouting, and so on. Well, that is what I wanted to convey, so I got a lot of old steam organ tapes, which played things like 'Stars and Stripes Forever' and Sousa marches, and chopped them up into one-foot sections. I then joined them together again, sometimes back to front. The whole thing was to create a sound that was unmistakably that of a steam organ which had no particular tune at all. By putting that in very quietly in the background it gave that sort of fairground, open air effect.

Question: Your studio equipment, very briefly, at the time of *Pepper*...

George: A Studer four-track, which used one-inch-wide tape. These were sort of standard machines made in Switzerland or Germany and mixed down on BTR twin-tracks. We had Fairchild compressors that we still use today, by the way. Which are the old valve-operated compressors, awfully good, Neumann microphones where it was possible, because they just were coming out then. And the old antiquated EMI disc cutter in Number 2, which was pretty primitive.

Question: But obviously effective.

George: Oh yes, it was clean, that was the main thing.

Question: Geoff Emerick worked with you as engineer. Was anybody else directly involved on a notable level in that recording?

George: We had lots of second engineers. The main second engineer was Richard Lush, who I believe is now working in Australia. Phil McDonald was second engineer – he's now quite a well-known bigwig – and lots of other people. We even had maintenance engineers working on sessions as engineers. Quite often the Beatles would come in on a session without any warning and by this time they'd gotten pretty important. They would ring me up in the morning and say, 'Want to come in tonight at eight o'clock?' And if the guy wasn't around, we just used whoever was. In fact, Dave Harris who is our technical director of the AIR Group here, was maintenance engineer at Abbey Road in those days. And he reminded me that on the first recording of 'Strawberry Fields,' he did the engineering; Geoff Emerick and I weren't there because we were attending a Cliff Richard opening. And we arrived about eleven o'clock at night, after he had done the first track. So that was the kind of thing that happened.

Question: Was Ken Townsend involved?

George: Yes, he was, because Ken, alongside Dave Harris, was maintenance engineer, in fact, senior to Dave. Ken was always involved in creating toys for us to play with. I don't think he actually did any direct recordings, if I remember, but he was always around in case something went wrong.

Question: And for the record, of course, you would say that Ken is now general manager of Abbey Road and still there after all these many years.

George: Indeed he is.

Question: Did the Beatles themselves ever become interested in studio technicalities?

George: Not in technical terms. They never wanted to know how a thing worked, they just wanted to know that it *did* work and what it did. George was the most technical one, he is the bloke who could mend a fuse. The others weren't, really. John, the least of all. John never bothered with the intricacies of things, he just wanted it down and was rather impatient.

Question: On a slightly more delicate subject, EMI and maybe for the Beatles themselves: relationships at that time were possibly getting strained, certainly between the Beatles and EMI. Were you aware of any such tensions? Is tension part of the magic mix of *Sgt Pepper?*

George: Well, they themselves, the Beatles, I don't think were very strained. I think the strain of fame and touring had taken its toll. I think they were going through a period when they secretly wanted not to be famous and go back to being ordinary people again. Which is maybe a psychological explanation of why *Sgt Pepper* existed in the first place, because it was a band they could refer to, like the Beatles. They often refer to the Beatles as being somebody quite separate. In the same way that Paul, I, and George look back on those days as though it were other people doing it rather than ourselves. Between the Beatles and EMI, they were always antiestablishment. Even when I first met them in 1962, it was them against the world. And anybody who existed in any authority was someone they wanted to be contemptuous of. It was part of their makeup. Fortunately I didn't come into that category because I was already a maverick with EMI, so they kind of sided with me, in a way.

Question: And after *Sgt Pepper*, how many more albums were there?

George: After *Sgt Pepper*, then the next one, of course, was the White Album, *Magical Mystery Tour, Let It Be*, and then *Abbey Road*. In between that were all the odd singles. The next immediate thing that I remember after *Sgt Pepper* was 'All You Need Is Love,' which was the first live television broadcast to over two hundred million people.

Question: You double-tracked a lot of vocals on the Beatle records, didn't you?

George: That all started in the early days with the Beatles when I was recording not only them, but Billy J. Kramer and Gerry and the

Pacemakers, and so on. I started double-tracking voices way back in 1962. I thought it was a useful technique for getting different sounds. John, in particular, was always wanting his voice changed, so we did quite a lot of double-tracking. But I used it quite a bit with Billy J. Kramer as his voice sounded very good double-tracked. When it came to the Beatles, they had gotten a little bit fed up with having to double-track everything physically and they said to me, 'Why can't we just tell you when we want our voice doubled?' It seemed so simple. I spoke to Ken Townsend about it, discussed the problem and said, 'Couldn't we effect some kind of double image by playing about with tape speed or something?' And he went away and worked on it. He came back with a huge machine which was a valve-operated frequency controller. By taking the sound off a playback head, and putting it back again, delaying it, bringing it into line with the live recording, he was able to shift the image or create two images. If you think of it in photographic terms, and imagine two negatives, if you had them overlapping so they're completely identical, then it becomes one and you only hear one sound. If you move one away slightly, and we found that if we moved them away by as much as a ten milliseconds, you get a kind of echoey, what I call a telephone-box effect. Then widen them a bit and you get to about twenty milliseconds, and you get what we think of as ADT or two voices. Widen them still further to about eighty milliseconds or one hundred milliseconds and you get a kind of Elvis Presley echo. We found that out by experiment. The great thing about Ken's device was that his variation of the gap between the two images was done by speed control with this huge power-operated device, which got very hot and it was done manually. There was no automatic wiggling a little knob trying to keep it more less in space. And the very fact that you physically controlled it, that it varied the pitch slightly and gave you a better artificial double-tracking than we have ever heard since. All the devices you have which are digitally controlled now are not as good as those early days.

Question: In fact, you pointed to a difference in what it's called, because you thought of it as 'artificial double-tracking.' Somewhere along the line, presumably when it became automatic.

George: There's another word like that which came into use called 'flanging,' because when John Lennon first heard about artificial double-tracking (and we used it a great deal) he thought it was a knockout. And he said, 'How do you do it, George?' Joking, I said, 'It's very simple, John. Listen carefully. What we do is to take the original ridge and split it through the double-wire vacators flushing plan. Then we bring it back into double-negative feedback.' All he could remember about that was double-wire vacators flushing plan. He said, 'You're pulling my leg, aren't you? Well, let's flange it again.' After that, whenever he wanted ADT, he would ask for his voice reflanged. So *flanged* is a word I've used a great deal. Many years later I was in America and a fellow said, 'George, should we flange the vocals?' I said, 'Where did you hear that word?' And he said it was a word that comes about from people putting their thumb on the flange of a tape machine. So that's it.

Jackie Lomax, Los Angeles, 1991

Question: When Brian Epstein took over managing the Beatles and they later had their first hit with 'Love Me Do' and they became a national sensation, did the other Liverpool groups like the Undertakers believe the same could or should happen for them too?

Jackie: I thought that was great for them, but I'm not sure we felt that was going to have a trickle-down effect. Yet, we would be offered more money to go play somewhere just because we were a Liverpool band. And people thought there was some special kind of music, something new, coming out of there. But it wasn't new, really. The German promoters came over to check out what we were doing and said, 'The Beatles have got a record coming out. We're not going to be able to get them as many times as we'd like. Could you come over and play?' This was a direct result of the Beatles putting out a record. In four and a half years of touring we covered the whole of England, Scotland and Wales. We did every gig there was to do. We had some great times, we did some great gigs. Certain nights can be remembered forever. That's the important part of music. We had no idea at all about business. It came down to us having a chance to go to New York in 1965 and by doing that we kind of broke up the band. Because the guy who made us the offer asked us not to get any gigs. We stopped gigging for a while and our manager was paying us a wage each month. We had no concept of what we were doing, I don't think anybody did in those days. We went to our manager and asked him to split up the money among us that we'd made over the past four and a half years and, of course, he said, 'Well, there isn't any.'

Question: How did you become a solo artist, and how did your association with Apple Records come about?

Jackie: I met Cilla Black at a party and she said, 'Brian Epstein's looking for you.' Well, Brian was a big name, this was 1966. I said, 'Well, where is he?' She told me and I got in touch with him. He said, 'I'm looking for a solo singer. Are you interested?' You got to be a fool to say no! This is the biggest guy in the world right now. So, I said, 'I have a band here right now. Come down and see us rehearse. If you like the band, take the band. And if you don't like the band I'll go with you anyway. No problem.' We were rehearsing in some cheesy, funky dance studio on 8th Avenue in New York and he actually agreed to come down and hear us. When I think about it now, to get Brian Epstein to come hear a band rehearse, it was like impossible. Why I didn't think it was impossible, I don't know. Anyway, he came and he liked us. We went back to London and started doing gigs there. We were called the Lomax Alliance. That's when Epstein had the Savile Theatre, we played it. That's where Hendrix made his debut, Cream, all this stuff going on. It was a great time. But then, of course, Brian died. We had recorded an album, produced by John Simon, with all original songs, but it was never released. I don't think it was a great album, but we had all started writing.

Question: What happened after Brian died? As far as you were concerned?

Jackie: He left me as a legacy to NEMS Enterprises, his company, which was run by Robert Stigwood. And Stigwood wasn't particularly impressed with me. So, I couldn't get an album out. He gave me a chance for a single, provided I record a Bee Gees song on the B side, which I did. I put out a single, written by an American, called 'Genuine Imitation Life'. And the other side was 'One Minute Woman' by the Bee Gees, my version. Nobody knew what to do with it. I don't think it was released over here. So I was kind of hanging around, waiting for something to happen.

Question: That was when George Harrison suggested you do a solo album, with him producing?

Jackie: Right, but he told me he just wanted to produce it, not talk to the press about it or anything. We came to Los Angeles and stayed in Zsa Zsa Gabor's house in Beverly Hills, which was great for me. We recorded seven tracks here with great musicians. Hal Blaine played drums, Joe Osbourne played bass and then there was me and George messing about as well. I played guitar on all of them, but George would play the significant guitar and over-dub all the lead stuff. The title cut was 'Is This What You Want' and Larry Knechtel's piano is great on that. We did some stuff back in London too. Clapton did, like, five tracks with us. Which was, to me, incredibly generous. I knew Eric quite well, but I could not have used my influence to get him into the studio to record with me. George could, of course. So it was a great opportunity for me and I'm still very appreciative of that. Eric was great, he worked for hours. We had Ringo on drums, Paul played bass on one thing, this was going on during the same time the Beatles were recording the White Album. So, George might say, 'We'll work on your songs.' Well, of course, it would run over and I'd be sitting there hearing stuff that was blowing my mind. The White Album is very special to me because I was at a lot of those sessions. I was there for 'Revolution' and 'While My Guitar Gently Weeps' and I actually sing on 'Dear Prudence'. When the Beatles say to you, 'Why don't you come out here and sing?', it's like, all of a sudden, you ain't got no voice! I ended up singing really low, which is unusual for me. I've got a high voice. It works good on the record. We were trying to get a single to break out for me. 'Sour Milk Sea' was released at the same time as 'Hey Jude' and the Mary Hopkin song, 'Those Were The Days', so mine didn't get much notice. I did a song with Mal Evans called 'New Day Dawning'. It was added to the album later on a second release. I was quite proud of that. George came back from India and put some great guitar work on it. I even did a session with Paul as producer when George was away. He picked this Drifters' song, 'Thumbin' a Ride' for me. But that song was never released. George also came up with this tune written by Mickie Most's brother, 'How the Web was Woven'. We had Leon Russell involved in that, who I was quite fond of. He played almost all the instruments on that. Later on, Elvis Presley recorded it and he must have used my record for the demo, because I don't think anybody else did it but me.

Question: How did things wind up with Apple?

Jackie: Allen Klein had taken over and nobody knew what the hell was going on. I tried to get in to see him three times, but each time it was cancelled. So I joined a blues band called Heavy Jelly. We went on the road and I wrote a whole bunch of new tunes in the blues vein. And it was fun! During that period I received a letter from Jackie Simon and he said, 'I'm living in Woodstock and I have all these musicians, but no singers. Can you get over here?' Well, that's a big question, right? So, I ended up in Woodstock with Jackie Simon and this record deal with Warner Brothers cropped up. I met the Band, Bob Dylan, all those people. I ended up producing the first Warners' album myself, which was a heavy responsibility at the time. Simon worked on the second one. I felt good because I was touring nationally, mostly clubs. But I really like clubs, it's much more of an intimate atmosphere than theatres. Touring was good for me, because it gave me a perspective of this country.

Singer/songwriter Jackie Lomax was in the Undertakers, and recorded one album and several singles for Apple Records. None of them reportedly did a thing. He lives in Los Angeles.

Peter Asher, Los Angeles, March 1993

Question: How did the duo of Peter and Gordon materialise?

Peter Asher: We started singing together when we were at Westminster School in London and continued when I entered university. After playing for two or three years at parties and clubs we got offered a record contract. We were playing at a place called the Pickwick Club and were approached by this A&R guy, your traditional guy in a shiny suit. It turned out to be Norman Newell, a very nice man whom I haven't seen for many years. He bought us a drink and asked if we would be interested in making a record, if we'd like to come and do an audition at EMI. We said, fine, love to. So we went over and recorded three or four of the songs we did in our show and he said, 'Yes, we'd like to give you a recording contract. Let's choose some songs for the first session.' He asked us to sign on the dotted line and that was it.

Question: You recorded some Lennon/McCartney tunes, didn't you?

Peter: Yes, quite a number of them. Nominally they were Lennon/McCartney, but they were actually Paul's songs. At that point in time, even if they wrote separately, they were construed as written together. Paul had written 'World Without Love', but the Beatles didn't want to do it. I had heard him sing it in passing, because we were friends and spent time together, even before we had passed our audition with EMI. I liked it a lot, but it was unfinished, didn't have a bridge. When we were picking songs for the first session, I told Paul if he could finish it, we'd like to do it. He wrote the bridge and it was one of the three or four songs we cut on our first recording session. That was the first single and it went to number one all over the world. We got off to a very rapid and fortunate start.

Question: Let's jump to 1968 and your new job as head of A&R at Apple Records. How did this transition happen?

Peter: I remained friends with Paul throughout that period and he told me a lot about his plans for Apple, what the company was supposed to be and what they were trying to accomplish. He was aware that I was interested in producing records, indeed I had produced a couple after I stopped recording.

The first record I produced was with Paul Jones, who used to be the lead singer with Manfred Mann, 'Do Wah Diddy' and all those great tracks. I owe him a lot because he was the first person who said he liked my ideas and asked if I would produce his record. A bold step on his part, for which I am grateful. Actually, the first track I produced was a Bee Gees song called 'And the Sun Will Shine'. It's interesting in retrospect because the rhythm section was Paul Samwell-Smith from the Yardbirds playing bass; Jeff Beck on guitar; Nicky Hopkins piano and Paul McCartney playing drums. It was a good record, actually, minor hit in England, but didn't do anything in America.

Based on that experience and from working with me on various things, Paul initially asked if I would produce some records for Apple. He also asked if I would like to be the head of A&R to run that aspect of the label. They also hired a man named Ron Kass, who was a real record company executive, an American who used to run Liberty Records. Good man; now, sadly, dead. Ron was the boss and I was second in command to him, running the artistic aspect of the label, in conjunction with whatever quorum of Beatles was in the building at the time.

Question: Why did you leave England in 1970 to start your management firm?

Peter: Apple had started to get pretty weird. It was crumbling and there was a lot of dissension among the Beatles. Allen Klein had come in and was changing the character of Apple, John was all for him and Paul was against him. All this weird stuff was going on and it became clear that Apple was on its last legs. James [Taylor] wanted to go back to America anyway and I followed shortly after and became his manager. We agreed we didn't know who else should undertake this task, so it made sense for me to try. Based on advice from people I knew, I started managing James and set out to get him a record deal in America.

Peter Asher is the brother of Paul McCartney's former fiancée, Jane Asher, and was head of A&R at Apple Records.

Ravi Shankar, London, 1968

Question: When and how did the sitar boom of the mid sixties come about?

Ravi Shankar: What I term the great sitar explosion began in early 1966. At least, that is when I became aware of it, when I went to England. All the big publicity came about when the Rolling Stones and the Beatles used it on some of their records.

Question: How did you come to meet the Beatles?

Ravi: I must tell you I never actually heard any records by these groups but I suppose I vaguely knew they were immensely popular young musicians from the West. Then in June 1966 I met Paul McCartney and George Harrison at a friend's home in London. I found them to be very charming and polite young men, not at all what I expected.

Question: And what about George Harrison?

Ravi: He told me how very impressed he was with the instrument and my playing. I then asked him if he would show me what he'd learned on the sitar and he very humbly told me it was 'not very much'. I was struck by both his sincerity and his deep humility. Tapping into his knowledge of the guitar he had experimented a bit on his own but expressed the desire to properly learn to play.

Question: But surely learning to play the sitar 'properly' is a lifelong process. It seems doubtful that a young pop star could ever muster the devotion necessary for such a high ideal.

Ravi: Of course, I explained all this to him, making sure he understood that before even a single note is played one must spend years learning all the basics. He said he understood and so I invited him and his sweet wife Pattie to India to spend some time with us. Before he left, however, I joined him at his home in Esher where I gave him his very first lesson. Actually, I visited Mr Harrison once more before returning home and played privately for the other Beatles.

Question: And how did the two of you finally get together in India?

Ravi: After I returned to India, George wrote and said he would be able to come and spend six weeks with me. I wrote back telling him to grow a moustache and cut his hair a bit so that he would not be recognised. When we went to pick up George and Pattie in September, we found that trick had worked and no one recognised either him or Pattie although there had been a lot of publicity about their visit in the press. They registered for a suite at the Taj Mahal Hotel under a false name, but as it turned out, a bell boy happened to spot them and within twenty-four hours all of Bombay came to know that one of the Beatles was there.

Question: One imagines it rather quickly became complete chaos.
Ravi: Huge crowds of teenagers gathered in front of the hotel, headlines appeared in the papers about George's arrival, and my telephone started to ring non-stop. One caller even pretended to be 'Mrs Shankar' and demanded to talk to George. She changed her mind when I took the telephone myself. I couldn't believe it when I saw this mad frenzy of young people, mostly girls from about twelve to seventeen. I would have believed it in London or Tokyo or New York – but in India!

Virtuoso sitarist Pundit Ravi Shankar was great friends with all the Beatles, but especially George Harrison.

Vivian Stanshall and 'Legs' Larry Smith, Chertsey, Surrey, 1983 (interview by Geoffrey Giuliano)

Question: How did the Bonzos' appearance as the house band in the *Magical Mystery Tour* come about?

Vivian Stanshall: Brian Epstein used to own a place called the Savile Theatre, and Paul and John used to sneak in occasionally to see us, because we supported Cream a couple of times and the Bee Gees. Yes, I think the *Mystery Tour* was just dropped on us. Paul suddenly phoned up and said, 'Do you fancy it?'

'Legs' Larry Smith: We were doing a week's cabaret in somewhere wonderful like Darlington, which is up in the north of England, and our roadie came rushing back from the telephone and said, 'You're not going to believe this.' It was an almost definite confirmation that we'd got the *Mystery Tour*. The Beatles had personally invited us to perform.

Vivian: Someone nicked all our instruments, though, didn't they, from outside that alley, don't you remember? All the saxes went, your kit went; we had to hire everything to do the film.

Larry: It was pretty rushed because, as I said, we were doing a week in Darlington. And believe it or not, the manager we had at the time was wondering whether we could get out of doing the gig, if I recall. And we had to rush around to find a substitute to play. We got Gene Pitney, as he was flying over.

Question: You must have been personal favourites of the Beatles, or you wouldn't have been asked.

Larry: Surely, yeah. That's very nice to know.

Question: Were you around on the bus with them and all that?

Vivian: Oh no, we just did that one bit, and it was *finito*. Then they had that ruddy great party wherever the hell it was, where they all . . .

Larry: At the Lancaster Hotel.

Vivian: Oh, we had a great jam that night, didn't we? God, I wish I had that on tape.

Question: Who was involved?

Vivian: Well, I was up on stage with Lennon doing vocals on 'Lawdie Miss Clawdy', 'Long Tall Sally', you know, all the oldies. We screamed our heads off. Who was on the kit? Must have been Ringo, I should think, and Klaus Voorman played bass.

Larry: George got up and blew some saxophone.

Vivian: That's right. By God, it was a great row!

Larry: I remember going out into the lobby and overhearing Lulu speaking on the phone: 'Hello, Mother? I'm in London having a great time. I just can't come home just yet. I'm with the Beatles!' For me the most wonderful costume event of the evening was George Martin and his wife storming the cocktail area as Prince Philip and the Queen. For a moment everyone thought, 'Can it really be them?' I mean, they just looked so right.

Question: Tell me how Paul got involved in producing the band.

Vivian: Well, they wouldn't let him back into Poland. Actually I was more chummy with John myself, riding around in that absurd psychedelic Rolls of his. I think I just phoned Paul up and said, 'Look, I think we could do with a hit record.' So he said, 'What have you got?' And so we sent him over some stuff, and when he heard 'Urban Spaceman' he said, 'That's the one. I'll come and do it, you fix up the studio,' and he came down and we did it. Just to put us at our ease, he sat down and said, 'I've just knocked this song off, what do you think of it?' and he played us 'Hey Jude'. So I said it was all right, apart from the verse!

Larry: And I told him religion will never be a hit. You can't write about that! Anyway, we worked really efficiently, it was quite nice. We did the whole thing in about five hours. I don't know why he wanted to be called Apollo C. Vermouth on the record, though.

Vivian: That was my idea. I didn't want the thing to sell on his name alone. It was nothing to do with anything contractual on his side, he was quite happy to have it out there with his name on it, but I just didn't think that would be a fair measure.

Question: Do you know he put out a few tunes under the name of Bernard Webb? He also penned a few songs for other artists that Epstein had, under assumed names, just to see if they would sell on their own or if everything was just selling because he was Paul McCartney. And he had a big number one hit. Tell me about this relationship with Lennon.

Vivian: There's not a lot to tell, really. Just the absurd anomalies of the time. We'd wind up at the Speakeasy or some other God-awful club, get sloshed, and he'd say, 'Want a ride home, wack?' I'd say, 'Okay, John,' so he'd drop me off in my crabby basement in Islington that I was rat-hunchbacked in, and he'd be in his Rolls full of birds and things and just drive off!

Larry: And I'd have been up two hours worrying where he'd been all night.

Vivian Stanshall, the other-worldly headmaster of the fabled Bonzo Dog Doo-Dah Band, co-starred in the Beatles' film Magical Mystery Tour *and went on to become chums with John Lennon and George Harrison.*

'Legs' Larry Smith was a founder member of the Bonzo Dog Doo-Dah Band.

Neil Innes, London, 1984 (interview by Geoffrey Giuliano)

Question: You actually met the Beatles at Abbey Road during the Bonzos' first session there, didn't you?

Neil Innes: Not to talk to. It was those days when they looked like the Blues Brothers – they all had dark glasses on, dark suits, and they're coming through the wall grinning . . . 'Did you see that? That was the Beatles!' 'Oh yeah, that was the Beatles,' blah blah blah.

Question: What do you remember about the filming of *Magical Mystery Tour*?

Neil: I remember Ringo was filming his own version, he called it the 'Weybridge version', and George was saying that we ought to release 'Death Cab for Cutie' as a single. I said, 'They'd never play it, George, come on, what are you talking about?' Paul was very nice about the album – he particularly liked the 'Music from the Head Ballet'. John was a bit quiet that day, I seem to remember. I don't think John was very keen on the film . . . as it turns up in the Rutles, which was 'not the best idea for a film – four Oxford University professors on a hitch-hiking tour of tea shops in Great Britain', or whatever. But I thought it was a good idea. It had some terrific songs in it – I've always loved 'Fool on The Hill'.

Question: It stands as one of the very few appearances of the Bonzos on film.

Neil: I know, the irony of it. The Bonzos were such a visual act, and there's very little evidence of that and a whole new generation has grown up, it seems, listening to the records, never having seen them.

Question: Tell me about Paul's involvement in producing 'Urban Spaceman'.

Neil: Viv [Stanshall] met Paul McCartney at a club one night – Viv was always one for the clubs and things – and was bemoaning our sorry plight in the record business. Everyone in the business had rather enjoyed 'Gorilla', people like Hendrix and Clapton, and all those people we'd rubbed shoulders with over the years. Paul offered to produce 'Urban Spaceman', so we said, 'You're on.' So the great day came and the magic man arrived and was very quick at putting everyone at ease – he sat down at the piano and said, 'I've just written a song,' and was going (*sings*): 'Hey Jude, don't make it bad.' And I'm looking at my watch, saying, 'Come on, Paul, who needs a ballad like this at a time like this? Can't we get on with it?' Only when the record came out did I realise, 'Hey, that's what he played us in the studio that day; isn't it funny how you don't really listen?' But it was perfect, because when we got to make the thing, Paul just got on the controls . . .

Question: You mean Mr Vermouth?

Neil: Apollo C. Vermouth. Paul was playing Viv's ukelele on the rhythm track, and afterwards our manager's wife said, 'What's that you've got there, a poor man's violin?' He said, 'No, a rich man's ukelele.' Anyway ... when Viv wanted to do his big garden-hose plastic-funnel trumpet sound at the end, the engineer was saying, 'Well, I don't really know how you can record a thing like that.' Paul said, 'Yes, you can, you just put a microphone at each corner of the studio.' So it went down. We wanted to keep it a secret that Paul had produced it because we wanted to see what the record would do on its own merits. It did grab a few people's attention, got quite a lot of airplay, and it sort of crept up the charts. We were in Holland somewhere and heard it was number 36, came back and it was number 32; then it got to number 24 or something, then the powers that be couldn't resist it and leaked the fact that Apollo C. Vermouth was Paul McCartney and it immediately shot up to number 4. But it was in the charts for a long, long time – in England I think it sold well over 250,000. But that was it, that was our hit, the one that got away.

Question: Tell me about how the Rutles' project came about and, specifically, how you did the soundtrack music.

Neil: By the time we'd formulated the idea of doing the Rutles, I'd made a couple of inroads in the songwriting brief. We needed about fourteen Beatle-style songs which ran the whole gamut of the Beatles' stuff, from 'I Want to Hold Your Hand' to the psychedelic stuff – the whole bit. A curse in a way, because I've been labelled as a parodist ever since. But it was a real labour of love, because I listened to nothing – I just thought, 'Ah, I remember that kind of song,' and I just started writing them up . . . The group, the Rutles, got together and I thought, This is one of the few astute things I've done I my career': to insist that we rehearse together for a fortnight as a group in a grotty little place in Hendon, so we more or less went through the experience . . . the rags to riches thing. By the time we left the rehearsal place, we felt like a group, it was really good, because we had none of the inhibitions about desperately having to make it . . . we knew we were going to make it (*laughing*), because we were going to make a film in a few weeks' time! So everyone was very up – we made the record in two weeks – in fact, the only part of the project that came in under budget was the album!

Question: Certainly George being involved in the production validated it, didn't it?

Neil: George liked the idea of it, I think, because . . .

Question: It burst the bubble of the myth?

Neil: In many ways, the story needed to be told. There's lots of things that are too heavy about the real story to make it entertaining at the end of the day. So the Rutles, the Pre-Fab Four in *All You Need Is Cash*, was a pretty good way of saying from their side what it was like, but without making it too heavy. It must be quite gruelling, because you've made some popular records and you're a rock'n'roll band, that people will bring people in wheelchairs up to you so you can touch them and make them better, you know. On the whole it doesn't make for a very healthy ego, but I think all the Beatles survived the madness of it really quite well. You can't do it with any other group – people were saying, 'I suppose you'll do the Rutland Stones next.' We said, 'Nope.' 'What about a live gig at Shea Stadium?' 'Nope.' People couldn't understand why we weren't going to rip this thing off. Because the Beatles hold a very special plateau in the history of the sixties.

Bonzo Dog alumnus, Neil Innes is a long-time associate of the Beatles. In 1978 he played Ron Nasty (John Lennon) of the Rutles in All You Need Is Cash, *the top-drawer parody of the Beatles' incredible life and times.*

The Lost Beatles Interviews

Donovan, Toronto, June 1986 (interview by Geoffrey Giuliano)

Question: I have many pictures of you in Rishikesh at the Maharishi's ashram. Can you give me just a quick feeling of that time?

Donovan: Here's a nice story that comes to mind concerning my time with the Beatles. It was 1968 in India, we were all gathered together in the Maharishi's bungalow, four Beatles, one Beach Boy, Mia Farrow and me. Maharishi was on the floor, sitting cross-legged, but the rest of us were all still standing around as we'd just arrived. Anyway, there was a kind of embarrassed hush in the room and John Lennon (always the funny one) decided to break the silence, so he walked up to the Maharishi, patted him on the head and quietly said, 'There's a good guru.'

Question: How do you remember Lennon?

Donovan: John certainly had a wicked tongue all right, but he was honest to a fault. His work proved that. Therefore, many people considered him to be very hard and forward. Actually, that's how he protected his sensitivities, by saying exactly what he felt. He was a very sensitive man inside and it was a great loss to the world. Everyone remembers exactly where they were when it happened. As far as I'm concerned he ranks with Kennedy, Martin Luther King and Gandhi as a figure for peace in the world. His passing produced a great shockwave across the world and people felt it right to the bone. You never know what you've got until you lose it. Like in the old blues tune, they sing, 'You never miss your water till your well runs dry.' And that's what happened. We didn't miss John until he'd gone. We didn't really appreciate him until he'd gone.

Singer/songwriter Donovan Leitch was one of the select few to be invited to accompany the Fabs to the Maharishi's mountain-top ashram in Rishikesh in 1968. He has recorded individually with at least three of the Beatles who have graciously returned the favour by showing up as back-up vocalists on one or two of his tracks.

You're my Idol . . .

When I first saw the Beatles I didn't think they'd make it. I remember Brian Epstein booked me to play the Cavern with them. A couple of weeks later he had me headlining a big concert at a theatre in Liverpool. They were a support band with the Swinging Blue Jeans, Cilla Black and Gerry and the Pacemakers. The Beatles went on and sang 'Love Me Do'. They couldn't do my numbers, 'Lucille' and 'Long Tall Sally' because I was there. When they came off Brian Epstein said to me, 'Richard, I'll give you fifty per cent of the Beatles.' I couldn't accept because I never thought they would make it. Brian Epstein said, 'Take the masters [of Beatle songs] back to America with you and give them to the record company for me.' I didn't do that, but I did call up some people for them. I phoned Art Rupe and I also got in touch with Vee Jay, but I didn't take a piece of them.

So then I was booked for a tour of clubs in Hamburg for Don Arden and I took the Beatles with me. We spent two months in Hamburg. John, Paul, George and Ringo, they would stay in my room every night. They'd come to my dressing room and eat there every night. They hadn't any money, so I paid for their food. I used to buy steaks for John.

Paul would come in, sit down and just look at me. He wouldn't move his eyes. And he'd say, 'Oh, Richard! You're my idol. Just let me touch you.' He wanted to learn my little holler, so we sat at the piano going 'Ooooh!' until he got it.

I threw my shirt in the audience and Paul went and got one of his best shirts. A flash shirt, a beautiful shirt, and he insisted, 'Please take it. I'll feel bad if you don't take it. Just think, Little Richard's got on my shirt. I can't believe it.'

I developed an especially close relationship with Paul McCartney, but John and I couldn't make it. John had a nasty personality. He was different from Paul and George, they were sweet. George and Paul had humbler personalities. You know, submissive. John and Ringo had strange personalities.

Little Richard

Loose Talk

I never signed a contract with the Beatles. I had given my word about what I intended to do and that was enough. I abided by the terms and no one ever worried about me not signing it. (Brian Epstein)

I arranged for the Beatles to come to the gym to see Cassius Clay, and he didn't know who they were. He had some idea they were rock stars from England, but that's all. When he met them, they were all up in the ring together, talking about how much money they made. So Cassius pulls out a line he uses all the time. He looked at them and said, 'You guys ain't as dumb as you look.' And John Lennon looked him right in the eye and told him, 'No, but you are.' (Harold Conrad, fight promoter)

I suppose there are two things I miss: I often think it would have been nice to have had a mother when I was a little boy, and yes, sometimes I think it would be quite nice to be considered a good guy. (Allen Klein)

I tell you, my friends, it [Beatlemania] is like a sickness, which is not a cultivated hallucinatory weakness, but something that derives from a lamentable and organic imbalance. If our children can listen avariciously to the Beatles it must be because through our genes we have transmitted to them a tendency to some disorder of the kind. What was our sin? Was it our devotion to Frank Sinatra? How could that be? We who worshipped at the shrine of purity. What then, gods and goddesses, was our sin, the harvest of what we now are reaping? We may not know what it was, even as Oedipus did not know during all those years, the reasons why he was cursed. (William F. Buckley, Jr.)

The Word on the Street

John Lennon and Yoko Ono's services to the cause of furthering Communist aggression in Indo-China and weakening this country's will to resist will undoubtedly win for them Hanoi's highest honours. (Victor Lasky, US syndicated columnist)

In the hot July of 1969, I became an 'Apple Scruff', a general Beatle name for the kids who had become fixtures outside Apple's offices and EMI studios. I was sixteen and in love, in love with an American 'Apple Scruff' called Becky and in love with the sixties. It was our time – thanks to the Beatles, everything was possible – world peace, an end to starvation and a Utopian existence.

For days, at Abbey Road, kids from literally all over the world congregated to actually meet the Beatles and, depending on what kind of mood they were in, as they arrived from their separate homes, they talked to the 'hang-on-every-word' kids.

As the days progressed, I gradually became aware of one fact. They were fallible, human and completely down-to-earth. But did it destroy any illusions? Indeed no, but it did strengthen the belief that they engendered that 'Joe Soap' was important and yes, you too could have something to say.

I was lucky enough to watch them record and be invited to Paul's house. (Through my determined girlfriend, we entered the 'Holy of Holies', a Beatle home!) So I feel that I've been very fortunate and although I'm now thirty and have a lovely wife and daughter, I still like to think that I'm always an 'Apple Scruff'. And what helps me to hold on to those days is to play my Beatle records, close my eyes and remember how it was. (Alex Millen, Newark, Cambridgeshire)

When the Beatles came along, I was ripe for the plucking. Basically I'm a melody freak and they were the masters. You went out and bought a Beatles album, listened from cut one to the end and liked them all. I started writing real Beatley-sounding songs on my own. (Billy Joel)

What I saw impressed me. The Beatles looked sharp, especially compared to the silly, juvenile striped shirts and white pants the Beach Boys were wearing on stage. I suddenly felt unhip, as if we looked more like golf caddies than rock'n'roll stars. Mike was equally concerned. Both of us saw them as a threat. (Brian Wilson)

They were doing things nobody was doing. Their chords were outrageous, just outrageous, and their harmonies made it all valid. Everybody else thought they were for the teeny boppers, that they were gonna pass right away. But it was obvious to me that they had staying power. I knew they were pointing to the direction where music had to go. (Bob Dylan)

What we admired about the Beatles was that they kept their personal and artistic integrity, and all their success didn't blow them away, like it killed Elvis. (Kris Kristofferson)

If it hadn't been for the Beatles, there wouldn't be anyone like us around. (Jimmy Page)

The Beatles changed American consciousness, introduced a new note of complete masculinity allied with complete tenderness and vulnerability. And when that note was accepted in America, it did more than anything or anyone to prepare us for some kind of open-minded, open-hearted relationship with each other, and the rest of the world. (Allen Ginsberg)

Rubber Soul just took hold of me, unlocked something in my imagination that I had never experienced in popular music. I can remember it so vividly. I just couldn't resist it. It was like a tidal wave of enthusiasm, ideas, and alternatives. You just had to take part in it, and before that, I was never someone who took part. I usually stood on the sidelines and watched, because I was cynical, never engaged by popular personalities. There was a certain amount of manufacture behind them. But with the Beatles you couldn't see the seam. (Bette Midler)

I resented [The Beatles] at first because it wasn't a fad I discovered for myself. I wasn't a Beatles fan until I listened to the White Album and became an instant convert. (Steven Spielberg)

I wanted to be a famous painter, that was my ambition. There aren't too many successful painters, though. Most of them ended up being very unsuccessful. So then I saw these four lads coming out of the blue called John, Paul, George and Ringo. My God, it was simply astounding! Somehow or other they were able to conquer the entire world on the sheer force of their music. I was very impressed. Obviously this is the way to do it if you're going to become successful. I figured that music must be easier. (Cat Stevens)

There was a cultural revolution where the best and the popular were identical. And that is a very rare occurrence in history. Musical groups like the Beatles made music they'll be listening to two hundred years from now. The effect of something like *Sgt Pepper's Lonely Hearts Club* album on me and other activists, organisers and counterculture people around the world was one of incredible impact, like starting a fire in a fireworks factory. (Abbie Hoffman)

Three bars of 'A Day in the Life' still sustain me, rejuvenate me, inflame my senses and sensibilities. They are the best songwriters since Gershwin. (Leonard Bernstein)

For me and my generation that song I watched John Lennon creating at the Abbey Road studios ['Revolution'] was an honest statement about social change, really coming out and revealing how he felt . . . It was the truth, but now it refers to a running shoe. (James Taylor)

Remembering John

If John had been killed by Elvis, it would at least have had meaning. (George)

John's watching over us, you know. (Ringo)

We were going through Regents Park on our way to North London to do a session. We were in John's big Rolls-Royce and we'd just come from his house in Weybridge. Suddenly we pulled up behind Brian [Jones]; he had a hat on and all his outfit. John had a microphone set up in his car with a speaker underneath, like a police set-up. John was a very funny guy and he shouted through the microphone, 'Brian Jones, do not move! You are under surveillance, you are under arrest,' and Brian leapt up about eight feet and went as white as a sheet, going, 'Oh, my God. Oh, my God.' Then he saw it was us. 'You bunch of bastards!' It nearly killed him that day, John was so official-sounding.

After sessions we'd be careening through these villages on the way to Weybridge, shouting 'Wey hey!' and driving much too fast at two or three in the morning. George would be in his little Ferrari or something – he was quite a fast driver – and John and I would be following in the Rolls or the Princess. John would have his mike on and he'd be shouting to George in front, 'It is foolish to resist, it is foolish to resist, pull over!' It was insane. All the lights would go on in the houses as we went past, it must have freaked everybody out.

When John went to make *How I Won the War* in Spain, he took the same car, which he virtually lived in. It had blacked-out windows and you could never see who was in it, so it was just perfect. John didn't come out of it, he just used to talk to the people outside through the microphone: 'Get away from the car, get away.' (Paul)

When the Beatles split, things got very bitter between us. We were putting out some publicity for the last album and it had a wedding photo of me and Linda, only John had crossed out the word 'wedding' and written 'funeral'. That was too bitter. He went through a messed-up period – he was into heroin – and he thought people were ignoring him and favouring me. I think there were people turning him against me. But towards the end, we got over all that and were able to talk to each other about 'How's your kids?' and 'How's your cats?' He liked cats an awful lot, John. His Aunt Mimi had a lot of cats.

I still can't cope with his death. I got slagged off at the time because I just went to work like a robot and someone stuck a microphone in the car and said, 'What do you think about John's death?' I can't cope with emotional stuff that easily and all I could say was, 'It's a drag.' It must have sounded so flippant to people when they read it in the newspapers, but I went home and we wept many buckets, that night and on many nights after that. John's death caused me great grief. I loved him and still do. (Paul)

I saw him a couple of times. I didn't often go to New York, but when I was there, I'd go see him and he was nice. He was always enthusiastic. That period where he was cooking bread and stuff, I always got an overpowering feeling from him. Almost a feeling that he wanted to say much more than he could, or than he did. You could see it in his eyes. But it was difficult. Well, you'd read all these stories – and they kept coming out all the time – about how the Beatles weren't actually anything. That they didn't mean a thing. That he [John] was the only one who had a clue about anything. (George)

Look, [John] was a great guy, great sense of humour and I'd do it all again. I'd go through it all again and have him slagging me off again just because he was so great; those are all the down moments, there was much more pleasure than has really come out. I had a wonderful time with one of the world's most talented people. (Paul)

Looking back on John, you know, he was a really great guy. I always idolised him. We always did, the group. I don't know if the others will tell you that, but he was very much our idol. (Paul)

He and Yoko came over to our hotel [November 1980] and we had a great time saying hello again. His head was together. His album was done and we worked it out that come January, we were going into the studio together. Even though he was always treated in the press as a cynical 'put down' artist, John had the biggest heart of all of us. He was so up, so happy then, he blew me away. (Ringo)

Seven months after our visit with John and Yoko, while sitting in my prison cell, I was astonished to hear the local rock station play a new song by the Beatles entitled 'Come Together'. Although the new version was certainly a musical and lyrical improvement on my campaign song, I was a bit miffed that Lennon had passed me over this way. (I must explain that even the most good-natured persons tend to be a bit touchy about social neglect while in prison.) When I sent a mild protest to John, he replied with typical Lennon charm and wit that he was a tailor and I was a customer who had ordered a suit and never returned. So he sold it to someone else.

Lennon presented his version of this misunderstanding in the final *Playboy* interviews, which were so poignantly prophetic of his own sudden mortality.

During my exile years John and Yoko always remained most generous and supportive. They sent a sum of money ($5,000?) through the Weathermen lawyers. The fact that I never got the money wasn't their fault. (Timothy Leary, remembering John composing 'Come Together' as Leary's campaign song for the Governorship of California.)

He's the only person in this business I've ever looked up to, the only person. (Elton John)

I refuse to be a leader and I'll always show my genitals or do something which prevents me from being Martin Luther King or Gandhi and getting killed. (John)

I'm not afraid of dying. . . I'm prepared for death because I don't believe in it. I think it's just getting out of one car and getting into another. (John)

I told Sean what happened. I showed him the picture of his father on the cover of the paper and explained the situation. I took Sean to the spot where John lay after he was shot. Sean wanted to know why the person shot John if he liked John. I explained that he was probably a confused person. Sean said we should find out if he was confused or if he really had meant to kill John. I said that was up to the courts. He asked what court— a tennis court or a basketball court? That's how Sean used to talk with his father. They were buddies. John would have been proud of Sean if he had heard this. Sean cried later. He also said, 'Now Daddy is part of God. I guess when you die you become much more bigger because you're part of everything.'

I don't have much more to add to Sean's statement. The Silent Vigil will take place 14 December at 2 p.m. for ten minutes.

Our thoughts will be with you.

> Love,
> Yoko & Sean
> 10 Dec. '80
> N.Y.C.

The killing of John Lennon altered everything . . . Like fifty million other people, I cared about Lennon. (Norman Mailer)

The Lost Beatles Interviews

The Last Word . . .

Look, guys, if you're just going to sit there and stare at me, I'm going to bed. (Elvis to the Beatles)

Contributing
Journalists

A. C. BHAKTIVEDANTA SWAMI PRABHUPADA and the Beatles, Ascot, Berkshire, conversation, 11 September, 1969. Copyright The Bhaktivedanta Book Trust (BBT), used by permission.

RINGO STARR, interview, Los Angeles, 1990. Copyright 1992 North-east Scene, Inc. Reprinted from *Cleveland Scene* magazine, June 4–10, 1992.

MARY 'MIMI' SMITH, interview, Bournemouth, 1970. Copyright Alanna Nash, used by permission.

GEORGE MARTIN, interview, London, 1987. Copyright Mr Bonzai, used by permission.

PETER ASHER, interview, Los Angeles, March, 1993. Copyright 1994 David Goggin, aka 'Mr Bonzai.' Originally published in *Mix* magazine.

JACKIE LOMAX, interview, Los Angeles, 1991. Copyright Steve Roeser, editor, *Note for Note* magazine.

Index

Index

Index

Index

Index